# RELATED KAPLAN BOOKS

# SAT*

## MATH WORKBOOK

BY THE STAFF OF
KAPLAN EDUCATIONAL CENTERS

SIMON & SCHUSTER

Kaplan Books
Published by Kaplan Educational Centers and Simon & Schuster
1230 Avenue of the Americas
New York, NY 10020

Executive Director, Pre-College Programs: Seppy Basili
Editor: Donna Ratajczak
Cover Design: Cheung Tai
Production Editor: Maude Spekes
Desktop Publishing Manager: Michael Shevlin
Managing Editor: Brent Gallenberger
Executive Editor: Del Franz

Special thanks to: Laura Barnes, Maureen Blair, Michael Cader, David Cameron, Gerard Capistrano, Kate Foster, Amparo Graf, Jay Johnson, Liza Kleinman, Alison May, Kiernan McGuire, Marie Mockett, Krista Pfeiffer, John Polstein, and Jobim Rose.

Manufactured in the United States of America
Published simultaneously in Canada

July 1998
10 9 8 7 6 5 4 3 2 1

ISBN 0-684-84983-6
ISSN 1081-0900

# CONTENTS

Since a great way to prepare yourself for the SAT is to practice answering testlike questions, this workbook gives you hundreds of sample problems to work on. The first chapter gives you an overview of the three question types, some tips on calculator use, and Kaplan's general approach to SAT Math.

## PRACTICE SETS

Each of the 18 Practice Sets is devoted to a math concept tested on the SAT and is followed by detailed explanations. There's a brief introduction to each Practice Set that lists the essential math skills you need to solve the problems, which are cross-referenced with the SAT Math in a Nutshell, found at the end of this book. Use the answer ovals to grid in your answers, or write in the space provided. We also recommend timing each set, using a calculator, and writing out your scratchwork on a separate sheet of paper.

## ORDER OF DIFFICULTY

The questions in each Practice Set are arranged according to level of difficulty—basic, medium, and hard—and the distribution of Regular Math, Quantitative Comparison or QC, and Grid-in questions is representative of the SAT. Use the Scorecard area to track your progress each time you practice.

## SAMPLE TESTS

This workbook also contains the Math sections from two sample SAT tests—for a total of six Math sections. You should take these under timed, testlike conditions.

## MATH REFERENCE

Finally, there's an SAT Math in a Nutshell section at the end of the book covering the math you need to know for the SAT. You can refer to this reference section as you work through the problems to review concepts that you can't recall or that you're having trouble with.

> Note: For more tips on SAT Math, pick up Kaplan's *SAT & PSAT*. For a last-minute, well-organized practice, look for Kaplan's *SAT & PSAT Essential Review*. If you have any questions about the SAT, or if you want more information about Kaplan, call us at 1-800-KAP-TEST.

Approximately 500,000 international students pursued academic degrees at the undergraduate, graduate, or professional school level at U.S. universities during the 1997–1998 academic year, according to the Institute of International Education's Open Doors report. Almost 50 percent of these students were studying for a bachelor's or first university degree. This trend of pursuing higher education in the United States is expected to continue well into the next century. Business, management, engineering, and the physical and life sciences are particularly popular majors for students coming to the United States from other countries.

If you are not from the United States, but are considering attending a U.S. college or university, here's what you'll need to get started:

- If English is not your first language, start there. You'll probably need to take the computerized or paper-and-pencil version of the Test of English as a Foreign Language (TOEFL), or show some other evidence that you are fully proficient in English in order to complete an academic degree program. Colleges and universities in the United States will differ on what they consider to be an acceptable TOEFL score. A minimum TOEFL score of 550 or better is often expected by the more prestigious and competitive institutions. Because American undergraduate programs require all students to take a certain number of general education courses, all students, even math and computer science students, need to be able to communicate well in spoken and written English.

- You may also need to take the Scholastic Assessment Test (SAT) or the American College Test (ACT). Many undergraduate institutions in the United States require both the SAT and TOEFL of international students.

- There are over 2,700 accredited colleges and universities in the United States, so selecting the correct undergraduate school can be a confusing task for anyone. You will need to get help from a good advisor or at least a good college guide that explains the different types of programs and gives you some information on how to choose wisely. Since admission to many undergraduate programs is quite competitive, you may also want to select three or four colleges and complete applications for each school.

- You should begin the application process at least a year in advance. An increasing number of schools accept applications year round. In any case, find out the application deadlines and plan accordingly. Although September (the fall semester) is the traditional time to begin university study in the United States, at most schools you can also enter in January (the spring semester).

- Finally, you will need to obtain an I-20 Certificate of Eligibility in order to obtain an F-1 Student Visa to study in the United States. This you will request from the university. The school will send you the I-20 document once you have been accepted.

For details about the admissions requirements, curriculum, and other vital information on top colleges and universities, see Kaplan's *Guide to College Selection*.

## ACCESS AMERICA ENGLISH LANGUAGE PROGRAMS

If you need more help with the complex process of undergraduate school admissions and information about the variety of programs available, you may be interested in Kaplan's Access America® program.

Kaplan created Access America to assist students and professionals from outside the United States who want to enter the U.S. university system. The program was designed for students who have received the bulk of their primary and secondary education outside the United States in a language other than English. Access America also has programs for obtaining professional certification in the United States. Here's a brief description of some of the help available through Access America.

## THE ACCESS ENGLISH COURSE

At the heart of the Access America program is the intensive Access English program. This comprehensive academic English course prepares students to achieve a high level of proficiency in English in order to successfully complete an academic degree. The course covers all areas necessary to gain admission to and succeed in a university program—reading, writing, listening, conversation, grammar, and TOEFL test-taking strategies. The Access English course combines personalized instruction with guided self-study to help students gain this proficiency in a short time. Certificates of Achievement in English are awarded to certify each student's level of proficiency.

## UNDERGRADUATE SCHOOL/ACT PREPARATION

If your goal is to complete a bachelor of arts (B.A.) or bachelor of science (B.S.) degree in the United States, Kaplan will help you prepare for the SAT or ACT, while helping you understand the American system of education.

## APPLYING TO ACCESS AMERICA

To get more information, or to apply for admission to any of Kaplan's programs for international students or professionals, you can write to us at:

Kaplan Educational Centers
International Admissions Department
888 Seventh Avenue, New York, NY 10106

Or call us at 1-800-527-8378 from within the United States, or 01-212-262-4980 outside the United States. Our fax number is 01-212-957-1654. Our E-mail address is world@kaplan.com. You can also get more information or even apply through the Internet at http:/www.kaplan.com/intl.

# Getting Ready for the SAT

## HOW SAT MATH IS SET UP

There are three scored Math sections on the SAT:
- One 30-minute section with 25 Regular Math questions
- One 30-minute section with 15 Quantitative Comparisons (QCs) and 10 Grid-ins
- One 15-minute section with 10 Regular Math questions

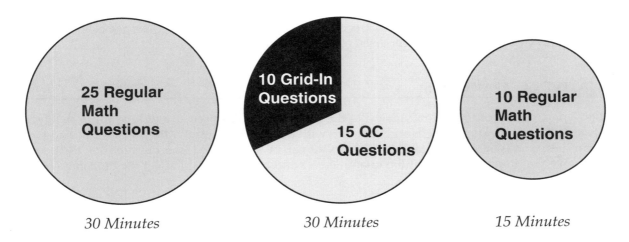

There also may be an "experimental" Math section. This section won't earn you points, but there's no sure way to identify it. Your best bet is to treat all sections as if they count toward your score.

## DIFFICULTY LEVEL

All sets of Math questions start off with basic questions and gradually increase in difficulty.

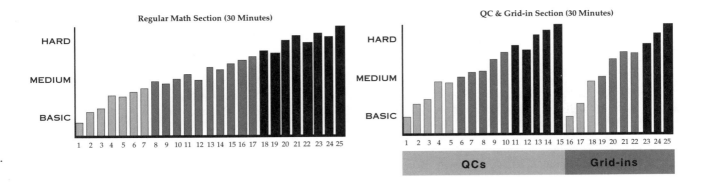

*Note: The questions in the 15-minute Regular Math section also increase in difficulty.*

Be aware of the difficulty level as you go through a question set. Hard problems call for different strategies than do basic ones. The harder the question, the more likely you are to encounter a trap. If you know you're dealing with a hard question (even though it may look basic), you'll be prepared.

## REGULAR MATH

Of the three different kinds of Math questions that appear on the SAT, you are probably most familiar with the Regular Math question type. It is simply a question followed by five answer choices, one of which is correct. Regular Math questions make up the bulk of the Math part of the SAT—35 of the 60 math questions you'll see appear in this format.

Often, Regular Math questions can be solved by indirect techniques. This is because you are given the correct answer—you simply have to select it from the five choices. Kaplan has developed techniques, such as picking numbers, to allow you to eliminate the incorrect answers. These special techniques are covered in full in Kaplan's *SAT & PSAT 1998* and the Kaplan courses.

## QUANTITATIVE COMPARISONS

Quantitative Comparisons, or QCs, don't look like the problems you're used to working on in high school. Instead of asking you to solve a problem and come up with a numerical answer, the 15 QCs ask you to compare two quantities. Once you get used to their format, QCs can be among the easier questions on the test.

Some QCs give you information about the quantities—"conditions" that will affect the outcome—centered above the problem.

QCs have only four possible answer choices:
(A)   The quantity in Column A is greater
(B)   The quantity in Column B is greater
(C)   The quantities are equal
(D)   It's impossible to determine which is greater

Since the answer choices are the same for all QCs, they are not listed after each problem. They are given in the instructions at the top of the page.

Note: Although there are five ovals on the answer sheet for QCs, there is no answer choice (E) for a QC. An (E) response will be treated as an omission.

While choices (A), (B), and (C) represent definite relationships between the columns, choice (D) represents a relationship that cannot be determined. You can be sure the answer is (D) if you find more than one possible relationship between the columns.

| Column A | | Column B |
|----------|--|----------|
| | $x > 0$ | |
| $x^2$ | | $x^3$ |

If $x = 1$, Column A and Column B both contain 1 and are equal. But if $x$ is any number greater than 1—say, $x = 2$, Column B will be greater. Since more than one relationship is possible, (D) is correct.

> **HINT:**   *If both columns contain only numbers, choice (D) can't be right. Relationships between numbers remain constant.*

Here are some things to remember when working on QCs:

**Compare, don't calculate.** QCs are supposed to be answered more quickly than Regular Math or Grid-in questions. That's because they call for less arithmetic and more reasoning than the other kinds of questions. If you find yourself doing lots of computation, you're probably using the wrong approach.

**Know when to use your calculator.** QCs are not about doing lots of calculating. If you find yourself punching lots of buttons, you're probably missing the shortcut solution. In general, you should avoid using your calculator on QCs.

**Avoid making assumptions that could be false.** Many problems involving "practical" situations or visualizing are really testing to see if you can think of less obvious possibilities. Look at the following example:

| Column A | Column B |
|----------|----------|

Points $X$, $Y$, and $Z$ lie on a line. Point $X$ is twice as far from $Z$ as it is from $Y$.

| The distance from $X$ to $Y$. | The distance from $Y$ to $Z$. |
|----------|----------|

The false assumption is that the points are in alphabetical order. If they are, the columns are equal.

But points $Y$ and $Z$ could be on opposite sides of $X$ and still fit the conditions.

In this case, Column B is greater than Column A. Since both situations are possible, (D) is the answer.

**Be suspicious on later QCs.** The problems get harder toward the end of the section. So a seemingly obvious answer at the beginning of the section is probably the right answer, but a seemingly obvious answer at the end is probably wrong.

## GRID-INS

There will be 10 Grid-ins, or questions without answer choices to pick from, on the SAT. Grid-ins follow the QCs in a 30-minute section of the test.

The main difference between Grid-ins and Regular Math is that the Regular Math answer choices can be a big help in finding the answer. Grid-ins don't give you the option of working backward from the choices.

Another thing that makes Grid-ins different: *There may be more than one correct answer to a question.* Some questions will have several possible answers, which is usually made clear in the problem. When that's the case, just find one answer that works and put it down. The computer that "reads" your answer grid will be programmed to accept any of the correct answers.

### Guessing on Grid-ins

There's no penalty for a wrong answer on Grid-ins. You have nothing to lose by guessing if you get stuck. Of course, try to make an educated guess; if you can narrow the possibilities down, you might get lucky and hit on the right answer.

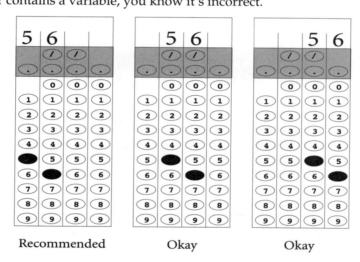

The Grid

**The Answer Grid**

You need to be careful to fill in the grids correctly. Note that there are boxes across the top of each grid for you to write in your answer. The computer reads only the bubbled-in circles, but writing in the answer can help ensure that you grid the right number or symbol in each column. You don't have to write in your answer first, but since gridding an answer correctly can be tricky, it's a good idea to do so.

There are four columns and boxes, but not every answer will take up four places. If the answer doesn't require four columns, you can start gridding anywhere, as long as the complete answer fits. For instance, if the answer were 56, you could grid a 5 in the first column and a 6 in the second, or use the second and third columns, or use the third and fourth columns (see the grids below). The computer will read all of these as an answer of "56." But it makes the most sense to start in the first column on the left, since some answers will need all four columns. The exception is zero—you have to start gridding in the second column because there is no zero in the first. In general, we recommend that you start in the first column on the left so you don't even have to think about it.

The grids include slash marks for gridding in fractions, and decimal points for decimal answers. Note that there isn't any way to grid a negative answer, or an answer with variables in it. If you get an answer that's negative or contains a variable, you know it's incorrect.

Recommended                Okay                Okay

**KAPLAN**

## How to Grid in Fractions

To grid in a fraction, grid the numerator, then a slash, and then the denominator. The slash gets its own column. Likewise, with a decimal answer, the decimal point gets its own column. A decimal answer can start with the decimal point, too; that's okay. You don't need to start with a zero—to grid in 0.5, leave off the zero and start with the decimal point.

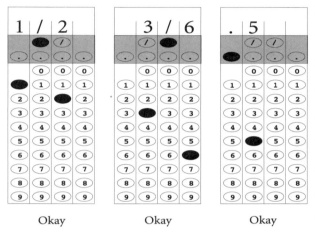

Okay       Okay       Okay

Note: You can express your answer as a fraction in any form that fits (in other words, you don't have to reduce a fraction to its simplest form), or as a decimal; the computer will accept it either of these ways. So if your answer is $\frac{1}{2}$, you can grid it in as "1-slash-2," "3-slash-6," or "point-5." (Putting a zero after the "point-5" isn't necessary, but it wouldn't make your answer wrong, either.) The easiest thing to do is to grid your answer in the form that you find, but you do have the option of putting it in a different form.

If you answer is a fraction that's too large to fit in the grid, say 27/32, use you calculator to convert it to a decimal. You'd get .84375, and you could grid either .843 or .844.

## The Mistakes to Avoid

Two potentially tricky gridding situations arise when your answer is a mixed number (such as $3\frac{1}{2}$) or when your answer is a repeating decimal (such as 0.33333). **The computer will not recognize a mixed number.** So if your answer is $3\frac{1}{2}$, do not grid 3-1-slash-2. The computer will read it as 31 halves, not three and a half. When your answer is a mixed number you must translate it into an improper fraction or a decimal. So $3\frac{1}{2}$ would become $\frac{7}{2}$, a fraction the computer will read correctly, or 3.5. **Watch out for this trap!**

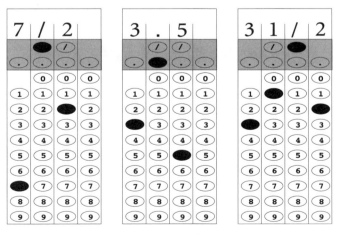

In both cases, the computer reads $3\frac{1}{2}$

**WRONG!**
This is $15\frac{1}{2}$

The other tricky situation occurs when your answer is a decimal with several digits after the decimal point. The rule is that you must grid your answer as accurately as possible, which means **you must include as many digits as will fit on the grid.** So if the answer were one-third, in decimal form, which equals 0.3333333 (and so on), .3 or even .33 would not be considered correct answers. You must grid .333, the longest version of the correct answer that will fit in the grid. This is another good reason to start your answer in the first column on the left; if it's a decimal, you'll automatically grid as many digits as is possible, and avoid this problem. You could also avoid this difficulty by simply gridding the fraction $\frac{1}{3}$.

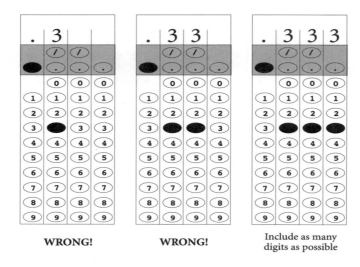

WRONG!          WRONG!          Include as many
                                digits as possible

## CALCULATORS AND THE SAT

If you use them properly, calculators can save you time on certain SAT problems. But while it's tempting to think you can rely on your calculator to solve problems for you, it's not true. SAT math questions test a lot more than your ability to do computation. In many cases, using a calculator will actually slow you down. And there are common mistakes many people make when using a calculator. You can't afford to make those kinds of mistakes on the SAT.

### To Bring or Not to Bring
Definitely bring a calculator with you on Test Day. Studies have shown that students who use calculators score an average of 10 to 20 points higher than students who don't use them.

### Choosing a Calculator
What kind should you bring? Well, you're allowed to bring any of these kinds of calculators:
- 4-function calculator (that simply adds, subtracts, multiplies, and divides)
- Scientific calculator (designed to do more complex operations with radicals, exponents, etcetera)
- Graphing calculator (able to display the graph of an equation in a coordinate plane)

Here's what you're not allowed to bring:
- Any calculator that prints out your calculations

**KAPLAN**

- Hand held minicomputer or laptop computer
- Any calculator with typewriter keypad
- Calculators with tilted screens
- Calculators that make noise
- Calculators that require an external power source

These would distract other students or allow you to take information concerning the test out of the room with you, which is forbidden by ETS.

Every calculator is different. Whatever calculator you decide to bring, make sure you practice using it before Test Day.

Does it matter how powerful your calculator is? Well, a calculator that can find square roots, powers, or percents can come in handy on a few problems. And some scientific calculators can help you make sure you do operations in the right order. But most of what you'll be doing is just speeding up ordinary multiplication and division. So having a scientific calculator can be an advantage, but only if you are thoroughly familiar with it.

**When to Use Your Calculator**
You can sometimes use your calculator to help speed up the arithmetic when using alternative problem-solving methods like picking numbers and backsolving. These methods involve plugging in different numbers to see what works, and that often requires doing extra arithmetic. Again, you have to decide whether the calculator will speed things up or slow them down.

But while a calculator may help speed up the arithmetic, it won't tell you how to set up the problem. In fact, trying to use the calculator when it's not appropriate can really mess things up. So the big rule for using your calculator is: First, think your way through the problem and look for the fastest and easiest way to solve it. *Then*, if you decide it's appropriate, use the calculator to help find the answer. For example, consider the following Grid-in problem:

> The sum of all the integers between 1 and 44, inclusive, is subtracted from the sum of all the integers between 7 and 50, inclusive. What is the result?

Don't just grab for your calculator. Think first. The SAT never requires you to do that much calculation. If you stop to think, you'll realize that each number in the first set is 6 fewer than a corresponding number in the second set (1 and 7, 2 and 8, etcetera). Since the first set runs from 1 to 44, there are 44 pairs of numbers, and each pair of numbers has a difference of 6. Therefore the difference between the sum of the first set and the sum of the second set must be 44 times 6. *Now* use your calculator! $6 \times 44 = 264$, the correct answer.

Using your calculator to find the sum of the first set, and the sum of the second set, and then subtracting them would take quite a bit of time. And punching in all those numbers, you're likely to hit a wrong key and wind up with the wrong answer.

**The Most Common Calculator Mistake**
Students who haven't done a lot of work with calculators often forget about PEMDAS (see number five in our SAT Math in a Nutshell section near the end of this book) and just punch in numbers in the order in which they appear on the page. That's fine if you're just multiplying two numbers together, but in a more complicated situation, you need to follow the order of operations.

For example, suppose you want to use your calculator to find the value of the fraction $\frac{6}{4 \times 9}$ in decimal form. This fraction stands for 6 divided by the product of 4 and 9, or 6 divided by 36, which equals $\frac{1}{6}$. But if you simply enter the numbers into your calculator in the order they appear, you get 6 divided by 4, times 9, which equals 13.5.

## HOW TO APPROACH SAT MATH

To maximize your Math score, you need to learn to use your time efficiently. Then you won't get bogged down on a single hard question and miss other problems you could have solved.

You'll save some time in the Math sections by already knowing the directions on Test Day. Sample tests at the end of the book have directions like those you'll find on the SAT. Once you're familiar with the directions, you can skip them and go straight to the questions.

Another key is to work systematically: Think about the question before you look for the answer. A few seconds spent up front looking for traps, thinking about your approach, and deciding whether to solve the problem now or come back to it later will pay off in SAT points. On easy problems, you may know what to do right away. But on hard problems, the few extra seconds is time well spent.

**Doing Math Questions the Kaplan Way**
1. Read through the whole question.
2. Decide whether to solve the problem now or return to it later.
3. If you decide to tackle the problem, look for the fastest approach.
4. If you get stuck, make an educated guess.

Now we'll apply our basic approach to the problem below:

12 At a certain diner, Joe orders 3 doughnuts and a cup of coffee and is charged $2.25. Stella ordered 2 doughnuts and a cup of coffee and is charged $1.70. What is the price of two doughnuts?
   (A)  $0.55
   (B)  $0.60
   (C)  $1.10
   (D)  $1.30
   (E)  $1.80

**1. Read through the question.**
This means the whole question. If you try to start solving the problem before reading it all the way through, you may end up doing unnecessary work.
   • Assess the difficulty level. Math questions are arranged in order of difficulty. Within a set, the first questions are basic, the middle ones are moderately difficult, and the last ones are hard. Problem number 12 above is a moderately difficult word problem.
   • Make sure you know what's being asked. Problem number 12 looks straightforward, but read through it carefully and you'll see a slight twist. You're asked to find the cost of two doughnuts, not one. Many people will find the price of a single doughnut and forget to double it.

**2. Decide whether to do the problem or return to it later.**
   • If you have no idea what to do, skip the problem and circle it in your test booklet. Spend your time on the problems you can solve.
   • If you think you can solve it, but it will take a lot of time, skip it. Circle the question in your test booklet and make a note to come back to it later if you have time.
   • If you can eliminate one or more answer choices, do so and make an educated guess. Note that you guessed in your test booklet, and try solving later if time permits.

**3. If you decide to tackle the problem, look for the fastest approach.**

• Look for hidden information. On a basic question, all of the information you need to solve the problem may be given up front, in the stem or in a diagram. But when you get to a harder question, you may need to look for hidden information that will help you solve the problem.

• Look for shortcuts. Sometimes the obvious way of doing a problem is the long way. If the method you choose involves lots of calculating, look for another route. There's usually a shortcut you can use that won't involve tons of arithmetic.

In problem number 12, for example, the cost of doughnuts and coffee could be translated into two distinct equations using the variables $d$ and $c$. You could find $c$ in terms of $d$, then plug this into the other equation. But if you think carefully, you'll see there's a quicker way: The difference in price between 3 doughnuts and a cup of coffee and two doughnuts and a cup of coffee is the price of one doughnut. So one doughnut costs $2.25 − $1.70 = $0.55. Remember, you have to find the price of two doughnuts. Twice $0.55 is $1.10.

**4. If you get stuck, make an educated guess.**

• If you're not sure what to do, or if you've tried solving but have gotten stuck, cut your losses. Eliminate answer choices that couldn't possibly be right, and make an educated guess.

Let's say it's taking too long to solve the doughnut problem. Can you eliminate any answer choices? The price of two doughnuts and a cup of coffee is $1.70. That means the cost of two doughnuts alone can't be $1.80, which eliminates choice (E). Now you can choose between the four remaining choices, and your odds of guessing correctly have improved considerably.

Remember, your goal is to answer correctly as many questions as possible; for most people, that means skipping or guessing on some problems. Practice using this approach whenever you try a problem. That way, come Test Day, the whole process should be automatic.

## PICKING NUMBERS

There are two alternative methods that come in handy when you don't see how to solve a problem on the SAT: picking numbers and backsolving.

### Kaplan's 5-Step Method for Picking Numbers
You can pick numbers on a wide variety of problems, including:
- Ratios
- Rates
- Odd/even questions
- Factors, multiples, and remainders
- Algebra problems
- Some percent problems

*THE KEY*: If there are variables in the answer choices, try picking numbers.

Here's how picking numbers works:
1. Pick numbers for the variables.
2. Plug the numbers into the question.
3. Find the value.
4. Substitute your numbers for the variables in all the answer choices.
5. Figure out the answer choices.

If two or more answer choices yield the same result, try another number or guess. The correct answer choice matches the value you solved for. For example, suppose you were given the following problem:

If $s$ skirts cost $d$ dollars, how much would $s - 1$ skirts cost?

(A) $d - 1$

(B) $d - s$

(C) $\dfrac{d}{s - 1}$

(D) $\dfrac{d(s - 1)}{s}$

Step 1. **Pick numbers for $s$ and $d$.** Choose numbers that are easy to work with, say $s = 3$ and $d = 15$.

Steps 2 and 3. **Plug these numbers into the question and find the value.** If 3 skirts cost \$15, each skirt costs \$5 and 2 would cost \$10.

Steps 4 and 5. **Plug $s = 3$ and $d = 15$ into the answer choices to see which gives you 10.**

Choice (A): $d - 1 = 15 - 1 = 14$. Discard.

Choice (B): $d - s = 15 - 3 = 12$. Discard.

Choice (C): $\dfrac{d}{s - 1} = \dfrac{15}{3 - 1} = \dfrac{15}{2} = 7.5$. Discard.

Choice (D): $\dfrac{d(s - 1)}{s} = \dfrac{15(3 - 1)}{3} = \dfrac{15 \times 2}{3} = \dfrac{30}{3} = 10$. This works.

Choice (E): $\dfrac{ds}{s - 1} = \dfrac{15 \times 3}{3 - 1} = \dfrac{45}{2} = 22.5$. Discard.

Only (D) works, so it must be correct. If more than one choice gives the desired result, pick new numbers and try them in those choices until just one matches.

**HINT:** *In questions with two variables, pick a different number for each. Avoid picking 0 and 1, as these often give several "possibly correct" answers.*

## BACKSOLVING

You can try working backward from the answer choices on some Math questions. Plug the choices back into the question until you find the one that works.

Backsolving works best:
- When the question is a complex word problem and the answer choices are numbers
- When the alternative is setting up multiple algebraic equations

Don't backsolve:
- If the answer choices include variables
- On algebra questions or word problems that have ugly answer choices (radicals, fractions, etcetera). Plugging them in takes too much time.

**KAPLAN**

**How Backsolving Works**

Two packages have a combined weight of 120 pounds. If the weight of one package is $\frac{1}{4}$ the weight of the other package, how many pounds does the lighter package weigh?

(A)   12
(B)   16
(C)   20
(D)   24
(E)   30

You're looking for the weight of the lighter package, so try plugging the answer choices back into the question stem. The choice that gives a total weight of 120 pounds, with one package $\frac{1}{4}$ the weight of the other, is the correct answer.

To save time, start with the middle-range number. Since answer choices are always listed in increasing or decreasing order, that means starting with choice (C). If (C) is too large, move to the smaller choices. If it's too small, move to the bigger ones.

Plugging in choice (C) gives you 80 pounds as the weight of the heavier package, for a total weight of 80 + 20, or 100 pounds. The total is too small, so the weight of the package must be greater than 20 pounds. Eliminate choices (A), (B), and (C).

Either (D) or (E) will be correct. Plugging in (D) gives you 96 pounds as the weight of the heavier package, for a total of 120 pounds. Choice (D) is correct.

# SAT Math
# Practice

# NUMBER OPERATIONS—PRACTICE SET 1

The ability to perform the standard arithmetic operations on all kinds of real numbers is fundamental for SAT Math. A few questions specifically test your adeptness at finding sums, differences, products, quotients, powers, and roots. Beyond those, however, the vast majority of SAT Math questions presume a solid grasp of arithmetic fundamentals.

The questions in this practice set are based primarily on the following skills (listed in the SAT Math in a Nutshell section near the back of this book):
1.   Integer/Noninteger
2.   Rational/Irrational Numbers
3.   Adding/Subtracting Signed Numbers
4.   Multiplying/Dividing Signed Numbers
5.   PEMDAS
18.   Reducing Fractions
19.   Adding/Subtracting Fractions
20.   Multiplying Fractions
21.   Dividing Fractions
22.   Converting a Mixed Number to an Improper Fraction
23.   Converting an Improper Fraction to a Mixed Number
24.   Reciprocal
25.   Comparing Fractions
26.   Converting Fractions to Decimals
27.   Converting Decimals to Fractions

You cannot expect to get a good SAT Math score without these basic skills.

## PRACTICE SET

### BASIC

1  Which of the following is less than $\frac{1}{6}$?

(A)   0.1667

(B)   $\frac{3}{18}$

(C)   0.167

(D)   0.1666

(E)   $\frac{8}{47}$

Ⓐ Ⓑ Ⓒ Ⓓ Ⓔ

2  Which of the following lists three fractions in ascending order?

(A)   $\frac{9}{26}, \frac{1}{4}, \frac{3}{10}$

(B)   $\frac{9}{26}, \frac{3}{10}, \frac{1}{4}$

(C)   $\frac{1}{4}, \frac{9}{26}, \frac{3}{10}$

(D)   $\frac{1}{4}, \frac{3}{10}, \frac{9}{26}$

(E)   $\frac{3}{10}, \frac{9}{26}, \frac{1}{4}$

Ⓐ Ⓑ Ⓒ Ⓓ Ⓔ

**3** Which of the following is not equal to $\dfrac{36}{45}$?

(A) $\dfrac{4}{5}$

(B) $\dfrac{12}{15}$

(C) $\dfrac{20}{25}$

(D) $\dfrac{24}{35}$

(E) $\dfrac{48}{60}$     Ⓐ Ⓑ Ⓒ Ⓓ Ⓔ

**4** Which of the following is equal to
25(27 + 29 + 31)?
(A)   25(27 + 29) + 31
(B)   25(27) + 29 + 31
(C)   25(27) + (29 + 31)(25)
(D)   25 + (27)(29)(31)
(E)   25(27 + 29) + 25(29 + 31)     Ⓐ Ⓑ Ⓒ Ⓓ Ⓔ

**5**  $1.04 \overline{)0.079}$ =

(A)   $10.4 \overline{)0.0079}$

(B)   $104 \overline{)0.79}$

(C)   $10.4 \overline{)0.79}$

(D)   $0.104 \overline{)0.79}$

(E)   $104 \overline{)0.0079}$     Ⓐ Ⓑ Ⓒ Ⓓ Ⓔ

**6**  $\dfrac{12}{\frac{1}{4}}$ =

## MEDIUM

**7**  $\dfrac{7}{5} \times \left( \dfrac{3}{7} - \dfrac{2}{5} \right) =$

(A)   $\dfrac{1}{165}$

(B)   $\dfrac{1}{35}$

(C)   $\dfrac{1}{25}$

(D)   $\dfrac{9}{15}$

(E)   1     Ⓐ Ⓑ Ⓒ Ⓓ Ⓔ

**8** Which of the following is closest in value to the decimal 0.40?

(A)   $\dfrac{1}{3}$

(B)   $\dfrac{4}{7}$

(C)   $\dfrac{3}{8}$

(D)   $\dfrac{5}{9}$

(E)   $\dfrac{1}{2}$     Ⓐ Ⓑ Ⓒ Ⓓ Ⓔ

Compare the quantity in Column A with the quantity in Column B. Select answer choice
(A)  if Column A is greater;
(B)  if Column B is greater;
(C)  if the columns are equal; or
(D)  if more information is needed to determine the relationship.
An (E) response will be treated as an omission.

| Column A | Column B |
| --- | --- |
| $a$, $b$, and $c$ are positive integers. | |
| **9**  $-c\,(a + b)$ | $b\,(a - c)$ |

Ⓐ Ⓑ Ⓒ Ⓓ Ⓔ

Column A      Column B

**10**   $\dfrac{1}{2}+\dfrac{3}{2\times 6+3^2}\times(17\times 2)$     $(17\times 2)\dfrac{3}{2\times(6+3^2)}+\dfrac{1}{2}$

Ⓐ Ⓑ Ⓒ Ⓓ Ⓔ

**11**   $\dfrac{6}{11}$ of 11               $\dfrac{11}{6}$ of 6

Ⓐ Ⓑ Ⓒ Ⓓ Ⓔ

**12**   $\dfrac{3}{5}\times\dfrac{5}{7}\times\dfrac{7}{9}\times\dfrac{9}{11}$     $\dfrac{3}{4}\times\dfrac{4}{5}\times\dfrac{5}{6}\times\dfrac{6}{11}$

Ⓐ Ⓑ Ⓒ Ⓓ Ⓔ

**13**   $[(12-11)-(10-9)]-[(12-11-10)-9]=$

$$\frac{5}{9}, \frac{5}{12}, \frac{23}{48}, \frac{11}{24}, \frac{3}{7}$$

**14** What is the positive difference between the largest and smallest of the fractions above?

## HARD

**15** For which of the following expressions would the value be greater if 160 were replaced by 120?

     I.   $1,000 - 160$

     II.   $\dfrac{160}{1+160}$

     III.   $\dfrac{1}{1-\dfrac{1}{160}}$

(A)   None
(B)   I only
(C)   III only
(D)   I and II
(E)   I and III       Ⓐ Ⓑ Ⓒ Ⓓ Ⓔ

**16** If $w$, $x$, $y$, and $z$ are all integers greater than 2, which of the following is greatest?
(A)   $x + yz + w$
(B)   $(x + y)z + w$
(C)   $x + y(z + w)$
(D)   $x + (yz + w)$
(E)   $(x + y)(z + w)$     Ⓐ Ⓑ Ⓒ Ⓓ Ⓔ

| SCORECARD | |
|---|---|
| Number of Questions Right: | |
| Number of Questions Wrong: | |
| Number of Questions Omitted: | |
| Number of Correct Guesses: | |
| Number of Wrong Guesses: | |
| Time Used: | |

## ANSWERS AND EXPLANATIONS

### BASIC

**1** **D**—We are asked which of the five values is less than $\frac{1}{6}$.

Choice (A): Since $\frac{1}{6} = 0.166\bar{6}$ (the bar indicates that the 6 repeats), $0.1667 > \frac{1}{6}$. No good.

Choice (B): $\frac{3}{18} = \frac{1 \times 3}{6 \times 3} = \frac{1}{6}$. No good.

Choice (C): $0.167 > 0.16\bar{6}$. No good.

Choice (D): $0.1666$ is less than $0.1666\bar{6}$. That means it is less than $\frac{1}{6}$, so this is the correct answer.

Choice (E): $\frac{1}{6} = \frac{8}{48}$ and $\frac{8}{47} > \frac{8}{48}$; therefore, $\frac{8}{47} > \frac{1}{6}$. No good.

**2** **D**—The same three fractions appear in each answer choice, and we need to arrange these in ascending order.

Convert fractions to decimals, using your calculator:

$\frac{1}{4} = 0.25$.

$\frac{3}{10} = 0.3$. This is a little less than $\frac{1}{3}$, but more than $\frac{1}{4}$.

$\frac{9}{26} = 0.346$. This is greater than $\frac{3}{10}$. The correct ascending order is $\frac{1}{4}, \frac{3}{10}, \frac{9}{26}$.

**3** **D**—Each fraction can be reduced to $\frac{4}{5}$ except (D), which cannot be simplified.

**4** **C**—Use the distributive law: $25(27 + 29 + 31) = 25(27) + 25(29) + 25(31) = 25(27) + (29 + 31)25$.

**5** **C**—To get the same quotient in a division problem, the decimal point must be moved the same number of places in the same direction for both numbers. This is the same as multiplying or dividing both numbers by the same power of 10, which won't change the number of times one goes into the other. Only choice (C) alters both decimal points the same way, multiplying each number by a factor of 10.

**6** **48**—Turn this division problem into multiplication by applying the "invert and multiply" rule:

$$12 \div \frac{1}{4} = 12 \times \frac{4}{1} = 48$$

### MEDIUM

**7** **C**—We could perform the subtraction within the parentheses and then multiply, but it's simpler to use the distributive law.

$$\frac{7}{5} \times \left( \frac{3}{7} - \frac{2}{5} \right) = \frac{7}{5} \times \frac{3}{7} - \frac{7}{5} \times \frac{2}{5}$$
$$= \frac{3}{5} - \frac{14}{25}$$
$$= \frac{3}{5} \times \frac{5}{5} - \frac{14}{25}$$
$$= \frac{15}{25} - \frac{14}{25} = \frac{1}{25}$$

**8** **C**—You can use your calculator to find the decimal equivalent of each answer choice, and then decide which is closest. Or, if you feel comfortable with the relative sizes of the choices, find the two choices that are closest to 0.40—one larger, one smaller, and then find which of those is closer.

Since $0.4 < \frac{1}{2}$, we can eliminate both $\frac{5}{9}$ and $\frac{4}{7}$ (since each is greater than $\frac{1}{2}$, both must be farther from 0.4 than $\frac{1}{2}$).

On the other hand, $\frac{3}{8} < 0.4$ the decimal equivalent of $\frac{3}{8}$ is 0.375), and since $\frac{1}{3} = \frac{3}{9} < \frac{3}{8}$, we can eliminate $\frac{1}{3}$.

So it comes down to $\frac{3}{8}$ or $\frac{1}{2}$. Since $\frac{3}{8} = 0.375$, it is 0.025 away from 0.4, which is much closer than $\frac{1}{2}$ (or 0.5, which is 0.1 away). So $\frac{3}{8}$ is the closest.

**9** **B**—Do the same thing to both columns, multiplying through the expression in each. In Column A you get $-ac - bc$, and in Column B, $ab - bc$. Since $-bc$ appears in both columns you can subtract it from each, and compare $-ac$ in Column A to $ab$ in Column B. Factoring out an $a$ from each leaves $-c$ in Column A and $b$ in Column B. Since there is a negative quantity in Column A and a positive quantity in Column B, Column B must be larger.

**10** **A**—Compare the columns piece by piece. Since $\frac{1}{2}$ is being added to both columns, subtract $\frac{1}{2}$ from both. Since the quantity $(17 \times 2)$ is being multiplied on both sides, divide both sides by $(17 \times 2)$. This leaves $\frac{3}{2 \times 6 + 3^2}$ in Column A and $\frac{3}{2 \times (6 + 3^2)}$ in Column B. If two fractions have the same numerator, the one with the smaller denominator is larger. So compare $2 \times 6 + 3^2$ to $2 \times (6 + 3^2)$. Be careful to follow the order of operations. (PEMDAS: **P**arentheses, then **E**xponents, then **M**ultiplication and **D**ivision, then **A**ddition and **S**ubtraction.) $2 \times 6 + 3^2 = 12 + 9 = 21$. $2 \times (6 + 3^2) = 2 \times (6 + 9) = 2 \times 15 = 30$. So Column

A is $\frac{3}{21}$ and Column B is $\frac{3}{30}$. Column A is larger and the answer is choice (A).

**11** **B**—In Column A: $\frac{6}{11}$ of $11 = \frac{6}{11} \times 11 = \frac{(6 \times 11)}{11} = 6$

In Column B: $\frac{11}{6}$ of $6 = \frac{11}{6} \times 6 = \frac{(11 \times 6)}{6} = 11$

**12** **C**—The hard way to do this one is to multiply all the fractions together. The easy way is to realize that the product of four fractions is equivalent to all four numerators multiplied together over all four denominators multiplied together. Thinking of the problem in this way, you can cancel factors of 5, 7, and 9 from both the numerator and the denominator in Column A, leaving a product of $\frac{3}{11}$. Likewise, in Column B you can cancel factors of 4, 5, and 6 from the numerator and the denominator, leaving the same product, $\frac{3}{11}$.

**13** **18**—Follow PEMDAS:

$[(12 - 11) - (10 - 9)] - [(12 - 11 - 10) - 9]$
$= [1 - 1] - [- 9 - 9]$
$= 0 - (- 18)$
$= 18$

**14** **.138 or .139 or 5/36**—With a calculator, convert each fraction to its decimal equivalent. Subtract the smallest from the largest to find the answer: 0.1388. Or you could realize that all the fractions are less than $\frac{1}{2}$ except for $\frac{5}{9}$. So $\frac{5}{9}$ is the largest. The $\frac{5}{12}$ is the fraction farthest away from $\frac{1}{2}$, so it is the smallest.

So $\frac{5}{9} - \frac{5}{12} = \frac{4 \times 5}{4 \times 9} - \frac{3 \times 5}{3 \times 12} = \frac{20 - 15}{36} = \frac{5}{36}$.

## HARD

**15** **E**—In statement I, if we were to subtract a smaller number from 1,000, our result would be larger. Since substituting 120 for 160 in this expression would produce a greater result, we can eliminate choices (A) and (C), which do not include statement I.

Statement II is equivalent to $\frac{160}{161}$. If we were to replace each 160 with 120, our result would be $\frac{120}{1+120}$ which is $\frac{120}{121}$. Which is greater? You can easily find out using your calculator, but if you prefer, you can think of each fraction's distance from 1. Both fractions are a tiny bit less than 1. Imagine a number line; $\frac{160}{161}$ is $\frac{1}{161}$ away from 1, while $\frac{120}{121}$ is $\frac{1}{121}$ away from 1. Since $\frac{1}{161}$ is less than $\frac{1}{121}$, that means $\frac{160}{161}$ must be *closer* to 1 than $\frac{120}{121}$. And that means $\frac{160}{161}$ is a little larger than $\frac{120}{121}$. So if we did replace 160 with 120, we would get a smaller result. Eliminate choice (D).

In statement III we're dividing 1 by a fraction, which is the same as multiplying 1 by the reciprocal of the fraction. In order to get a *larger* reciprocal, we need to start with a *smaller* fraction. Which is smaller, $1 - \frac{1}{160}$ or $1 - \frac{1}{120}$? $1 - \frac{1}{120}$ is smaller since it is farther to the left from 1 on the number line. By replacing 160 with 120 we get a smaller fraction in the denominator of our expression and, therefore, a *larger* reciprocal. That gives the expression a larger

value. So III is part of the correct answer. If this is difficult to see, we can actually do the math:

$$\frac{1}{1 - \frac{1}{160}} = \frac{1}{\frac{159}{160}} = 1 \times \frac{160}{159} = 1\frac{1}{159}$$

$$\frac{1}{1 - \frac{1}{120}} = \frac{1}{\frac{119}{120}} = 1 \times \frac{120}{119} = 1\frac{1}{119}$$

$$1\frac{1}{119} > 1\frac{1}{159}$$

Statements I and III are larger when 160 is replaced with 120, so the answer is choice (E).

**16** **E**—It's possible to solve this one by picking numbers for the variables, but it's not necessary. Since all the variables are greater than 2, multiplying any two of them together will produce a greater value than either variable alone would have. If you multiply out each answer choice and eliminate the parentheses, then you get:

(A) $x + yz + w$
(B) $xz + yz + w$
(C) $x + yz + yw$
(D) $x + yz + w$
(E) $xz + xw + yz + yw$

A piece-by-piece comparison shows that choice (E) must have the greatest value.

# NUMBER PROPERTIES—PRACTICE SET 2

Some SAT Math questions test not so much your ability to perform an operation or solve a problem as your understanding of the special characteristics of the various classes of numbers: integers and nonintegers; positives and negatives; odds and evens; prime numbers; factors, multiples, and remainders.

Questions in this number properties category test the following skills (see the SAT Math in a Nutshell section near the back of this book).
7.   Factor/Multiple
8.   Prime Factorization
9.   Relative Primes
10.   Common Multiple
11.   Least Common Multiple (LCM)
12.   Greatest Common Factor (GCF)
13.   Even/Odd
14.   Multiples of 2 and 4
15.   Multiples of 3 and 9
16.   Multiples of 5 and 10
17.   Remainders
28.   Repeating Decimal

## PRACTICE SET

### BASIC

**1** How many odd integers are between $\frac{10}{3}$ and $\frac{62}{3}$?
(A)   Nineteen
(B)   Eighteen
(C)   Ten
(D)   Nine
(E)   Eight                    Ⓐ Ⓑ Ⓒ Ⓓ Ⓔ

**2** If the sum of three different prime numbers is an even number, what is the smallest of the three?
(A)   2
(B)   3
(C)   5
(D)   7
(E)   It cannot be determined from the information given.          Ⓐ Ⓑ Ⓒ Ⓓ Ⓔ

**3** If the product of 3 consecutive odd integers is 15, what is the smallest of the three integers?

| Column A | Column B |
|----------|----------|

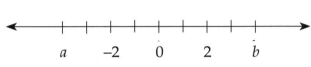

**4**   $ab$          $a + b$

Ⓐ Ⓑ Ⓒ Ⓓ Ⓔ

---

$0 < x < 1$

**5**   $x^2$          $\dfrac{1}{\frac{1}{x}}$

Ⓐ Ⓑ Ⓒ Ⓓ Ⓔ

**6** What is the greatest integer that will divide evenly into both 36 and 54?

## MEDIUM

**7** If the integer $P$ leaves a remainder of 4 when divided by 9, all of the following must be true EXCEPT

(A) The number that is 4 less than $P$ is a multiple of 9.

(B) The number that is 5 more than $P$ is a multiple of 9.

(C) The number that is 2 more than $P$ is a multiple of 3.

(D) When divided by 3, $P$ will leave a remainder of 1.

(E) When divided by 2, $P$ will leave a remainder of 1.

Ⓐ Ⓑ Ⓒ Ⓓ Ⓔ

**8** How many three-digit integers can be divided by 2 to produce a new integer with the same tens' digit and units' digit as the original integer?

(A) None

(B) One

(C) Two

(D) Three

(E) Four

Ⓐ Ⓑ Ⓒ Ⓓ Ⓔ

**9** On a number line, point $B$ is at a distance of 5 from point $C$, and point $D$ is at a distance of 7 from point $C$. What is the distance from point $B$ to point $D$ ?

(A) 2

(B) 5

(C) 7

(D) 12

(E) It cannot be determined from the information given.

Ⓐ Ⓑ Ⓒ Ⓓ Ⓔ

**10** If $a$ and $b$ are integers and the sum of $ab$ and $b$ is odd, which of the following could be true?

    I. $a$ and $b$ are both odd.

    II. $a$ is even and $b$ is odd.

    III. $a$ is odd and $b$ is even.

(A) I only

(B) II only

(C) III only

(D) I and II

(E) I and III

Ⓐ Ⓑ Ⓒ Ⓓ Ⓔ

| Column A | Column B |
|----------|----------|
| $a > b > 0 > c > d$ | |

**11**    $(ab)(cd)$          $(ac)(bd)$

Ⓐ Ⓑ Ⓒ Ⓓ Ⓔ

When $a$ is divided by 3 the remainder is 2 and $a$ is a positive integer greater than 6.

**12** The remainder when       2
     $a$ is divided by 6

Ⓐ Ⓑ Ⓒ Ⓓ Ⓔ

**13** In a certain shop, each customer takes a number to be served. If the first customer of the day took number 14, and the last customer took number 314, how many customers were there that day?

**14** What is the smallest integer greater than 1 that leaves a remainder of 1 when divided by any of the integers 6, 8, and 10?

**HARD**

15 If both the product and sum of four integers are even, which of the following could be the number of even integers in the group?
    I. 0
    II. 2
    III. 4
(A) I only
(B) II only
(C) III only
(D) II and III only
(E) I, II, and III    Ⓐ Ⓑ Ⓒ Ⓓ Ⓔ

16 How many positive integers less than 60 are equal to the product of a positive multiple of 5 and an even number?
(A) Four
(B) Five
(C) Nine
(D) Ten
(E) Eleven    Ⓐ Ⓑ Ⓒ Ⓓ Ⓔ

17 Which of the following is the greatest integer less than 630,000 that can be written using all of the digits from 1 to 6?
(A) 629,999
(B) 654,321
(C) 624,531
(D) 621,543
(E) 625,431    Ⓐ Ⓑ Ⓒ Ⓓ Ⓔ

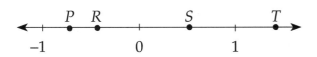

18 Points $P$, $R$, $S$, and $T$ lie on a number line, as illustrated above. Which of the following statements could be true?
(A) $R \times S = P$
(B) $P \times R = T$
(C) $R \times S = T$
(D) $R \times T = P$
(E) $P \times T = S$    Ⓐ Ⓑ Ⓒ Ⓓ Ⓔ

| Column A | Column B |
|---|---|

19 The number of distinct prime factors of $15^2$ / The number of distinct prime factors of $64^3$

Ⓐ Ⓑ Ⓒ Ⓓ Ⓔ

$$rstu < 0$$
$$rst > 0$$

20    $rs$    $tu$

Ⓐ Ⓑ Ⓒ Ⓓ Ⓔ

21 In the repeating decimal 0.097531097531..., what is the 44th digit to the right of the decimal point?

22 A wire is cut into three equal parts. The resulting segments are then cut into 4, 6, and 8 equal parts, respectively. If each of the resulting segments has an integer length, what is the minimum length of the wire?

| SCORECARD | |
|---|---|
| Number of Questions Right: | |
| Number of Questions Wrong: | |
| Number of Questions Omitted: | |
| Number of Correct Guesses: | |
| Number of Wrong Guesses: | |
| Time Used: | |

## ANSWERS AND EXPLANATIONS

### BASIC

**1** **E**—We're asked for the number of odd integers between $\frac{10}{3}$ and $\frac{62}{3}$, so let's be more clear about this range. $\frac{10}{3}$ is the same as $3\frac{1}{3}$, and $\frac{62}{3}$ is the same as $20\frac{2}{3}$. We count the odd integers between $3\frac{1}{3}$ and $20\frac{2}{3}$. We can't include 3 since 3 is less than $3\frac{1}{3}$. Similarly, we can't include 21 since it's larger than $20\frac{2}{3}$. This leaves the odd integers of 5, 7, 9, 11, 13, 15, 17, and 19. That's a total of 8.

**2** **A**—If the sum of three numbers is even, either all three are even or only one of the three is even. The sum of three odd numbers can *never* be even, nor can the sum of one odd and two evens. Remember, we're dealing with three different *prime* numbers. There's only one even prime: 2; all the rest are odd. Therefore, only one of our group can be even, and that must be 2. Since 2 is the smallest prime, it must also be the smallest of the three.

**3** **1**—Trial and error is the best way to find the answer here. Consecutive odd integers include –3, –1, 1, 3, 5, 7, 9, 11..., and so on. 15 is obviously the product of 5 and 3, so we can say that 15 is the product of the three consecutive odd integers 1, 3, and 5, the smallest of which is 1.

**4** **B**—It's not hard to tell that $a$ equals –4 and $b$ equals positive 4. Since a negative times a positive gives a negative result, the product $ab$ in Column A is –16. But adding 4 and –4 gives you 0 in Column B, which is greater than –16.

**5** **B**—Try making the columns look more alike by getting rid of the fraction in Column B. Dividing by a fraction is the same as multiplying by its reciprocal, so $\dfrac{1}{\left(\frac{1}{x}\right)}$ is the same as $1 \times \dfrac{x}{1}$ or $x$.

Since $x$ is a positive fraction less than 1, its square is less than the original number. So $x^2$ in Column A is less than $x$ in Column B.

**6** **18**—Check the factors of 36, in descending order, to see which is also a factor of 54. 36 is the largest factor of 36, but it doesn't divide into 54. The next largest factor is 18, and this does divide into 54, so it is also a factor of 54.

### MEDIUM

**7** **E**—We need to find the one choice that isn't *always* true. To find it, let's test each choice. Choice (A) is always true: Since $P \div 9$ has a remainder of 4, $P$ is 4 greater than some multiple of 9, so the number 4 less than $P$ is a multiple of 9. And if $P - 4$ is a multiple of 9, then the next multiple of 9 would be $(P - 4) + 9$, or $P + 5$; thus choice (B) is also true. With choice (C), we know that since $P - 4$ is a multiple of 9, it is also a multiple of 3. By adding 3s, we know that $(P - 4) + 3$, or $P - 1$, and $(P - 4) + 3 + 3$, or $P + 2$, are also multiples of 3. Choice (C) must be true. And since $P - 1$ is a multiple of 3, when $P$ is divided by 3, it will have a remainder of 1, and choice (D) is always true.

This leaves only choice (E). In simpler terms, choice (E) states that $P$ is always odd. Since multiples of 9 are alternately odd and even (9, 18, 27, 36...), $P - 4$ could be either even or odd, so $P$ also could be either even or odd. Choice (E) is not always true, so it is the correct answer choice.

If you have trouble thinking this way, try picking a number for $P$ that fits the description ("a remainder of 4 when divided by 9..."). You could pick 13, but if you try 13 in each answer choice, you'll find that all five seem to be true. You'll have to try a different number for $P$. How about 22? It fits the description, and it disproves the statement in choice (E). Picking numbers is not always the fastest method—sometimes you'll have to try many numbers before you find what you need—but it's a good tactic if you don't know what else to do.

**8** E—Only one digit can be divided by 2 to produce the same digit: 0. If the last two digits in a three-digit number are 0, it's possible to divide by 2 and still have the same last two digits. So the three-digit numbers worth considering are the hundreds: 100, 200, 300, 400, and so on. With a little thought you'll see that some of these don't work either. If the hundreds' digit is an odd number, dividing by 2 leaves a 5 in the tens' place. For example, 500 divided by 2 is 250. Therefore the only numbers that will work are 200, 400, 600, and 800.

**9** E—Do not assume that the points lie on the line in alphabetical order, since this is not stated. If $B$ and $D$ are on opposite sides of $C$, then the distance between them is 12. But they could be on the same side, in which case the distance between them would be 2. Since there's no way to tell which is the case, the correct answer is choice (E).

**10** B—Pick numbers. Statement I says $a$ and $b$ are both odd. Let $a = 1$ and $b = 3$. Then $ab + b = (1)(3) + 3 = 6$. Since the sum is even, statement I can't be correct. Statement II says $a$ is even and $b$ is odd. Let $a = 2$, and $b = 3$. Then $ab + b = (2)(3) + 3$, or 9. Since the sum is odd, this statement is true. Statement III says $a$ is odd and $b$ is even. Let $a = 3$ and $b = 2$. Then $ab + b = (3)(2) + 2$, or 8, which is not odd. So only statement II works, and choice (B) is indeed correct.

**11** C—Compare the columns piece by piece. Although the variables are grouped differently in each column, both contain the product of $a$, $b$, $c$, and $d$. So, by the commutative law of multiplication, $abcd = acbd$ and the columns are equal.

**12** D—Column A contains the remainder when $a$ is divided by 6, so test out some values of $a$. It could equal 8, since it is greater than 6 and leaves a remainder of 2 when divided by 3. When 8 is divided by 6, the remainder is 2, which equals the quantity in Column B. But this isn't always the case; 11 also meets the conditions to be a possible value of $a$. When 11 is divided by 6 the remainder is 5, which would make Column A greater than Column B. Since more than one relationship between the columns is possible, the correct answer is choice (D).

**13** 301—It's tempting to simply subtract the starting number from the final number, but that gives you the difference between the numbers. To

find the total number of customers you need to include the first customer as well, the one who took number 14. For instance, if the first number taken was 2 and the last number taken was 4, three people were served (number 2, number 3, and number 4) not $4 - 2$, or 2. So if the first customer had number 14 and the last 314 there were $314 - 14 + 1 = 301$ customers.

**14** 121—We are asked for the smallest integer greater than 1 that leaves a remainder of 1 when divided by 6, 8, and 10. If we find the smallest integer that is a common multiple of these three numbers, we can add 1 to that number to get our answer. To find the least common multiple of 6, 8, and 10, we find the prime factors of each, and eliminate the shared factors.

$$6 = 2 \times 3$$
$$8 = 2 \times 2 \times 2$$
$$10 = 2 \times 5$$

We drop one factor of 2 from 10 and from 6, since they are already present in the factors of 8.

$$2 \times 2 \times 2 \times 3 \times 5 = 120; \quad 120 + 1 = 121$$

## HARD

**15** D—Since these four integers have an even product, at least one of them must be even, so statement I, 0, is impossible. Is it possible for exactly 2 of the 4 to be even? If there are 2 odds and 2 evens, the sum is even, since odd + odd = even and even + even = even. Also, if there's only 1 even among the integers, the product is even, so statement II *is* possible. Similarly, statement III gives an even product and even sum, so our answer is II and III only.

**16** B—Here we want to determine how many numbers between 0 and 60 are even multiples of 5. All even multiples of 5 must be multiples of 10. So the multiples of 10 between 0 and 60 are 10, 20, 30, 40, and 50. That's 5 altogether.

**17** E—To arrange the digits into the largest number, you want to put the biggest digits in the highest-value places. For the number to be less than 630,000, it must start with 62. The next largest digit, 5, must go in the thousands' place, and 4 in the hundreds' place. Three goes in the tens' place, and since 2 is already used, 1 is left for the ones' place. This gives us 625,431, answer choice (E).

**18** **D**—Approximate the value of each point and see what happens. $P$ could be around $-\frac{3}{4}$; $R$ might be $-\frac{1}{2}$; $S$ looks like positive $\frac{1}{2}$; and $T$ is about $1\frac{1}{2}$.

Now you can try each answer choice.

(A): $R \times S = P$ becomes $\left(-\frac{1}{2}\right)\left(\frac{1}{2}\right)=\left(-\frac{3}{4}\right)$. Not true.

(B): $P \times R = T$ becomes $\left(-\frac{3}{4}\right)\left(-\frac{1}{2}\right)=1\frac{1}{2}$. Not true.

(C): $R \times S = T$ becomes $\left(-\frac{1}{2}\right)\left(\frac{1}{2}\right)=1\frac{1}{2}$. Not true.

(D): $R \times T = P$ becomes $\left(-\frac{1}{2}\right)\left(1\frac{1}{2}\right)=-\frac{3}{4}$. True.

(E): $P \times T = S$ becomes $\left(-\frac{3}{4}\right)\left(1\frac{1}{2}\right)=\frac{1}{2}$. Not true.

Choice (D) is correct.

**19** **A**—Since the columns ask for the number of distinct prime factors, all you need to do is find the prime factors of the base of the exponential expressions; raising the number to a power will only repeat the same set of prime factors. In Column A, the prime factorization of 15 is $3 \times 5$, while the prime factorization of $15^2$ or 225 is $3 \times 3 \times 5 \times 5$ (that is, the prime factors of 15 times the prime factors of 15). There are still only two distinct prime factors: 3 and 5. Bearing this in mind as you approach Column B, simply find the prime factorization of 64, which is $2 \times 2 \times 2 \times 2 \times 2 \times 2$. So there is only one distinct prime factor in Column B, while there are two in Column A, and answer choice (A) is correct.

**20** **D**—If $rstu$ is negative but $rst$ is positive, $u$ must be negative. But this doesn't mean that $r$, $s$, and $t$ must all be positive. They could be, but $rst$ would still be positive even if two of them were negative, since a negative times a negative produces a positive. If they are all positive, the product of $r$ and $s$ in Column A would yield a positive result, while the positive $t$ multiplied by the negative $u$ in Column B would have a negative product, making

Column A larger than Column B. But if two of the variables are negative, say $s$ and $t$, in Column A there would be a positive $r$ times a negative $s$ resulting in a negative product, while in Column B a negative $t$ times a negative $u$ would result in a positive, making Column B greater than Column A. Since more than one possibility exists, the correct answer is choice (D), more information is needed to determine the relationship.

**21** **9**—First we have to identify the pattern. It consists of the same 6 numerals, 0, 9, 7, 5, 3, and 1, in that order, repeating infinitely. Our job is to identify the 44th digit to the right of the decimal point. Since the pattern of 6 numerals will continually repeat, every 6th digit of the digits to the right of the decimal point will be the same, namely the numeral 1. So 1 will be the 6th, 12th, 18th, and 24th (and so on) digit. Since 44 is just 2 more than 42, which is a multiple of 6, the 44th digit will be the digit 2 places to the right of 1. That's 9.

**22** **72**—Each third of the wire is cut into 4, 6, and 8 parts respectively, and all the resulting segments have integer lengths. This means that each third of the wire has a length that is evenly divisible by 4, 6, and 8. The smallest positive integer divisible by 4, 6, and 8 is 24, so each third of the wire has a minimum length of 24. So the minimum length of the whole wire is three times this, or 72.

# Averages—Practice Set 3

Averages questions appear on virtually every SAT. Mastery of the following skills will guarantee you some points. The questions in this set test the following skills (from the SAT Math in a Nutshell section near the back of this book).

39.     Average Formula
40.     Average of Evenly Spaced Numbers
41.     Using the Average to Find the Sum
42.     Finding the Missing Number
43.     Median
44.     Mode

## PRACTICE SET

### BASIC

**1** If the average (arithmetic mean) of $a$ and $-5$ is 10, then $a =$
(A)   25
(B)   15
(C)    5
(D)   $-5$
(E)   $-15$     Ⓐ Ⓑ Ⓒ Ⓓ Ⓔ

**2** The average (arithmetic mean) of 6 consecutive integers is $18\frac{1}{2}$. What is the average of the first 5 of these integers?

(A)   $12\frac{1}{2}$
(B)   15
(C)   16
(D)   $17\frac{1}{2}$
(E)   18     Ⓐ Ⓑ Ⓒ Ⓓ Ⓔ

| NAME | WEIGHT IN POUNDS |
|---|---|
| Chris | 150 |
| Anne | 153 |
| Malcolm | 154 |
| Paul | 157 |
| Sam | 151 |

**3** What is the average (arithmetic mean) weight of the five people whose weights are listed in the table above?

(A)   152
(B)   153
(C)   $153\frac{1}{2}$
(D)   154
(E)   155     Ⓐ Ⓑ Ⓒ Ⓓ Ⓔ

**4** A certain store stocks five different brands of ice cream, and sells a pint of each for $2.75, $3.25, $2.50, $3.25, and $3.00, respectively. What is the positive difference between the mode price and the median price?
(A)  $0.05
(B)  $0.25
(C)  $0.30
(D)  $0.50
(E)  $0.75          Ⓐ Ⓑ Ⓒ Ⓓ Ⓔ

---

| Column A | Column B |
|---|---|

Cathy plans the following study schedule:

Monday, Wednesday, and Friday—3 hours daily

Tuesday and Thursday—2 hours daily

Saturday and Sunday—4 hours daily

**5** The average (arithmetic mean) of the number of hours Cathy plans to study each day | The median of the number of hours Cathy plans to study each day

Ⓐ Ⓑ Ⓒ Ⓓ Ⓔ

---

The average (arithmetic mean) of $x$ and $y$ is 14.

**6**   $x$                $y$

Ⓐ Ⓑ Ⓒ Ⓓ Ⓔ

---

Herman's test scores in a certain class were 79, 84, 85, 90, and 92.

**7** The average (arithmetic mean) of Herman's test scores | The median of Herman's test scores

Ⓐ Ⓑ Ⓒ Ⓓ Ⓔ

**8** A violinist practices 1 hour a day from Monday through Friday. How many hours must she practice on Saturday in order to average 2 hours a day for the 6-day period?

## MEDIUM

**9** The average (arithmetic mean) of 6 numbers is 6. If 3 is subtracted from each of 4 of the numbers, what is the new average?
(A)  $1\frac{1}{2}$
(B)  2
(C)  3
(D)  4
(E)  $4\frac{1}{2}$          Ⓐ Ⓑ Ⓒ Ⓓ Ⓔ

**10** What is the average (arithmetic mean) of $n$, $n + 1$, $n + 2$, and $n + 3$?

(A)  $n + 1$

(B)  $n + 1\frac{1}{2}$

(C)  $n + 2$

(D)  $n + 2\frac{1}{2}$

(E)  $n + 6$          Ⓐ Ⓑ Ⓒ Ⓓ Ⓔ

**11** The average (arithmetic mean) of two numbers is $3n - 4$. If one of the numbers is $n$, then the other number is
(A)  $2n - 4$
(B)  $3n - 4$
(C)  $5n - 8$
(D)  $5n + 8$
(E)  $6n - 8$          Ⓐ Ⓑ Ⓒ Ⓓ Ⓔ

**12** If the average (arithmetic mean) of $x + 2$, $x + 4$, and $x + 6$ is 0, then $x =$
(A)  −4
(B)  −3
(C)  −2
(D)  −1
(E)   0          Ⓐ Ⓑ Ⓒ Ⓓ Ⓔ

13  In a certain class there are 12 boys and 18 girls. If the class average for an algebra exam is 90 and the boys' average score is 87, what is the girls' average score?
(A)  88.5
(B)  91
(C)  92
(D)  93
(E)  94.5    Ⓐ Ⓑ Ⓒ Ⓓ Ⓔ

| Column A | Column B |
|---|---|

The average (arithmetic mean) of $r$, $s$, and 12 is 18.

14  The average (arithmetic mean) of $r$ and $s$     21

Ⓐ Ⓑ Ⓒ Ⓓ Ⓔ

15  The average (arithmetic mean) of 100, 101, and 103     The median of 100, 101, and 103

Ⓐ Ⓑ Ⓒ Ⓓ Ⓔ

16  The average (arithmetic mean) of 12, 15, and 21     The average (arithmetic mean) of 12, 15, 21, and 26

Ⓐ Ⓑ Ⓒ Ⓓ Ⓔ

17  Jerry's average (arithmetic mean) score on the first three of four tests is 85. If Jerry wants to raise his average by 2 points, what score must he earn on the fourth test?

18  In a certain course, Lily received an average (arithmetic mean) score of 82 for her first 2 tests, 76 for her third test, and 92 for her fourth test. What grade must she receive on her next test if she wants an average (arithmetic mean) of 86 for all 5 tests?

## HARD

19  15 movie theaters average 600 customers per theater per day. If 6 of the theaters close down but the total theater attendance stays the same, what is the average daily attendance per theater among the remaining theaters?
(A)  500
(B)  750
(C)  1,000
(D)  1,200
(E)  1,500    Ⓐ Ⓑ Ⓒ Ⓓ Ⓔ

20  The average (arithmetic mean) of 6 positive numbers is 5. If the average of the least and greatest of these numbers is 7, what is the average of the other 4 numbers?
(A)  3
(B)  4
(C)  5
(D)  6
(E)  7    Ⓐ Ⓑ Ⓒ Ⓓ Ⓔ

21  If the average of $27 - x$, $x - 8$, and $3x + 11$ is $y$, what is the average of $2y$ and $\dfrac{2y}{3}$ ?

(A)  $4x + 40$

(B)  $x + 10$

(C)  $\dfrac{8x + 80}{3}$

(D)  $\dfrac{4x + 40}{3}$

(E)  $\dfrac{2x + 20}{3}$    Ⓐ Ⓑ Ⓒ Ⓓ Ⓔ

Column A          Column B

Carol exercises daily, alternating every other day between 30-minute and 60-minute workouts.

22  The mode                The average
    of Carol's             (arithmetic mean)
    daily workout          of Carol's daily
    times for 1            workout times
    week                   for 1 week

Ⓐ Ⓑ Ⓒ Ⓓ Ⓔ

23  George drives the first 30 miles of a trip at a constant rate of 40 miles per hour. If he drives the remaining 75 miles of the trip at a constant rate of 50 miles per hour, what is his average speed for the entire trip?

24  If the average (arithmetic mean) of 18 consecutive odd integers is 534, what is the least of these integers?

25  If the average (arithmetic mean) of $a$, $b$, and 7 is 13, what is the average of $a + 3$, $b - 5$, and 6?

| SCORECARD | |
|---|---|
| Number of Questions Right: | |
| Number of Questions Wrong: | |
| Number of Questions Omitted: | |
| Number of Correct Guesses: | |
| Number of Wrong Guesses: | |
| Time Used: | |

## ANSWERS AND EXPLANATIONS

### BASIC

**1** **A**—We can plug everything we are given into the standard formula for an average of two numbers and then solve for $a$. Since we know the average of –5 and $a$ is 10:

$$\frac{\text{Sum of terms}}{\text{Number of terms}} = \text{Average of terms}$$
$$\frac{-5+a}{2} = 10$$
$$-5+a = 20$$
$$a = 20+5$$
$$a = 25$$

A much faster method is to balance the numbers: Since –5 is 15 less than the average, 10, $a$ must be 15 *more* than the average, or 10 + 15 = 25.

**2** **E**—The average of evenly spaced numbers is the middle number. The average of 6 such numbers lies halfway between the third and fourth numbers. Since $18\frac{1}{2}$ is the average, the third number must be 18 and the fourth number 19. The six numbers are:

16, 17, 18, 19, 20, 21.

Since the first 5 numbers are also evenly spaced, their average is be the middle (third) number, 18.

**3** **B**—To find the average, add the weights and divide by the number of people.

$$\text{Average} = \frac{150+153+154+157+151}{5} = \frac{765}{5} = 153.$$

**4** **B**—The mode of a group of terms is the value that occurs most frequently. The only price that occurs more than once is $3.25, so it is the mode price. The median is the middle term in a group arranged in numerical order. If the prices are listed in either ascending or descending order, the third and middle term is $3.00. So the difference between the mode and median prices is $3.25—$3.00 = $0.25.

**5** **C**—Find Cathy's average (arithmetic mean) study time with the formula:

$$\text{average} = \frac{\text{sum of the terms}}{\text{number of terms}}$$

During this 7-day period she studies for 3 hours on 3 days, 2 hours on 2 days, and 4 hours on 2 days:

$$\text{average} = \frac{3(3)+2(2)+2(4)}{7}$$
$$= \frac{9+4+8}{7}$$
$$= \frac{21}{7}$$
$$= 3 \text{ hours}$$

The median is the middle value in a consecutively ordered group. Arranging the terms in order—2, 2, 3, 3, 3, 4, 4—the median is also 3, so Columns A and B are equal.

**6** **D**—The average = $\frac{\text{sum of the terms}}{\text{number of terms}}$. So if the average of $x$ and $y$ is 14, then $\frac{x+y}{2} = 14$ and $x + y =$ 28. However, you still know nothing about $x$ and $y$ individually. More than one relationship between the columns is possible, so choice (D) is correct.

**7** **A**—Be careful not to confuse the mean with the median; they are not necessarily equal.

To find the average of Herman's test scores, use the

average formula: $\text{average} = \frac{\text{sum of the terms}}{\text{number of the terms}}$.

So the average of his test scores is $\frac{79+84+85+90+92}{5}$,

or $\frac{430}{5}$, which is 86.

The median is the middle term in a list of numerically ordered terms. Therefore, Herman's median test score is 85. So Column A is greater than Column B, and choice (A) is correct.

**8** 7—To average 2 hours a day over 6 days, the violinist must practice 2 × 6, or 12 hours. From Monday through Friday, the violinist practices 5 hours, 1 hour each day. To total 12 hours, she must practice 12 – 5, or 7, hours on Saturday.

## MEDIUM

**9** D—If 6 numbers have an average of 6, their sum is 6 × 6, or 36. To subtract 3 from 4 of the numbers, we subtract 4 × 3, or 12, from the sum. The new sum is 36 – 12, or 24; the new average is $\frac{24}{6}$, or 4.

**10** B—Don't let the $n$s bother you; the arithmetic performed is the same.

*Method I:*

Add the terms and divide by the number of terms. Since each term contains $n$, we can ignore the $n$ and add it back at the end. Without the $n$s, we get $\frac{0+1+2+3}{4} = \frac{6}{4} = 1\frac{1}{2}$.

The average is $n + 1\frac{1}{2}$.

*Method II:*

These are just evenly spaced numbers (regardless of what $n$ is). Since there are 4 of them, the average is midway between the second and third terms: midway between $n + 1$ and $n + 2$, or $n + 1\frac{1}{2}$.

**11** C—This can be done two ways. In the first method, we can use the average formula and label the other number $x$:

$$\frac{(n+x)}{2} = 3n - 4$$
$$n + x = 2(3n - 4)$$
$$n + x = 6n - 8$$
$$x = 6n - 8 - n$$
$$x = 5n - 8$$

A second way to do this is to pick numbers. Let's say that $n$ is 10. Then $3n - 4$ is $3(10) - 4$ or 26. If the average of 10 and some number is 26, then since 10 is 16

less than 26, the other number must be 16 more than 26. So, the other number must be 42. Plug in 10 for $n$ in each answer choice to see which one gives us 42. If more than one answer choice gives us 42, we have to try another number. Choice (A) gives us 16; no good. Choice (B) gives us 26; no good. Choice (C) works, since 5 times 10, minus 8 is 42. Choice (D) gives us 58 and choice (E) gives us 52. Since only choice (C) gave us 42, this must be correct.

**12** A—The fastest way to solve this problem is to recognize that $x + 2$, $x + 4$, and $x + 6$ are evenly spaced numbers, so that the average equals the middle value, $x + 4$. We're told that the average of these values is zero, so:
$$x + 4 = 0$$
$$x = -4$$

**13** C—The class average is equal to the number of boys times the boys' average, plus the number of girls times the girls' average, divided by the total number of students. Let $x$ = the girls' average.
$$\frac{12(87)+18(x)}{30} = 90$$

Cross multiplying:
$$12(87) + 18(x) = 30(90)$$
$$1,044 + 18x = 2,700$$
$$18x = 1,656$$
$$x = 92$$

**14** C—The average = $\frac{\text{sum of the terms}}{\text{number of the terms}}$. So if the average of $r$, $s$, and 12 is 18, then $\frac{r+s+12}{12} = 18$, or $r + s + 12 = 54$, which simplifies to $r + s = 42$. Therefore, the average of $r$ and $s$ is $\frac{42}{2}$, or 21. So the columns are equal, and answer choice (C) is correct.

**15** A—The median of a group of numbers is the "middle number"; it is the value above which half of the numbers in the group fall, and below which the other half fall. If you have an even number of values, the median is the average of the 2 "middle" numbers; if you have an odd number of values, the median is the middle value. Here, in Column B, the median is 101. In Column A, if the numbers were 100, 101, and 102, the average would also be 101, but since the third number, 103, is larger than 102, the average must be larger than 101. Column A is greater than 101, and Column B equals 101. Choice (A) is correct.

**16** **B**—3 of the numbers appear in both columns. The only one that doesn't is 26 in Column B. Since 26 is larger than any of the other numbers, it will raise the average in Column B above the average in Column A. Therefore, choice (B) is correct.

**17** **93**—Jerry's average score is 85. His total number of points for the 3 tests is the same as if he had scored 85 on each of the tests: 85 + 85 + 85, or 255. He wants to average 87 over 4 tests, so his total must be 87 + 87 + 87 + 87 = 348. The difference between his total score after 3 tests and the total that he needs after 4 tests is 348 – 255, or 93. Jerry needs a 93 to raise his average over the 4 tests to 87.

Another way of thinking about the problem is to "balance" the average around 87. Imagine Jerry has 3 scores of 85. Each of the first 3 is 2 points below the average of 87. So together, the first 3 tests are a total of 6 points below the average. To balance the average at 87, the score on the fourth test will have to be 6 points more than 87, or 93.

**18** **98**—Plug the information about Lily's first four test grades into the average formula to find what grade on a fifth test would result in an overall average of 86. Lily averaged 82 on her first and second tests. This is mathematically equivalent to her scoring 82 on each of these 2 tests. Let $x$ = the fifth test grade.

$$86 = \frac{76 + 92 + 2(82) + x}{5}$$

$$86 = \frac{332 + x}{5}$$

$$430 = 332 + x$$

$$98 = x$$

## HARD

**19** **C**—The key to this problem is that the total theater attendance stays the same after 6 theaters close. No matter how many theaters there are:

Total attendance = (number of theaters) × (average attendance).

We know that originally there are 15 theaters,

and they average 600 customers per day. Plug these values into the formula above to find the total theater attendance:

Total attendance = (15) × (600) = 9,000.

Even after the 6 theaters close, the total attendance remains the same. Now, though, the number of theaters is only 9:

New average attendance

$$= \frac{\text{Total attendance}}{\text{New number of theaters}}$$

$$= \frac{9,000}{9}$$

$$= 1,000$$

**20** **B**—We can't find individual values for any of these 6 numbers. However, with the given information we can find the sum of the 6 numbers, and the sum of just the largest and smallest. Subtracting the sum of the smallest and largest from the sum of all 6 will leave us with the sum of the 4 others, from which we can find *their* average.

The sum of all 6 numbers = (average of all 6 numbers) × (number of values) = 5 × 6, or 30.

The sum of the greatest and smallest = (average of greatest and smallest) × 2 = 7 × 2 = 14.

The sum of the other 4 numbers
= (the sum of all six)
– (the sum of the greatest and smallest)
= (30 – 14) = 16.

Since the sum of the other 4 numbers is 16, their average is $\frac{16}{4}$, or 4.

**21** **D**—In terms of $y$, the average of $2y$ and $\frac{2y}{3}$ is

$$\frac{2y + \frac{2y}{3}}{2} = \frac{\frac{6y}{3} + \frac{2y}{3}}{2}$$

$$= \frac{8y}{3} \times \frac{1}{2}$$

$$= \frac{8y}{6}$$

$$= \frac{4y}{3}$$

Next, solve for $y$ as the average of $27 - x$, $x - 8$, and $3x + 11$:

$$y = \frac{27 - x + x - 8 + 3x + 11}{3}$$

$$y = \frac{30 + 3x}{3}$$

$$y = \frac{3(x + 10)}{3}$$

$$y = x + 10$$

Plug this into $\frac{4y}{3}$:

$$\frac{4(x + 10)}{3}$$

$$= \frac{4x + 40}{3}$$

**22** **D**—The mode is the term that occurs most frequently in a group of terms; the average is found by using the average $= \frac{\text{sum of the terms}}{\text{number of terms}}$ formula. If Carol starts the week with a 30-minute workout, she will perform a total of four 30-minute workouts and three 60-minute workouts, so the mode is 30. The mean is $\frac{4(30) + 3(60)}{7} = \frac{120 + 180}{7} = \frac{300}{7} = 42\frac{6}{7}$ minutes, and Column B is greater than Column A. But there is another possible schedule of workouts. If Carol does a 60-minute workout the first day, she will perform a total of four 60-minute workouts and only three 30-minute workouts, so in this case 60 is the mode. The mean is $\frac{4(60) + 3(30)}{7} = \frac{240 + 90}{7} = \frac{330}{7} = 47\frac{1}{7}$ minutes, and in this case Column A is

greater than Column B. Since more than one relationship is possible between the columns, the answer must be choice (D).

**23** **46.6 or 46.7**—To find the average speed for the entire trip, divide the total distance traveled by the total amount of time traveled. Use the formula:

Rate × Time = Distance

to find out how much time each part of the trip took. To drive 30 miles at 40 miles per hour would take

$$40 \times \text{Time} = 30,$$

$$\text{Time} = \frac{30}{40} = \frac{3}{4} \text{ hour.}$$

To drive 75 miles at 50 miles per hour would take

$$50 \times \text{Time} = 75,$$

$$\text{Time} = \frac{75}{50} = 1\frac{1}{2} \text{ hours.}$$

So the average speed:

$$= \frac{30 + 75 \text{ miles}}{\frac{3}{4} + 1\frac{1}{2} \text{ hours}} = 46\frac{2}{3} \text{ miles per hour.}$$

**24** **517**—The average of a group of evenly spaced numbers is equal to the middle number. In this problem, there is an even number of terms, 18, so the average is midway between the 2 middle numbers, the 9th and 10th terms. This tells us that the 9th consecutive odd integer here will be the first odd integer less than 534, which is 533. Once we have the 9th term, we can count backward to find the first.

10th: 535, Average: 534, 9th: 533, 8th: 531, 7th: 529, 6th: 527, 5th: 525, 4th: 523, 3rd: 521, 2nd: 519, 1st: 517.

**25** **12**—We need to find the average of $a + 3$, $b - 5$, and 6. If we could determine their sum, then all we'd need to do is divide this sum by 3 to find their average. Well, we don't know $a$ and $b$, but we can determine their sum. We are given the average of $a$, $b$, and 7. The sum of these 3 values is the average times the number of terms, or $13 \times 3 = 39$. If $a + b + 7 = 39$, then $a + b = 39 - 7$, or $a + b = 32$. Remember, we're asked for the average of $a + 3$, $b - 5$, and 6. The sum of these expressions can be rewritten as $a + b + 3 - 5 + 6$, or, as $a + b + 4$.

If $a + b = 32$, then $a + b + 4 = 32 + 4$, or 36.

Therefore, the sum is 36 and the number of terms is 3, so the average is $\frac{36}{3}$, or 12.

Ratios and rates are very common on the SAT. These are the essential skills (see the SAT Math in a Nutshell section near the back of this book):

34. Setting up a Ratio
35. Part-to-Part Ratios and Part-to-Whole Ratios
36. Solving a Proportion
37. Rate
38. Average Rate

## PRACTICE SET

### BASIC

**1** A subway car passes 3 stations every 10 minutes. At this rate, how many stations will it pass in one hour?

(A)  2
(B)  12
(C)  15
(D)  18
(E)  30          Ⓐ Ⓑ Ⓒ Ⓓ Ⓔ

**2** On a certain street map, $\frac{3}{4}$ inch represents one mile. What distance, in miles, is represented by $1\frac{3}{4}$ inches?

(A)  $1\frac{1}{2}$

(B)  $1\frac{3}{4}$

(C)  $2\frac{1}{3}$

(D)  $2\frac{1}{2}$

(E)  $5\frac{1}{4}$          Ⓐ Ⓑ Ⓒ Ⓓ Ⓔ

**3** The Greenpoint factory produced two-fifths of the Consolidated Brick Company's bricks in 1991. If the Greenpoint factory produced 1,400 tons of bricks in 1991, what was the Consolidated Brick Company's total output that year, in tons?

(A)  700
(B)  2,100
(C)  2,800
(D)  3,500
(E)  7,000          Ⓐ Ⓑ Ⓒ Ⓓ Ⓔ

**4** The ratio of $3\frac{1}{4}$ to $5\frac{1}{4}$ is equivalent to the ratio of

(A)  3 to 5
(B)  13 to 21
(C)  5 to 7
(D)  7 to 5
(E)  5 to 3          Ⓐ Ⓑ Ⓒ Ⓓ Ⓔ

**5** If a car travels $\frac{1}{100}$ of a kilometer each second, how many kilometers does it travel per hour?

(A)  $\frac{3}{5}$

(B)  $3\frac{3}{5}$

(C)  36

(D)  72

(E)  100          Ⓐ Ⓑ Ⓒ Ⓓ Ⓔ

Column A      Column B

The ratio of *a* to *b* is 10 to 12.

**6**    6*a*                5*b*

Ⓐ Ⓑ Ⓒ Ⓓ Ⓔ

---

A jar contains only dimes and quarters.

**7** The ratio of        The ratio of the
the value of         value of the quarters
the dimes to        to the value of the
the value of the     dimes
quarters

Ⓐ Ⓑ Ⓒ Ⓓ Ⓔ

---

**8** A certain box contains baseballs and golf balls. If the ratio of baseballs to golf balls is 2:3, and there are 30 baseballs in the box, how many golf balls are in the box?

(A)   15
(B)   18
(C)   20
(D)   36
(E)   45            Ⓐ Ⓑ Ⓒ Ⓓ Ⓔ

---

**9** After spending $\frac{5}{12}$ of his salary, a man has $140 left. What is his salary, in dollars?

## MEDIUM

**10** At garage *A*, it costs $8.75 to park a car for the first hour and $1.25 for each additional hour. At garage *B*, it costs $5.50 for the first hour and $2.50 for each additional hour. What is the difference between the cost of parking a car for 5 hours at garage *A* and parking it for the same length of time at garage *B* ?

(A)   $1.50
(B)   $1.75
(C)   $2.25
(D)   $2.75
(E)   $3.25        Ⓐ Ⓑ Ⓒ Ⓓ Ⓔ

---

**11** If a kilogram is equal to approximately 2.2 pounds, which of the following is the best approximation of the number of kilograms in one pound?

(A)   $\frac{11}{5}$

(B)   $\frac{5}{8}$

(C)   $\frac{5}{11}$

(D)   $\frac{1}{3}$

(E)   $\frac{1}{5}$        Ⓐ Ⓑ Ⓒ Ⓓ Ⓔ

---

**12** If the ratio of boys to girls in a class is 5 to 3, which of the following could not be the number of students in the class?

(A)   32
(B)   36
(C)   40
(D)   48
(E)   56        Ⓐ Ⓑ Ⓒ Ⓓ Ⓔ

---

**13** If a tree grew 5 feet in *n* years, what was the average rate, in inches per year, at which the tree grew during those years?

(A)   60*n*

(B)   $\frac{5}{n}$

(C)   $\frac{5}{12n}$

(D)   $\frac{12n}{5}$

(E)   $\frac{60}{n}$        Ⓐ Ⓑ Ⓒ Ⓓ Ⓔ

14  If a man earns $200 for his first 40 hours of work in a week and then is paid one-and-one-half times his regular hourly rate for any additional hours, how many hours must he work to make $230 in a week?

(A)  4
(B)  5
(C)  6
(D)  44
(E)  45          Ⓐ Ⓑ Ⓒ Ⓓ Ⓔ

15  In a certain class, 3 out of 24 students are in student organizations. What is the ratio of students in student organizations to students not in student organizations?

(A)  $\frac{1}{8}$

(B)  $\frac{1}{7}$

(C)  $\frac{1}{6}$

(D)  $\frac{1}{5}$

(E)  $\frac{1}{4}$          Ⓐ Ⓑ Ⓒ Ⓓ Ⓔ

16  A student's grade in a course is determined by 4 quizzes and 1 exam. If the exam counts twice as much as each of the quizzes, what fraction of the final grade is determined by the exam?

(A)  $\frac{1}{6}$

(B)  $\frac{1}{5}$

(C)  $\frac{1}{4}$

(D)  $\frac{1}{3}$

(E)  $\frac{1}{2}$          Ⓐ Ⓑ Ⓒ Ⓓ Ⓔ

Column A        Column B

$p$, $q$, and $r$ are positive integers.
The ratio of $p$ to $q$ is 4:3.
The ratio of $q$ to $r$ is 2:3.

17      $p$                          $r$

Ⓐ Ⓑ Ⓒ Ⓓ Ⓔ

Melinda mailed $\frac{1}{4}$ of her party invitations after lunch. She mailed $\frac{1}{2}$ of the remaining invitations after class.

18  The unmailed                   $\frac{1}{4}$
    fractionof the total
    number of invitations

Ⓐ Ⓑ Ⓒ Ⓓ Ⓔ

19  In a local election, votes were cast for Mr. Dyer, Ms. Frau, and Mr. Borak in the ratio of 4:3:2. If there were no other candidates and none of the 1,800 voters cast more than one vote, how many votes did Ms. Frau receive?

20  Ms. Smith recently drove a total of 700 miles on a business trip. If her car averaged 35 miles per gallon of gasoline and gasoline cost $1.25 per gallon, what was the cost in dollars of the gasoline for the trip?

21  If cement, gravel, and sand are to be mixed in the ratio of 3:5:7 respectively, and 5 tons of cement are available, how many tons of the mixture can be made? (Assume that enough gravel and sand are available to use all the available cement.)

## HARD

22  A student finishes the first half of an exam in $\frac{2}{3}$ of the time it takes him to finish the second half. If the entire exam takes him an hour, how many minutes does he spend on the first half of the exam?

(A)  20
(B)  24
(C)  27
(D)  36
(E)  40        Ⓐ Ⓑ Ⓒ Ⓓ Ⓔ

23  John buys $R$ pounds of cheese to feed $N$ people at a party. If $N + P$ people come to the party, how many more pounds of cheese must John buy in order to feed everyone at the original rate?

(A)  $\dfrac{NP}{R}$

(B)  $\dfrac{N}{RP}$

(C)  $\dfrac{N + P}{R}$

(D)  $\dfrac{P}{NR}$

(E)  $\dfrac{PR}{N}$        Ⓐ Ⓑ Ⓒ Ⓓ Ⓔ

24  Phil is making a 40-kilometer canoe trip. If he travels at 30 kilometers per hour for the first 10 kilometers, and then at 15 kilometers per hour for the rest of the trip, how many minutes longer will it take him than if he makes the entire trip at 20 kilometers per hour?

25  A sporting goods store ordered an equal number of white and yellow tennis balls. The tennis ball company delivered 30 extra white balls, making the ratio of white balls to yellow balls 6:5. How many tennis balls did the store originally order?

(A)  120
(B)  150
(C)  180
(D)  300
(E)  330        Ⓐ Ⓑ Ⓒ Ⓓ Ⓔ

26  If $x$ oranges cost the same as $y$ peaches and peaches cost 39 cents each, how many *dollars* does each orange cost?

(A)  $\dfrac{39x}{100y}$

(B)  $\dfrac{39y}{100x}$

(C)  $\dfrac{3,900}{xy}$

(D)  $\dfrac{39y}{x}$

(E)  $\dfrac{39x}{y}$        Ⓐ Ⓑ Ⓒ Ⓓ Ⓔ

27  If $\frac{1}{2}$ of the number of white mice in a certain laboratory is $\frac{1}{8}$ of the total number of mice, and $\frac{1}{3}$ of the number of gray mice is $\frac{1}{9}$ of the total number of mice, then what is the ratio of the number of white mice to the number of gray mice?

(A)  16:27
(B)  2:3
(C)  3:4
(D)  4:5
(E)  8:9        Ⓐ Ⓑ Ⓒ Ⓓ Ⓔ

Column A | Column B

Machine $M$ produces $p$ steel plates every 20 minutes. Machine $N$ produces $q$ steel plates every 15 minutes.

28 The number of steel plates produced by machine $M$ in 1 hour | The number of steel plates produced by machine $N$ in 1 hour

ⒶⒷⒸⒹⒺ

---

$\frac{2}{5}$ of the people in a certain room are male. After 2 females enter the room, the ratio of males to females is $\frac{1}{2}$.

29 The total number of people in the room after the females enter | 12

ⒶⒷⒸⒹⒺ

---

There are at least 200 apples in a grocery store. The ratio of the number of oranges to the number of apples is 9 to 10.

30 The number of oranges in the store | 200

ⒶⒷⒸⒹⒺ

---

April drives the first 100 miles of her trip at 50 miles per hour. She drives the next 100 miles of her trip at 40 miles per hour.

31 The average speed of her entire trip in miles per hour | 45

ⒶⒷⒸⒹⒺ

---

32 An oculist charges $30 for an eye examination, frames, and glass lenses, but $42 for an eye examination, frames, and plastic lenses. If the plastic lenses cost four times as much as the glass lenses, how much do the glass lenses cost?

| SCORECARD | |
|---|---|
| Number of Questions Right: | |
| Number of Questions Wrong: | |
| Number of Questions Omitted: | |
| Number of Correct Guesses: | |
| Number of Wrong Guesses: | |
| Time Used: | |

## ANSWERS AND EXPLANATIONS

### BASIC

**1** **D**—Since there are 60 minutes in an hour, the subway will pass $\frac{60}{10}$ or 6 times as many stations in 1 hour as it passes in 10 minutes. In 10 minutes it passes 3 stations; in 60 minutes it must pass $6 \times 3$ or 18 stations.

**2** **C**—In this question, the ratio is implied: For every $\frac{3}{4}$ inch of map there is 1 real mile, so the ratio of inches to the miles they represent is always $\frac{3}{4}$ to 1. Therefore, we can set up the proportion:

$$\frac{\text{\# of inches}}{\text{\# of miles}} = \frac{\frac{3}{4}}{1} = \frac{3}{4}$$

Now $1\frac{3}{4}$ inches $= \frac{7}{4}$ inches.

Set up a proportion:

$$\frac{\frac{7}{4}\text{inches}}{\text{\# of miles}} = \frac{3}{4}$$

Cross multiply:

$$\frac{7}{4} \times 4 = 3 \times \text{\# of miles}$$

$$7 = 3 \times \text{\# of miles}$$

$$\frac{7}{3} = \text{\# of miles}$$

$$\text{or } 2\frac{1}{3} = \text{\# of miles}$$

**3** **D**—*Method I:*
If *two*-fifths of Consolidated's output (the bricks produced by the Greenpoint factory) was 1,400 tons, *one*-fifth must have been half as much, or 700 tons. The entire output for 1991 was *five*-fifths or five times as much: $5 \times 700$ or 3,500 tons.

*Method II:*

We are asked for total output, so let's call the total output $T$. We are told that 1,400 tons represents $\frac{2}{5}$ of

$T$ or $\frac{2}{5} T$, so we can set up the following equation:

$$\frac{2}{5} T = 1,400$$

Multiply both sides by $\frac{5}{2}$ to solve for $T$:

$$\frac{5}{2} \times \frac{2}{5} T = 1,400 \times \frac{5}{2}$$

$$T = \frac{1,400 \times 5}{2} = 700 \times 5 = 3,500$$

**4** **B**—We are asked which of five ratios is equivalent to the ratio of $3\frac{1}{4}$ to $5\frac{1}{4}$. Since the ratios in the answer choices are expressed in whole numbers, turn this ratio into whole numbers:

$$3\frac{1}{4} : 5\frac{1}{4} = \frac{13}{4} : \frac{21}{4} = \frac{\frac{13}{4}}{\frac{21}{4}} = \frac{13}{4} \times \frac{4}{21} = \frac{13}{21} \text{ or } 13:21$$

**5** **C**—Find the number of seconds in an hour, and then multiply this by the distance the car is traveling each second. There are 60 seconds in a minute and 60 minutes in one hour; therefore, there are $60 \times 60$, or 3,600, seconds in an hour. In one second the car travels $\frac{1}{100}$ kilometers; in one hour the car will travel $3,600 \times \frac{1}{100}$, or 36 kilometers.

**6** **C**—We can rewrite the ratios as equivalent fractions: The ratio of $a$ to $b$ is 10 to 12 becomes $\frac{a}{b} = \frac{10}{12}$, and since $\frac{10}{12}$ can be reduced to $\frac{5}{6}$, we have $\frac{a}{b} = \frac{5}{6}$. Cross multiplying, we have $6a = 5b$, so the columns are equal, and choice (C) is correct.

**7** **D**—This question is lacking essential information. You don't know the number of dimes or the number of quarters. Therefore, you cannot determine either ratio, and choice (D) is correct.

**8** **E**—We can express the ratio of baseballs to the golf balls as $\frac{2}{3}$. Since we know the number of baseballs, we can set up a proportion: $\frac{2}{3} = \frac{30}{x}$, where $x$ is the number of golf balls. To solve, we cross multiply, and get $2x = 90$, or $x = 45$.

**9** **240**—If the man has spent $\frac{5}{12}$ of his salary, he still has $1 - \frac{5}{12}$, or $\frac{7}{12}$ of his salary. So \$140 represents $\frac{7}{12}$ of his salary. Set up a proportion, using $S$ to represent his salary:

$$\frac{7}{12} = \frac{140}{S}$$

Cross multiply:

$$7S = 12 \times 140$$
$$S = \frac{12 \times 140}{7}$$
$$S = 240$$

## MEDIUM

**10** **B**—We need to compute the cost of parking a car for 5 hours at each garage. Since the two garages have a split-rate system of charging, the cost for the first hour is different from the cost of each remaining hour.

The first hour at garage $A$ costs \$8.75
The next 4 hours cost $4 \times \$1.25 = \$5.00$
The total cost for parking at garage $A = \$8.75 + \$5.00 = \$13.75$
The first hour at garage $B$ costs \$5.50
The next 4 hours cost $4 \times \$2.50 = \$10.00$
The total cost for parking at garage $B$ = \$5.50 + \$10.00 = \$15.50
So the difference in cost = \$15.50 – \$13.75 = \$1.75.

**11** **C**—Here you can set up a direct proportion:

$$\frac{1 \text{ kilogram}}{2.2 \text{ pounds}} = \frac{x \text{ kilograms}}{1 \text{ pound}}$$

Cross multiply (the units drop out):

$$1(1) = 2.2x$$
$$x = \frac{1}{2.2} = \frac{10}{22} = \frac{5}{11}$$

If you have trouble setting up the proportion, you could use the answer choices to your advantage and take an educated guess. Since 2.2 pounds equals a kilogram, 1 pound must be a little less than $\frac{1}{2}$ kilogram. Of the possible answers, $\frac{11}{5}$ and $\frac{5}{8}$ are greater than $\frac{1}{2}$; $\frac{1}{3}$ and $\frac{1}{5}$ are too small. But $\frac{5}{11}$ is just under $\frac{1}{2}$, and so it should be the correct answer.

**12** **B**—The ratio 5 boys to 3 girls tells you that for every 5 boys in the class there must be 3 girls in the class. So the total number of students in the class must be a multiple of 8, since the smallest possible total is 5 + 3, or 8. Since 36 is not divisible by 8, 36 cannot be the total number of students.

**13** **E**—First find the rate at which the tree grew, in feet per year. It grew 5 feet in $n$ years, so it grew at an average rate of $\frac{5 \text{ feet}}{n \text{ years}}$.

But we were asked for the average amount it grew in inches per year, so we must convert. There are 12 inches in a foot, so the following can be set up.

$$\frac{5 \text{ feet}}{n \text{ years}} \times \frac{12 \text{ inches}}{1 \text{ foot}} = \frac{60 \text{ inches}}{n \text{ years}} = \frac{60}{n} \text{ inches per year.}$$

This is the average amount the tree grew in 1 year.
If the presence of the variable confuses you, another approach is to pick a number for $n$. The tree

grew 5 feet in $n$ years, so if we let $n = 5$, then the tree grew 5 feet in 5 years, or an average of 1 foot per year. 1 foot = 12 inches, so the tree grew an average of 12 inches a year. Now plug in our value of 5 for $n$ in each answer choice and see which ones give a value of 12.

Choice (A): $60n = 60 \times 5 \neq 12$. Discard.

Choice (B): $\dfrac{5}{n} = \dfrac{5}{5} \neq 12$. Discard.

Choice (C): $\dfrac{5}{12n} = \dfrac{5}{12 \times 5} \times 5 \neq 12$. Discard.

Choice (D): $\dfrac{12n}{5} = \dfrac{12 \times 5}{5} = 12$. Hold onto.

Choice (E): $\dfrac{60}{n} = \dfrac{60}{5} = 12$. Hold onto.

We now have two possibilities. Therefore we must try another value for $n$ to distinguish between the two. If $n = 10$ then the tree grew 5 feet in 10 years, or $\dfrac{1}{2}$ foot a year, which is 6 inches a year. In this case,

Choice (D): $\dfrac{12n}{5} = \dfrac{120}{5} \neq 6$. Discard.

Choice (E): $\dfrac{60}{n} = \dfrac{60}{10} = 6$. Okay.

(E) is the only answer choice that works in both cases.

**14** **D**—To learn the man's overtime rate of pay, we have to figure out his regular rate of pay. Divide the amount of money made, $200, by the time it took to make it, 40 hours: $200 ÷ 40 hours = $5 per hour. That is the normal rate. The man is paid $1\frac{1}{2}$ times his regular rate during overtime, so when working more than 40 hours he makes $\dfrac{3}{2} \times \$5$ per hour = $7.50 per hour. Now we can figure out how long it takes the man to make $230. It takes him 40 hours to make the first $200. The last $30 are made at the

overtime rate. Since it takes the man one hour to make $7.50 at this rate, we can figure out the number of extra hours by dividing $30 by $7.50 per hour. $30 ÷ $7.50 per hour = 4 hours. The total time needed is 40 hours plus 4 hours, or 44 hours.

**15** **B**—Since 3 out of 24 students are in student organizations, the remaining 24 – 3, or 21, students are not in student organizations. Therefore, the ratio of students in organizations to students not in organizations is

$$\dfrac{\text{\# in organizations}}{\text{\# not in organizations}} = \dfrac{3}{21} = \dfrac{1}{7}.$$

**16** **D**—The grade is decided by 4 quizzes and 1 exam. Since the exam counts twice as much as each quiz, the exam equals two quizzes, so we can say the grade is decided by the equivalent of 4 quizzes and 2 quizzes, or 6 quizzes. The exam equals two quizzes, so it represents $\dfrac{2}{6}$, or $\dfrac{1}{3}$, of the grade.

**17** **B**—The parts of the given ratios do not refer to the same whole. You must restate both ratios so that $q$ corresponds to the same number in both ratios. Then all the parts of the ratios will refer to the same whole. So $p{:}q = 4{:}3$ becomes $p{:}q = 8{:}6$ and $q{:}r = 2{:}3$ becomes $q{:}r = 6{:}9$. Therefore, $p{:}q{:}r = 8{:}6{:}9$, so $\dfrac{p}{r} = \dfrac{8}{9}$ and $p = \dfrac{8}{9}r$. Since $\dfrac{8}{9}r < r$, Column B is greater, and choice (B) is correct.

**18** **A**—The columns may appear equal at first, but this is not an easy question. Pick a number for the invitations. Suppose the total number of invitations is 80. If she mailed $\frac{1}{4}$ of them after lunch, she mailed $\frac{1}{4} \times 80$, or 20 invitations. So she had 80 − 20, or 60 invitations left to send. If she mailed $\frac{1}{2}$ of those, she sent $\frac{1}{2}$ x 60, or 30 invitations. So she had 60 − 30, or 30 invitations that remained. The fraction still unmailed is $\frac{30}{80}$, or $\frac{3}{8}$, and that's greater than $\frac{1}{4}$ in Column B. So answer choice (A) is correct.

**19** **600**—The ratio of parts is 4:3:2, making a total of 9 parts. Since 9 parts are equal to 1,800 votes, each part represents $\frac{1,800}{9}$, or 200 votes. Since Ms. Frau represents 3 parts, she received a total of 3 × 200, or 600 votes. (Another way to think about it: Out of every 9 votes, Ms. Frau gets 3, which is $\frac{3}{9}$ or $\frac{1}{3}$ of the total number of votes. $\frac{1}{3}$ of 1,800 is 600.)

We could also have solved this algebraically by setting up a proportion, with F as Ms. Frau's votes:

$$\frac{3}{9} = \frac{F}{1,800}$$

$$\frac{3}{9} \times 1,800 = F$$

$$600 = F$$

**20** **25**—If Ms. Smith's car averages 35 miles per gallon, she can go 35 miles on 1 gallon. To go 700 miles she will need $\frac{700}{35}$, or 20 gallons of gasoline. The price of gasoline was $1.25 per gallon, so she spent 20 × $1.25, or $25, for her trip.

**21** **25**—The ratio of cement to gravel to sand is 3:5:7. For every 3 portions of cement we put in, we get 3 + 5 + 7, or 15, portions of the mixture. So the recipe gives us $\frac{15}{3}$, or 5, times as much mixture as cement. We have 5 tons of cement available, so we can make 5 × 5, or 25, tons of the mixture.

## HARD

**22** **B**—The time it takes to complete the entire exam is the sum of the time spent on the first half of the exam and the time spent on the second half. We know the time spent on the first half is $\frac{2}{3}$ of the time spent on the second half. If S represents the time spent on the second half, then the total time spent is $\frac{2}{3}S + S$ or $\frac{5}{3}S$. We know this total time is one hour, or 60 minutes. So we can set up a simple equation and solve for S.

$$\frac{5}{3}S = 60$$

$$\frac{3}{5} \times \frac{5}{3}S = \frac{3}{5} \times 60$$

$$S = 36$$

So the second half takes 36 minutes. The first half takes $\frac{2}{3}$ of this, or 24 minutes. (You could also find the first half by subtracting 36 minutes from the total time, 60 minutes.)

**23** **E**—If John buys R pounds for N people, he is planning on feeding his guests cheese at a rate of $\frac{R \text{ pounds}}{N \text{ people}} = \frac{R}{N}$ pounds per person.

How much additional cheese must John buy for

the extra $P$ people? If John is buying $\frac{R}{N}$ pounds of cheese for each person, he will need $P \times \frac{R}{N}$, or $\frac{PR}{N}$ pounds for the extra $P$ people. We can check our answer by seeing if the units cancel out:

$$P \text{ people} \times \frac{R \text{ pounds}}{N \text{ people}} = \frac{PR}{N} \text{ pounds}$$

Another approach: Get rid of all those variables by picking numbers. Say John buys 10 pounds of cheese for 5 people (that is, $R = 10$ and $N = 5$). Then everyone gets 2 pounds of cheese. Also say 7 people come, 2 more than expected (that is, $P = 2$). Then he needs 14 pounds to have enough for everybody to consume 2 pounds of cheese. Since he already bought 10 pounds, he must buy an additional 4 pounds. Therefore, an answer choice that equals 4 when we substitute 10 for $R$, 5 for $N$, and 2 for $P$ is possibly correct:

Choice (A): $\frac{(5)(2)}{10} \neq 4$. Discard.

Choice (B): $\frac{5}{(10)(2)} \neq 4$. Discard.

Choice (C): $\frac{5+2}{10} \neq 4$. Discard.

Choice (D): $\frac{2}{(5)(10)} \neq 4$. Discard.

Choice (E): $\frac{(2)(10)}{5} = 4$. Correct.

Since only choice (E) gives us 4, that must be the correct answer.

**24** **20**—First find how long the trip takes him at each of the two different rates, using the formula $\text{time} = \frac{\text{distance}}{\text{rate}}$.

He travels the first 10 km at 30 km per hour, so he takes $\frac{10}{30} = \frac{1}{3}$ hour for this portion of the journey.

He travels the remaining 30 km at 15 km per hour, so he takes $\frac{30}{15} = 2$ hours for this portion of the journey.

So the whole journey takes him $2 + \frac{1}{3} = 2\frac{1}{3}$ hours. Now we need to compare this to the amount of time it would take to make the same trip at a constant rate of 20 km per hour. If he traveled the whole 40 km at 20 km per hour, it would take $\frac{40}{20} = 2$ hours.

This is $\frac{1}{3}$ hour, or 20 minutes, shorter.

**25** **D**—We can solve this algebraically. Let the number of yellow balls received be $x$. Then the number of white balls received is 30 more than this, or $x + 30$.

So $\frac{\# \text{ of white balls}}{\# \text{ of yellow balls}} = \frac{6}{5} = \frac{x+30}{x}$

Cross multiply: $6x = 5(x + 30)$

Solve for $x$: $6x = 5x + 150$

$x = 150$.

Since the number of white balls ordered equals the number of yellow balls ordered, the total number of balls ordered is $2x$, which is $2 \times 150$, or 300.

**26** **B**—Since the question asks for the answer in dollars, start by converting cents to dollars. There are 100 cents in a dollar, so 39 cents = $\frac{39}{100}$ dollars. Since each peach costs $\frac{39}{100}$ dollars, $y$ peaches cost $\frac{39}{100}y$ dollars. If $x$ oranges cost as much as $y$ peaches, $x$ oranges also cost $\frac{39}{100}y$ dollars or $\frac{39y}{100}$ dollars. Then one orange costs $\frac{1}{x}$ as much, or $\frac{39y}{100x}$ dollars.

This is an ideal problem to solve by picking numbers. Let's say that 5 oranges and 10 peaches cost the same; that is, $x = 5$ and $y = 10$. If peaches are 39 cents each, 10 of them will cost $3.90, so that's the cost of 5 oranges. That means each orange costs $\frac{\$3.90}{5}$ or $0.78. We try our numbers in each answer choice:

Choice (A): $\dfrac{(39)(5)}{(100)(10)} = \dfrac{195}{1,000}$ . Discard.

Choice (B): $\dfrac{(39)(10)}{(100)(5)} = \dfrac{390}{500} = \dfrac{39}{50} = 0.78$ . This may be

our answer.

Choice (C): $\dfrac{3900}{(5)(10)} = \dfrac{3900}{50} = 78$ . This is 78 dollars,

not 78 cents. Discard.

Choice (D): $\dfrac{(39)(10)}{5} = \dfrac{390}{5} = 78$ . Again, discard.

Choice (E): $\dfrac{(39)(5)}{10} = \dfrac{195}{10} = 19.5$ . Again, discard.

Since only choice (B) produced the correct result, it must be correct.

**27** C—In this question we cannot determine the number of white mice or gray mice, but we can determine their ratio.

*Method I:*

Since $\dfrac{1}{2}$ of the number of white mice makes up

$\dfrac{1}{8}$ of the *total* number of mice, the total number of

white mice must be double $\dfrac{1}{8}$ of the total number of

mice, or $\dfrac{1}{4}$ of the total number of mice.

Algebraically, letting W be the number of white

mice and $T$ the total number of mice, if $\dfrac{1}{2} \times W = \dfrac{1}{8} \times T$,

then $W = \dfrac{1}{4} \times T$. So $\dfrac{1}{4}$ of the total number of mice

are white. Similarly, since $\dfrac{1}{3}$ of the number of gray

mice is $\dfrac{1}{9}$ of the total number of mice, $3 \times \dfrac{1}{9}$ of all

the mice, or $\dfrac{1}{3}$ of all the mice, are gray mice.

Therefore, the ratio of the number of white mice to

the number of gray mice is $\dfrac{1}{4} : \dfrac{1}{3}$ , which is the same as

$\dfrac{3}{12} : \dfrac{4}{12}$ , or 3:4.

*Method II:*

Pick numbers. Whenever a problem gives us information about ratios and asks us to determine some other ratio, we can *pick a value* for one of the quantities and solve for the ratio based on this value. The result will be the same no matter what value we pick.

In this case, we can pick a number for the total number of mice. Pick one that will facilitate calculations. Let's try 72, since it's a multiple of all the denominators of the fractions in the ratios (2, 3, 8, and 9). Now we can get values for the number of white mice and gray mice by using the given information. For the white mice, we have:

$\dfrac{1}{2}$ the # of white mice = $\dfrac{1}{8}$ the total # of mice =

$\dfrac{1}{8} \times 72 = 9$.

If 9 is $\dfrac{1}{2}$ of the number of white mice, there must

be $2 \times 9$, or 18, white mice altogether. As for the gray

mice, the following applies.

$\dfrac{1}{3}$ the number of gray mice = $\dfrac{1}{9}$ the total # of mice

$= \dfrac{1}{9} \times 72 = 8$.

If 8 is $\dfrac{1}{3}$ of the number of gray mice, there must

be $3 \times 8$, or 24, gray mice altogether. The ratio of

white mice to gray mice, then, is 18:24, or 3:4.

**28** D—If machine M produces p steel plates every 20 minutes, it must produce 3p plates every 60 minutes, or hour. If machine N produces q steel plates every 15 minutes, it must produce 4q plates every 60 minutes, or every hour. However, you know nothing about the values of p and q. Therefore, there is more than one possible relationship between 3p and 4q. So choice (D) is the correct answer.

**29** C—Let $M$ be the number of men initially in the room and $W$ the number of women initially in the room. If $\frac{2}{5}$ of the people in the room are male, then $1-\frac{2}{5}$, or $\frac{3}{5}$, must be female. The ratio of men to women is initially $\frac{2}{5}:\frac{3}{5}$, or $\frac{2}{3}$, so $\frac{M}{W}=\frac{2}{3}$. Cross multiplying gives us $3M = 2W$. After 2 more women enter, the ratio becomes $\frac{1}{2}$, or $\frac{M}{W+2}=\frac{1}{2}$. Cross multiplying gives us $2M = W + 2$, or $W = 2M - 2$. Substituting this into the equation $3M = 2W$ gives us $3M = 2(2M - 2)$ or $3M = 4M - 4$, or $M = 4$. If $M = 4$, then $W = 2(4) - 2$, or 6. So there were originally 4 men and 6 women in the room; 2 more women entered for a total of 12 people.

**30** D—We know that the ratio of oranges to apples is 9 to 10, and that there are "at least" 200 apples. The ratio tells us that there are more apples than oranges. If there were 200 apples in the store, $\frac{\# \text{ of oranges}}{200}=\frac{9}{10}$, so # of oranges $=\frac{9}{10} \times 200 = 180$. In this case Column A is less than Column B. However, if there were 300 apples in the store, $\frac{\# \text{ of oranges}}{300}=\frac{9}{10}$, so # of oranges $=\frac{9}{10} \times 300 = 270$. Now Column A is greater than Column B; so the correct answer is choice (D).

**31** B—Be careful when averaging average rates or speeds; there's more to it than just finding the average. Remember, traveling the same distance at different speeds takes different amounts of time. To find her average speed for the entire trip, use the formula $\text{Average Rate} = \frac{\text{Total Distance}}{\text{Total Time}}$.

The total distance = 100 miles + 100 miles, or 200 miles. The total time is found by calculating the amount of time spent on each part of the trip. The first 100 miles: $\frac{100 \text{ miles}}{50 \text{ miles per hour}} = 2$ hours. The next 100 miles: $\frac{100 \text{ miles}}{40 \text{ miles per hour}} = 2\frac{1}{2}$ hours. So the total travel time is $4\frac{1}{2}$ hours. Therefore, the average speed $= \frac{200 \text{ miles}}{4\frac{1}{2}\text{hours}}$, or $44\frac{4}{9}$ miles. So Column B is greater than Column A, and choice (B) is correct.

**32** 4—In each case the examination and the frames are the same; the difference in cost must be due to the difference in the costs of the lenses. Since plastic lenses cost four times as much as glass lenses, the *difference* in cost must be *three* times the cost of the glass lenses.

Difference in cost = Cost of plastic − Cost of glass
= 4(cost of glass) − 1(cost of glass)
= 3(cost of glass)

The difference in cost is $42 − $30, or $12. Since this is 3 times the cost of the glass lenses, the glass lenses must cost $\frac{\$12}{3}$, or $4.

The test makers love percents. You'll find them all over the SAT. A few questions specifically test your understanding of percents, but many more SAT Math questions combine percents with other concepts. For a fast reference, look up the following items in our SAT Math in a Nutshell section:

30. Percent Formula
31. Percent Increase and Decrease
32. Finding the Original Whole
33. Combined Percent Increase and Decrease

## PRACTICE SET

### BASIC

1   If 48 of the 60 seats on a bus were occupied, what percent of the seats were not occupied?

(A)   12%
(B)   20%
(C)   25%
(D)   60%
(E)   80%                 Ⓐ Ⓑ Ⓒ Ⓓ Ⓔ

2   Four people shared a taxi to the airport. The fare was $36.00, and they gave the driver a tip equal to 25 percent of the fare. If they equally shared the cost of the fare and tip, how much did each person pay?

(A)   $9.00
(B)   $9.75
(C)   $10.25
(D)   $10.75
(E)   $11.25              Ⓐ Ⓑ Ⓒ Ⓓ Ⓔ

3   In a certain class, if Edie's average rose from 72 to 84, by what percent did her average increase?

(A)   12%

(B)   $14\frac{2}{7}\%$

(C)   $16\frac{2}{3}\%$

(D)   $66\frac{2}{3}\%$

(E)   $85\frac{5}{7}\%$        Ⓐ Ⓑ Ⓒ Ⓓ Ⓔ

4   If 60 percent of $W$ equals 20 percent of $T$, what percent of $T$ is $W$ ?

(A)   12%

(B)   $33\frac{1}{3}\%$

(C)   60%

(D)   120%

(E)   $133\frac{1}{3}\%$       Ⓐ Ⓑ Ⓒ Ⓓ Ⓔ

5   36 percent of 18 is 18 percent of what number?

(A)   9
(B)   24
(C)   36
(D)   40
(E)   48                 Ⓐ Ⓑ Ⓒ Ⓓ Ⓔ

6   A closet contains 24 pairs of shoes. If 25 percent of those pairs of shoes are black, how many pairs are NOT black?

(A)   4
(B)   6
(C)   12
(D)   18
(E)   20                 Ⓐ Ⓑ Ⓒ Ⓓ Ⓔ

**7** What is the percent discount on a jacket marked down from \$120 to \$100?

(A) $16\frac{2}{3}\%$

(B) 20%

(C) 30%

(D) $33\frac{1}{3}\%$

(E) 40%

Ⓐ Ⓑ Ⓒ Ⓓ Ⓔ

**8** A survey found that 80 percent of the apartments in City G have smoke alarms installed. Of these, 20 percent have smoke alarms that are not working. What percent of the apartments in City G were found to have working smoke alarms?

(A) 60%

(B) 64%

(C) $66\frac{2}{3}\%$

(D) 70%

(E) 72%

Ⓐ Ⓑ Ⓒ Ⓓ Ⓔ

| Column A | Column B |
|----------|----------|
| **9** $\frac{3}{7}\%$ of .819 | .819% of $\frac{3}{7}$ |

Ⓐ Ⓑ Ⓒ Ⓓ Ⓔ

A factory produced 2,400 staplers last year. The factory produces 25 percent more staplers this year.

**10** The number of staplers the factory produces this year

2,800

Ⓐ Ⓑ Ⓒ Ⓓ Ⓔ

**11** What is 10 percent of 20 percent of 30?

**MEDIUM**

**12** Bob took 20 math tests last year. If he failed 6 of them, what percent of the math tests did he pass?

(A) $37\frac{1}{2}\%$

(B) 60%

(C) $62\frac{1}{2}\%$

(D) $66\frac{2}{3}\%$

(E) 70%

Ⓐ Ⓑ Ⓒ Ⓓ Ⓔ

**13** In a certain box of gloves, 12 pairs are size 7 and 24 pairs are size 6. If all the gloves in the box are either size 6 or size 7, what percent of the gloves in the box are size 6?

(A) $33\frac{1}{3}\%$

(B) 50%

(C) $66\frac{2}{3}\%$

(D) 75%

(E) 200%

Ⓐ Ⓑ Ⓒ Ⓓ Ⓔ

**14** If 65 percent of $x$ is 195, what is 75 percent of $x$?

(A) 215
(B) 225
(C) 235
(D) 250
(E) 260

Ⓐ Ⓑ Ⓒ Ⓓ Ⓔ

**15** A 25-ounce solution is 20 percent alcohol. If 50 ounces of water are added to it, what percent of the new solution is alcohol?

(A) 5%

(B) $6\frac{2}{3}\%$

(C) 10%

(D) $13\frac{1}{3}\%$

(E) 20%

Ⓐ Ⓑ Ⓒ Ⓓ Ⓔ

16  A store sells a watch for a profit of 25 percent of the wholesale cost. What percent of the selling price of the watch is the store's profit?

(A)   12.5%
(B)   20%
(C)   25%
(D)   50%
(E)   75%           Ⓐ Ⓑ Ⓒ Ⓓ Ⓔ

| Column A | Column B |
|---|---|

$p$, $q$, and $r$ are positive.

$r$ is $p$ percent of $q$.

17    $pq$                    $r$

Ⓐ Ⓑ Ⓒ Ⓓ Ⓔ

$b > 0$

$a$ equals $\frac{1}{4}$ percent of $b$.

18    4% of $a$                 $b$

Ⓐ Ⓑ Ⓒ Ⓓ Ⓔ

19  The price of a newspaper rises from 5 cents to 15 cents. What is the percent increase in price?

(A)   50%
(B)   75%
(C)   100%
(D)   150%
(E)   200%          Ⓐ Ⓑ Ⓒ Ⓓ Ⓔ

20  After getting a 20 percent discount, Jerry paid $100 for a bicycle. How much, in dollars, did the bicycle originally cost?

**HARD**

21  A stock decreases in value by 20 percent. By what percent must the stock price increase to reach its former value?

(A)   15%
(B)   20%
(C)   25%
(D)   30%
(E)   40%           Ⓐ Ⓑ Ⓒ Ⓓ Ⓔ

22  The population of a certain town increases by 50 percent every 50 years. If the population in 1950 was 810, in what year was the population 160?

(A)   1650
(B)   1700
(C)   1750
(D)   1800
(E)   1850          Ⓐ Ⓑ Ⓒ Ⓓ Ⓔ

23  A man bought 10 crates of oranges for a total cost of $80. If he lost 2 of the crates, at what price would he have to sell each of the remaining crates in order to earn a total profit of 25 percent of the total cost?

(A)   $10.00
(B)   $12.50
(C)   $15.00
(D)   $100.00
(E)   $120.00       Ⓐ Ⓑ Ⓒ Ⓓ Ⓔ

24  In a certain school, 50 percent of all male students and 60 percent of all female students play a varsity sport. If 40 percent of the students at the school are male, what percent of the students DO NOT play a varsity sport?

(A)   44%
(B)   50%
(C)   55%
(D)   56%
(E)   60%           Ⓐ Ⓑ Ⓒ Ⓓ Ⓔ

25  The quantities $a$, $b$, and $c$ are positive and $ab$ equals $\frac{c}{4}$. If $a$ is increased by 50 percent and $b$ is decreased by 25 percent, then, in order for the equation to remain true, $c$ must be

(A)  decreased by 25%

(B)  decreased by $12\frac{1}{2}$%

(C)  increased by $12\frac{1}{2}$%

(D)  increased by 25%

(E)  increased by 50%

Ⓐ Ⓑ Ⓒ Ⓓ Ⓔ

---

Column A          Column B

The price of a certain stock increased by 20 percent and then decreased the next day by 20 percent of its new price.

26  The price of          The price of the
    the stock before      stock after the
    the increase          decrease

Ⓐ Ⓑ Ⓒ Ⓓ Ⓔ

---

Manny's weekly income is 72 percent of Fran's weekly income. Manny's weekly income is $648.

27  Fran's weekly          $900
    income

Ⓐ Ⓑ Ⓒ Ⓓ Ⓔ

28  A baseball team won 45 percent of the first 80 games it played. How many of the remaining 82 games will the team have to win in order to win exactly 50 percent of all the games it plays?

| SCORECARD | |
|---|---|
| Number of Questions Right: | |
| Number of Questions Wrong: | |
| Number of Questions Omitted: | |
| Number of Correct Guesses: | |
| Number of Wrong Guesses: | |
| Time Used: | |

## ANSWERS AND EXPLANATIONS

### BASIC

**1** **B**—If 48 out of 60 seats on a bus were occupied, then 60 – 48, or 12, seats were not occupied. Since percent $= \frac{\text{part}}{\text{whole}} \times 100\%$, the percent of seats not occupied $= \frac{12}{60} \times 100\%$, or $\frac{1}{5} \times 100\% = 20\%$. So choice (B) is correct.

**2** **E**—The total cost of the taxi ride equals $36.00 + (25\% \text{ of } \$36.00)$, or $\$36.00 + (\frac{1}{4} \times \$36.00) = \$36.00 + \$9.00 = \$45.00$. If four people split the cost equally, then each person paid $\frac{\$45.00}{4}$, or $11.25 each. So choice (E) is correct.

**3** **C**—Percent increase $= \frac{\text{amount of increase}}{\text{original whole}} \times 100\%$ So if Edie's average rose from 72 to 84, the amount of the increase is 84 – 72, or 12. The percent increase $= \frac{12}{72} \times 100\%$, or $16\frac{2}{3}\%$, and choice (C) is correct.

**4** **B**—The question asks us to find $W$ as a percent of $T$.
60% of $W$ = 20% of $T$
$.6W = .2T$
Now solve for $W$:
$$W = \frac{.2T}{.6}$$
$$W = \frac{1}{3}T$$
$\frac{1}{3}$ is $33\frac{1}{3}\%$, so $W$ is $33\frac{1}{3}\%$ of $T$.

**5** **C**—This question involves a principle that appears frequently on the SAT: $a\%$ of $b = b\%$ of $a$. You can show that with the following example:

36% of 18 $= \frac{36}{100} \times 18$
$= \frac{18}{100} \times 36$
$= 18\%$ of 36
The answer here is 36.

**6** **D**—If 25% of the shoes are black, then 100% – 25%, or 75% of the shoes are not black. 75% of $24 = \frac{3}{4} \times 24 = 18$.

**7** **A**—The percent discount equals the amount of discount divided by the *original* price (*not* the final price). The amount of discount is $120 – $100, or $20. The original price was $120.
Percent discount $= \frac{20}{120} \times 100\% = \frac{1}{6} \times 100\% = 16\frac{2}{3}\%$.

**8** **B**—If 20 percent of the apartments with smoke alarms were found to have smoke alarms that are not working, then the remaining 80 percent of the apartments with smoke alarms have smoke alarms that *are* working. Since 80 percent of all apartments in the city have smoke alarms, and 80 percent of these have working smoke alarms, 80 percent of 80 percent of all the apartments in the city have working smoke alarms. Converting to fractions, 80% of 80% $= \frac{8}{10} \times \frac{8}{10} = \frac{64}{100}$. $\frac{64}{100}$ is 64%.

Alternatively, since we are working with percents only, try picking numbers. Let the number of apartments in City $G$ be 100. If 80 percent of these have smoke alarms, then 80 percent of 100, or 80, apartments have smoke alarms. If 20 percent of these do not work, then 80 percent do work. Eighty percent of 80 is $\frac{8}{10} \times 80$ = 64 apartments. If 64 of the 100 apartments in City $G$ have working smoke alarms, then we come up with $\frac{64}{100}$, or 64 percent, that have working smoke alarms.

**9** C—You can use a calculator to find that $\frac{3}{7}$% of .819 = .00351, as does .819% of $\frac{3}{7}$. However, it's much faster if you know that $a$% of $b = b$% of $a$. Remember this tidbit or call it to mind by using numbers that are easier to work with (such as 10% of 50 = 5, and 50% of 10 = 5).

**10** A—If the factory produces 25% more staplers this year than last, that is an increase of 25%, or $\frac{1}{4} \times 2,400 = 600$ staplers. So 2,400 + 600 = 3,000 staplers in Column A, which is more than 2,800 in Column B.

**11** .6 OR 3/5—You are asked for 10% of 20% of 30. You can simply multiply this through on a calculator:
10% = 0.1; 20% = 0.2
So 10% of 20% of 30 becomes $0.1 \times 0.2 \times 30 = 0.6$.

## MEDIUM

**12** E—You can assume Bob either passed or failed each test; there's no third possibility. If Bob failed 6 tests out of 20, he passed the other 14. Bob passed $\frac{14}{20}$ of the tests. To convert $\frac{14}{20}$ to a percent, multiply numerator and denominator by 5; this will give us a fraction with a denominator of 100: $\frac{14}{20} \times \frac{5}{5} = \frac{70}{100}$ or 70%. (Or realize that since $\frac{1}{20} = 5\%$, $\frac{14}{20}$ must be 14 times as big, or $14 \times 5\%$, or 70%.) Bob passed 70% of his tests.

**13** C—First, you have to identify the *part* and the *whole*. You're asked what percent of the gloves in the box are size 6, so the *part* is the number of size 6 gloves, and the *whole* is the total number of gloves. You're told there are 12 size 7 pairs and 24 size 6 pairs, for a total of 36 pairs. Of those 36 pairs, 24 pairs are size 6, so $\frac{24}{36}$ are size 6. $\frac{24}{36} = \frac{2}{3}$, or $66\frac{2}{3}$%.

**14** B—You first need to find what $x$ is. If 65% of $x$ = 195, then

$(0.65)\,(x) = 195$

$x = \frac{195}{0.65} = 300$

75% of 300 = $0.75 \times 300 = 225$

**15** B—You're asked what percent of the new solution is alcohol. The *part* is the number of ounces of alcohol; the *whole* is the total number of ounces of the new solution. There were 25 ounces originally. Then 50 ounces were added, so there are 75 ounces of new solution. How many ounces are alcohol? Twenty percent of the original 25-ounce solution was alcohol. Twenty percent is $\frac{1}{5}$, so $\frac{1}{5}$ of 25, or 5 ounces are alcohol. Now you can find the percent of alcohol in the new solution:

$$\% \text{ alcohol} = \frac{\text{alcohol}}{\text{total solution}} \times 100\%$$

$$= \frac{5}{75} \times 100\%$$

$$= \frac{20}{3}\% = 6\frac{2}{3}\%$$

**16** B—The easiest approach is to pick a sample value for the wholesale cost of the watch, and from that, work out the profit and selling price. As usual with percent problems, it's simplest to pick 100. If the watch cost the store $100, then the profit will be 25% of $100, or $25. The selling price equals the cost to the store plus the profit: $100 + $25, or $125. The profit represents $\frac{25}{125}$ or $\frac{1}{5}$ of the selling price. The percent equivalent of $\frac{1}{5}$ is 20%.

**17** A—The centered information tells us that $r = p\%$ of $q$. So $\frac{p}{100} \times q = r$, or $\frac{pq}{100} = r$, or $pq = 100r$. Since $p$, $q$, and $r$ are positive and $pq = 100r$ in Column A, this is greater than $r$ in Column B.

**18** B—Picking numbers can help in making this comparison. If $b = 100$, then
$$\frac{1}{4}\% \times 100 = a, \quad \frac{\frac{1}{4}}{100} \times 100 = a, \quad \frac{1}{4} = a.$$
So 4% of $a$ in Column A is $\frac{4}{100} \times \frac{1}{4} = \frac{1}{100}$, versus 100 in Column B. Column B is larger.

Another approach: The centered information tells you that $a$ is a small percentage of $b$, so $a < b$. In Column A, 4% of $a$ must be much less than $b$.

**19** E—Percent increase $= \frac{\text{Amount of increase}}{\text{Original whole}} \times 100\%$
The original whole is the price *before* the increase. The amount of increase is the difference between the increased price and the original price. So the amount of increase is 15¢ − 5¢ = 10¢.
$$\% \text{ increase} = \frac{10¢}{5¢} \times 100\% = 2 \times 100\% = 200\%.$$

**20** 125—The bicycle was discounted by 20%; this means that Jerry paid (100% − 20%), or 80%, of the original price. Jerry paid $100, so you have the percent and the part and need to find the whole. Now plug the numbers into the percent formula:

Percent × Whole = Part

80% × Whole = $100

0.8 × Whole = $100

Whole $= \frac{\$100}{.8}$

Whole = $125

The bicycle originally sold for $125.

**HARD**

**21** C—The key is: While the value of the stock decreases and increases by the same *amount*, it doesn't decrease and increase by the *same percent*. When the stock first decreases, that amount of change is part of a larger whole. If the stock were to increase to its former value, that same amount of change would be a larger percent of a smaller whole.

Pick a number for the original value of the stock, such as $100. (Since it's easy to take percents of 100, it's usually best to choose 100.) The 20% decrease represents $20, so the stock decreases to a value of $80. Now in order for the stock to reach the value of $100 again, there must be a $20 increase. What percent of $80 is $20? It's $\frac{\$20}{\$80} \times 100\%$, or $\frac{1}{4} \times 100\%$, or 25%.

**22** C—Since the population increases by 50% every 50 years, the population in 1950 was 150%, or $\frac{3}{2}$, of the 1900 population. This means the 1900 population was $\frac{2}{3}$ of the 1950 population. Similarly, the 1850 population was $\frac{2}{3}$ of the 1900 population, and so on. You can just keep multiplying by $\frac{2}{3}$ until you get to a population of 160.

1950: $810 \times \frac{2}{3} = 540$ in 1900

1900: $540 \times \frac{2}{3} = 360$ in 1850

1850: $360 \times \frac{2}{3} = 240$ in 1800

1800: $240 \times \frac{2}{3} = 160$ in 1750

The population was 160 in 1750.

Another approach is to work forward from the population of 160 until reaching 810; then determine how far back the population of 160 must have been.

During each 50-year period, the population increases by 50 percent, or by $\frac{1}{2}$.

160: $160 + \frac{1}{2}(160) = 240$

240: $240 + \frac{1}{2}(240) = 360$

360: $360 + \frac{1}{2}(360) = 540$

540: $540 + \frac{1}{2}(540) = 810$

So, if the population was 810 in 1950, it must have been 540 in 1900, 360 in 1850, 240 in 1800, and 160 in 1750.

**23** **B**—The man paid $80 for 10 crates of oranges, and then lost 2 crates. That leaves him with 8 crates. You want to find the price per crate that will give him an overall profit of 25%. 25%, or $\frac{1}{4}$, of $80 is $20. So to make a 25% profit, he must bring in $80 + $20, or $100, in sales receipts. If he has 8 crates, that means that each crate must sell for $\frac{\$100}{8}$, or $12.50.

**24** **A**—First find what percent of the whole population *does* play a varsity sport. We can do this by finding out what percent of all students are male students who play a varsity sport, and what percent of all students are female students who play a varsity sport, and then summing these values. 40 percent of all students are male, so 60% of the students are female.

First, what percent of all students are males who play a varsity sport? 50% of the males play a varsity sport; that is, 50% (or half) of 40% = $.5 \times .4 = .20 = 20\%$ of all the students.

Now for the women. 60% of the females play a varsity sport; that is, 60% of 60% = $.6 \times .6 = .36 = 36\%$ of all the students.

Sum the percents of the males and females who play a varsity sport: 20% + 36% = 56% of the total student population.

The percent of all students who DO NOT play a varsity sport is 100% − 56% = 44%.

**25** **C**—You have the equation $ab = \frac{c}{4}$. Increasing $a$ by 50% is the same as multiplying $a$ by $\frac{3}{2}$. Decreasing $b$ by 25% is the same as multiplying $b$ by $\frac{3}{4}$. Performing both these operations gives $\frac{3}{2}a \times \frac{3}{4}b = \frac{9}{8}ab$.

Therefore, $ab$ has increased by $\frac{1}{8}$. If $ab$ increases by $\frac{1}{8}$, then in order for the equation to remain true, $\frac{c}{4}$ must also be increased by $\frac{1}{8}$. If $\frac{c}{4}$ is increased by $\frac{1}{8}$, $c$ is also increased by $\frac{1}{8}$.

An increase of $\frac{1}{8}$ is the same as an increase of $12\frac{1}{2}\%$.

You can make this a lot less algebraic by picking numbers. We'll pick values for $a$ and $b$, which will yield a particular value for $c$ (since its value is determined by $a$ and $b$). Then you will make the described changes to $a$ and $b$, and see what change this gives for $c$.

Since $a$, $b$, and $c$ are positive numbers, say $a$ is 2 and $b$ is 4.

$$ab = \frac{c}{4}$$
$$c = 4ab$$
$$c = 4(2)(4) = 32$$

If $a$ is increased by 50 percent, it becomes 2 + 1, or 3. Since $b$ is decreased by 25%, it becomes 4 − 1, or 3. The relationship between $a$, $b$, and $c$ remains the same, but we'll use capital letters to denote the new values:

$$AB = \frac{C}{4}$$
$$C = 4AB$$
$$C = 4(3)(3) = 36$$

Therefore, $C$ increases from 32 to 36, which is a change of 4. The percent increase is then $\frac{4}{32} \times 100\% = 12\frac{1}{2}\%$.

**26** A—You could use algebra to solve this problem, but it's easier and quicker to pick numbers. Since you're working with percents, pick 100.

Suppose the stock starts at $100, then increases by 20 percent. Twenty percent of $100 is $20, so the stock is now $120. The price then decreases by 20 percent of this new price, or 20 percent of $120. 20 percent is $\frac{1}{5}$ so the stock price is decreased by $\frac{1}{5} \times \$120 = \$24$, down to $120 − $24 = $96. The original price of the stock was greater, so the answer is (A). (It makes sense that the original price would be greater, since the 20 percent decrease was 20 percent of a larger whole.)

**27** C—Manny's income is 72% of Fran's, so $M = .72F$, or $648 = .72F$ if you plug in 648 for Manny's income. Solving for $F$, you find that $F = 900$. The two columns are equal.

**28** 45—In their season, the baseball team plays 80 + 82, or 162 games. To win exactly 50% or $\frac{1}{2}$ of their games, they must win 81 games. They have won 45% of their first 80 games. Since $45\% \times 80 = \frac{9}{20} \times 80 = 36$, they have won 36 games. To finish with 81 wins, they must win 81 − 36, or 45, of the remaining games.

You'll see positive integer exponents and square roots incidentally in many SAT Math questions. Questions that specifically test you on powers and roots tend to be among the more difficult on the test. These are the essential skills (which you will find referenced in our SAT Math in a Nutshell section near the back of the book):

47.   Multiplying and Dividing Powers
48.   Raising Powers to Powers
49.   Simplifying Square Roots
50.   Adding and Subtracting Roots
51.   Multiplying and Dividing Roots

## PRACTICE SET

### BASIC

**1**   $2^4 \times 4^3 =$

(A)   $8^{12}$
(B)   $8^7$
(C)   $6^7$
(D)   $2^{10}$
(E)   $2^7$            Ⓐ Ⓑ Ⓒ Ⓓ Ⓔ

**2**   $6\sqrt{9} \times 2\sqrt{16} =$

(A)        72
(B)      144
(C)      288
(D)      864
(E)   1,728            Ⓐ Ⓑ Ⓒ Ⓓ Ⓔ

**3**   If $x = 9a^2$ and $a > 0$, then $\sqrt{x} =$

(A)   $-3a$
(B)   $3a$
(C)   $9a$
(D)   $3a^2$
(E)   $81a^4$            Ⓐ Ⓑ Ⓒ Ⓓ Ⓔ

**4**   Which of the following is NOT equal to 0.0675?

(A)   $67.5 \times 10^{-3}$
(B)   $6.75 \times 10^{-2}$
(C)   $0.675 \times 10^{-1}$
(D)   $0.00675 \times 10^2$
(E)   $0.0000675 \times 10^3$            Ⓐ Ⓑ Ⓒ Ⓓ Ⓔ

| Column A | Column B |
|---|---|

**5**   $\sqrt{100-36}$          $\sqrt{100} - \sqrt{36}$

Ⓐ Ⓑ Ⓒ Ⓓ Ⓔ

$a$ and $b$ are positive integers and $a - b = 5$.

**6**   $\dfrac{4^a}{4^b}$          $4^5$

Ⓐ Ⓑ Ⓒ Ⓓ Ⓔ

**7**   $70^{140}$          $140^{70}$

Ⓐ Ⓑ Ⓒ Ⓓ Ⓔ

**8**   $\dfrac{4^3 - 4^2}{2^2} =$

Ⓐ Ⓑ Ⓒ Ⓓ Ⓔ

### MEDIUM

**9**   If $q$ is an odd integer greater than 1, what is the value of $(-1)^q + 1$?

(A)   $-2$
(B)   $-1$
(C)    0
(D)    2
(E)   It cannot be determined from the information given.

Ⓐ Ⓑ Ⓒ Ⓓ Ⓔ

**10** If $x > 0$, then $(4^x)(8^x) =$

(A)  $2^{9x}$
(B)  $2^{8x}$
(C)  $2^{6x}$
(D)  $2^{5x}$
(E)  $2^{4x}$         Ⓐ Ⓑ Ⓒ Ⓓ Ⓔ

---

**11** If $\dfrac{\sqrt{n}}{3}$ is an even integer, which of the following could be the value of $n$ ?

(A)  27
(B)  48
(C)  81
(D)  121
(E)  144         Ⓐ Ⓑ Ⓒ Ⓓ Ⓔ

---

**12** Which of the following is equal to $8^5$?
   I.   $2^5 \times 4^5$
   II.  $2^{15}$
   III. $2^5 \times 2^{10}$

(A)  II only
(B)  I and II only
(C)  I and III only
(D)  II and III only
(E)  I, II, and III         Ⓐ Ⓑ Ⓒ Ⓓ Ⓔ

---

| Column A | Column B |
|---|---|
| $r > 1$ | |

**13**   $\sqrt{r^{16}}$         $(r^4)^2$

Ⓐ Ⓑ Ⓒ Ⓓ Ⓔ

---

$n^5 = 81$

**14**   $n^3$         27

Ⓐ Ⓑ Ⓒ Ⓓ Ⓔ

---

$a^2 = 81$

**15**   $a$         $-a$

Ⓐ Ⓑ Ⓒ Ⓓ Ⓔ

---

**16** If $x = 2$, then $3^x + (x^3)^2 =$

### HARD

**17** If $xyz \neq 0$, then $\dfrac{x^2 y^6 z^{10}}{xy^3 z^5} =$

(A)  $xy^2 z^2$
(B)  $xy^3 z^5$
(C)  $x^2 y^2 z^2$
(D)  $x^2 y^3 z^5$
(E)  $x^3 y^9 z^{15}$         Ⓐ Ⓑ Ⓒ Ⓓ Ⓔ

---

**18** If $x^a x^b = 1$ and $x \neq \pm 1$, then $a + b =$

(A)  $x$
(B)  $-1$
(C)  $0$
(D)  $1$
(E)  It cannot be determined from the information given.

Ⓐ Ⓑ Ⓒ Ⓓ Ⓔ

---

| Column A | Column B |
|---|---|
| $p$ and $q$ are positive numbers and $p > q$. | |

$$\sqrt{p^2 + 2pq + q^2} = x$$

$$\sqrt{p^2 - 2pq + q^2} = y$$

**19**   $2p$         $x + y$

Ⓐ Ⓑ Ⓒ Ⓓ Ⓔ

---

**20** If $5^n > 10,000$ and $n$ is an integer, what is the smallest possible value of $n$ ?

| SCORECARD | |
|---|---|
| Number of Questions Right: | |
| Number of Questions Wrong: | |
| Number of Questions Omitted: | |
| Number of Correct Guesses: | |
| Number of Wrong Guesses: | |
| Time Used: | |

**KAPLAN**

## ANSWERS AND EXPLANATIONS

### BASIC

**1** **D**—To multiply two numbers with the same base, *add* the two exponents. Here, we have two different bases, 2 and 4. We must rewrite one of the numbers so that the bases are the same. Since 4 = $2^2$, we can easily rewrite $4^3$ as a power of 2: $4^3$ = $(2^2)^3$. To raise a power to an exponent, *multiply* the exponents, so $(2^2)^3 = 2^6$.

Therefore, $2^4 \times 4^3 = 2^4 \times 2^6$
$$= 2^{4+6}$$
$$= 2^{10}$$

**2** **B**—The expression $6\sqrt{9} \times 2\sqrt{16}$ can be simplified by taking the square roots of 9 and 16, respectively:

$6\sqrt{9} \times 2\sqrt{16} =$

$(6 \times 3) \times (2 \times 4) = 18 \times 8 = 144$

So choice (B) is correct.

**3** **B**—We can find the value of $\sqrt{x}$ by substituting $9a^2$ for $x$.

$\sqrt{x} = \sqrt{9a^2}$
$$= \sqrt{9} \times \sqrt{a^2}$$
$$= 3a$$

*Note:* We could do this only because we know that $a > 0$. The radical sign ($\sqrt{\ }$) refers to the positive square root of a number.

**4** **D**—To multiply or divide a number by a power of 10, we move the decimal point to the right or left, respectively, the same number of places as the number of zeros in the power of 10. Multiplying by a negative power of 10 is the same as dividing by a positive power. For instance: $3 \times 10^{-2} = \frac{3}{10^2}$. Keeping this in mind, let's go over the choices one by one. Remember: We are looking for the choice that is *not* equal to 0.0675.

Choice (A):  $67.5 \times 10^{-3} = 0.0675$. No good.
Choice (B):  $6.75 \times 10^{-2} = 0.0675$. No good.
Choice (C):  $0.675 \times 10^{-1} = 0.0675$. No good.
Choice (D):  $0.00675 \times 10^2 = 0.675$.
$0.675 \neq 0.0675$, so this is the correct answer.

Let's go over choice (E) for practice.
Choice (E): $0.0000675 \times 10^3 = 0.0675$. No good.

**5** **A**—Pay attention to the order of operations. In Column A, you have to perform the subtraction before you take the square root: $\sqrt{100 - 36} = \sqrt{64} = 8$. However, in Column B, you have to get the square roots before you perform the subtraction: $\sqrt{100} - \sqrt{36} = 10 - 6 = 4$. So Column A is greater than Column B, and choice (A) is correct.

**6** **C**—Make the columns look more similar by getting rid of the fraction in Column A. When dividing two powers with the same base, you subtract the exponents. And since a fraction is a way of representing division, Column A can be rewritten as $4^{a-b}$. Since you are told that $a - b = 5$, Column A is $4^5$, and equal to Column B.

**7** **A**—The numbers in this problem are too large for a calculator to handle, so you need to use the laws of exponents to make the columns look more similar and easier to compare. Column A can be rewritten as $70^{70} \times 70^{70}$, since when multiplying two exponential expressions with the same base you add the exponents. Rewrite Column B: $140^{70} = (70 \times 2)^{70} = 70^{70} \times 2^{70}$. Since each column contains $70^{70}$ you can divide both sides by it. You are left comparing $70^{70}$ in Column A to $2^{70}$ in Column B, so Column A is obviously greater

**8** **12**—If you use your calculator on this question, be very careful in following the order of operations. In this case, remember to find the values of the exponential terms first.

A different approach: When you divide powers with the same base, keep the base and subtract the exponent of the denominator from the exponent of the numerator. First get everything in the same base. Since $2^2 = 4 = 4^1$, then

$$\frac{4^3 - 4^2}{2^2} = \frac{4^3 - 4^2}{4^1}$$
$$= \frac{4^3}{4^1} - \frac{4^2}{4^1}$$
$$= 4^{3-1} - 4^{2-1}$$
$$= 4^2 - 4^1$$
$$= 16 - 4$$
$$= 12$$

## MEDIUM

**9** **C**—The product of two negatives is positive, and the product of three negatives is negative. In fact, if we have any odd number of negative terms in a product, the result will be negative; any even number of negative terms gives a positive product. Since $q$ is odd, we have an odd number of factors of $-1$. Therefore, the product is $-1$. Adding 1 to $-1$, we get 0.

**10** **D**—Remember the rules for operations with exponents. First you have to get both powers in terms of the same base so you can combine the exponents. Note that the answer choices all have base 2. Start by expressing 4 and 8 as powers of 2:

$(4^x)(8^x) = (2^2)^x \times (2^3)^x$

To raise a power to an exponent, multiply the exponents:

$(2^2)^x = 2^{2x}$
$(2^3)^x = 2^{3x}$

To multiply powers with the same base, add the exponents:

$2^{2x} \times 2^{3x} = 2^{(2x + 3x)}$
$= 2^{5x}$

**11** **E**—If $\dfrac{\sqrt{n}}{3}$ is an even integer, then $\sqrt{n}$ must be a multiple of 2 and 3 and therefore $n$ must be a perfect square and an even multiple of 3. Looking at the answer choices, you can immediately eliminate choices (A) and (B) because they are not perfect squares. Out of the remaining choices, only choice (E), 144, is both a perfect square and an even multiple of 3. Check it to make sure it works. If $n = 144$, then $\dfrac{\sqrt{144}}{3} = \dfrac{12}{3} = 4$. So 144 fits the given conditions, and choice (E) is correct.

**12** **E**—You can easily raise 8 to the 5th power using your calculator and see that it equals 32,768. Plugging each of the three statements into your calculator, being wary of the order of operations, you will see that each statement also equals 32,768. So answer choice (E) is correct.

Alternatively, look at this question as a good review of the rules for the product of exponential expressions. In order to make the comparisons easier, transform $8^5$ and each of the three options so that they have a common base. Since 2 is the smallest base among the expressions to be compared, let it be your common base. Since $8^5 = (2^3)^5 = 2^{3 \times 5} = 2^{15}$, look for options equivalent to $2^{15}$.

I: $2^5 \times 4^5 = 2^5 \times (2^2)^5 = 2^5 \times 2^{2 \times 5} = 2^5 \times 2^{10}$ $= 2^{5+10} = 2^{15}$. Okay.

II: $2^{15}$. Okay.

III: $2^5 \times 2^{10} = 2^{5+10} = 2^{15}$. Okay.

Again, all three are equivalent to $2^{15}$ or $8^5$.

**13** **C**—To find $\sqrt{r^{16}}$ in Column A, we can work backward. That is, $r$ to what power, squared, gives us $r^{16}$? $(r^8)^2 = r^{8 \times 2} = r^{16}$. So in Column A, we have $r^8$. In Column B, you have $(r^4)^2$, which is $r^{4 \times 2}$, or $r^8$ as well. Since the two columns are equal, choice (C) is correct.

**14** **B**—If you know how to use the function keys on your calculator, you can find the value of $n$, and then raise it to the third power to find that Column A equals 13.96661, which is less than 27 in Column B. Without a calculator, you can recognize 81 as a power of 3—that is, $3^4$. If $n^5 = 81$, then n must be less than 3. Since $3^3$ is 27, and if n is less than 3, then $n^3$ in Column A must be less than 27, and Column B is greater.

**15** **D**—Since $a^2 = 81$, $a$ could equal 9 or $-9$. If $a = 9$, Column A is 9 while Column B is $-9$, making Column A greater. But if $a = -9$, Column A contains $-9$ and Column B contains $-(-9)$, or 9, making Column B greater. Since more than one relationship is possible, the correct answer must be choice (D).

**16** **73**—Substitute 2 for $x$, and then solve by following PEMDAS.

$3^x + (x^3)^2 = 3^2 + (2^3)^2$
$x = 3^2 + 8^2$
$= 9 + 64$
$= 73$

## HARD

**17** **B**—First break up the expression to separate the variables, transforming the fraction into a product of three simpler fractions:

$$\frac{x^2 y^6 z^{10}}{xy^3 z^5} = \left(\frac{x^2}{x}\right)\left(\frac{y^6}{y^3}\right)\left(\frac{z^{10}}{z^5}\right)$$

Now carry out each division by keeping the base and subtracting the exponents.

$$\frac{x^2}{x} = x^{2-1} = x$$

$$\frac{y^6}{y^3} = y^{6-3} = y^3$$

$$\frac{z^{10}}{z^5} = z^{10-5} = z^5$$

The answer is the product of these three terms, or $xy^3 z^5$.

**18** **C**—We are told that $x^a \times x^b = 1$. Since $x^a x^b = x^a + x^b$, we know that $x^{a+b} = 1$. If a power is equal to 1, either the base is 1 or $-1$, or the exponent is 0. Since we are told $x \neq 1$ or $-1$, the exponent must be 0; therefore, $a + b = 0$.

**19** **C**—The difficult part of this problem is recognizing the expressions beneath the radicals. The left side of the first equation can be factored:

$\sqrt{(p+q)(p+q)} = \sqrt{(p+q)^2}$ . So $x = \sqrt{(p+q)^2} = (p+q)$.

The second equation can be factored in a similar way: $\sqrt{p^2 - 2pq + q^2} = y$ becomes $\sqrt{(p-q)(p-q)} = y$,

or $\sqrt{(p-q)^2} = y$. So $y = p - q$. Since you're comparing the value of $x + y$ in Column B to $2p$ in Column A, substitute $p + q$ and $p - q$ for $x$ and $y$, respectively:

$x + y = p + q + p - q$, or $x + y = 2p$. So the columns are equal, and choice (C) is correct.

**20** **6**—Use your calculator to test values of $n$. Raise 5 to successive exponents to see which is the smallest power such that $5^n > 10,000$. Alternatively, try approximating to find $n$. $5^2 = 25$, $5^3 = 125$, so $5^3 > 100$.

Then $5^4 > 100 \times 5$, or $5^4 > 500$

$5^5 > 500 \times 5$, or $5^5 > 2,500$

$5^6 > 2,500 \times 5$, or $5^6 > 12,500$

$5^6$ must be greater than 10,000, but $5^5$ clearly is a lot less than 10,000. So, in order for $5n$ to be greater than 10,000, $n$ must be at least 6.

Most SATs include one or two data interpretation questions. You'll see a table, a pie chart, a line graph, or a bar graph, and you'll be asked to extract some piece of information. The key is to read the question and all labels extra carefully, ignore extraneous data, and zero in on what's asked for.

## PRACTICE SET

Questions 1 and 2 refer to the following table.

LUNCHEON SPECIALS

| MEAL | PRICE |
|------|-------|
| Hamburger | $3.00 |
| Chicken | $2.75 |
| Tuna Salad | $2.50 |
| Pasta Salad | $2.25 |
| Pizza | $1.50 |

1 If the table above represents the luncheon prices at a certain cafeteria, what is the average (arithmetic mean) price for a meal at this cafeteria?

(A) $2.40
(B) $2.50
(C) $2.60
(D) $2.70
(E) $2.80

2 If three people each ordered a different meal, which of the following could not be the total cost of the meals, excluding tax?

(A) $7.50
(B) $7.00
(C) $6.75
(D) $6.25
(E) $6.00          Ⓐ Ⓑ Ⓒ Ⓓ Ⓔ

ANNUAL APPLICATIONS TO COLLEGE W
1987 – 1992

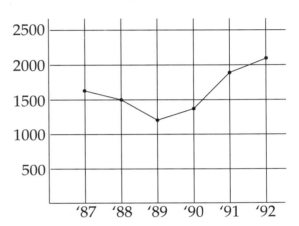

3 The graph above represents the number of applications submitted to College W each year for a six-year period. If applications increase by approximately the same percent from 1992 to 1993 as they decreased from 1988 to 1989, approximately how many applications will College W receive in 1993?

(A) 2,100
(B) 2,300
(C) 2,520
(D) 2,625
(E) 2,800          Ⓐ Ⓑ Ⓒ Ⓓ Ⓔ

DISTRIBUTION OF GRADES FOR MATH EXAM

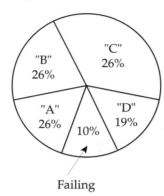

Failing

**4** If 180 students passed the test, how many received a grade of B?

ANNUAL TOURISM REVENUE IN CITY X
1986 –1992

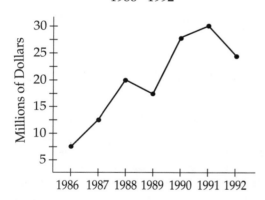

**5** The graph above represents the annual revenue from tourism in City X over a seven-year period. During which of the following periods was the change in tourism revenues greatest?

(A)   1986–1987
(B)   1987–1988
(C)   1989–1990
(D)   1990–1991
(E)   1991–1992          Ⓐ Ⓑ Ⓒ Ⓓ Ⓔ

**6** By what percent did tourism revenues decrease from 1988 to 1989?

(A)   10%

(B)   $12\frac{1}{2}\%$

(C)   25%

(D)   $37\frac{1}{2}\%$

(E)   50%          Ⓐ Ⓑ Ⓒ Ⓓ Ⓔ

MAJORS OF JUNIOR CLASS AT COLLEGE W

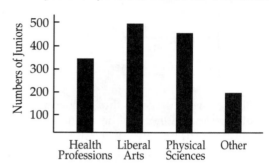

**7** If the graph above represents the majors of the entire junior class, what is the ratio of juniors majoring in Physical Sciences to all juniors enrolled?

(A)   3:7
(B)   5:13
(C)   1:3
(D)   3:10
(E)   3:26          Ⓐ Ⓑ Ⓒ Ⓓ Ⓔ

SUMMER PLANS FOR SOPHOMORE CLASS

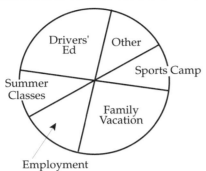

100% = 240 Students

| Column A | Column B |
| --- | --- |
| 8 The number of students in the class who plan to take driver's education | 100 |

Ⓐ Ⓑ Ⓒ Ⓓ Ⓔ

AMOUNT IN DOLLARS CONTRIBUTED BY A
SCHOOL TO FIVE STUDENT ORGANIZATIONS

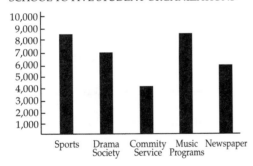

9 How much more money did the school contribute to the drama society than to the community service organization?

(A) $4,000
(B) $3,500
(C) $3,000
(D) $2,500
(E) $2,000

Ⓐ Ⓑ Ⓒ Ⓓ Ⓔ

10 If the school provided 80% of the budget of the newspaper, what was the newspaper's total budget?

(A) $4,800
(B) $6,800
(C) $7,200
(D) $7,500
(E) $8,750

Ⓐ Ⓑ Ⓒ Ⓓ Ⓔ

| SCORECARD | |
| --- | --- |
| Number of Questions Right: | |
| Number of Questions Wrong: | |
| Number of Questions Omitted: | |
| Number of Correct Guesses: | |
| Number of Wrong Guesses: | |
| Time Used: | |

## ANSWERS AND EXPLANATIONS

**1** **A**—To find the average price for a meal, use the formula: average $= \dfrac{\text{sum of terms}}{\text{number of terms}}$

$= (\$3.00 + \$2.75 + \$2.50 + \$2.25 + \$1.50) \div 5$

$= \$12.00 \div 5$

$= \$2.40$

**2** **E**—The three lowest-priced meals—pizza at $1.50, pasta salad at $2.25, and tuna salad at $2.50—total $6.25. So it is not possible that a combination of three different meals could cost less than $6.25. Since choice (E), $6.00, is less than this, it could not be the total cost of three different meals.

**3** **C**—The number of applications received in a particular year is represented as the vertical distance from the bottom of the graph to the line above that year. In 1988 College W received 1,500 applications, and in 1989 only 1,200. This is a decrease of 300 applications, so from 1988 to 1989 applications decreased by $\dfrac{300}{1,500} = \dfrac{1}{5} = 20\%$. (Remember, when figuring a percent increase/decrease, put the amount of change over the *original* amount, in this case 1,500; if you put it over the amount you end up with, you'd get $\dfrac{300}{1,200} = \dfrac{1}{4} = 25\%$, and you'd answer the problem incorrectly.) In 1992 College W received 2,100 applications. If between 1992 and 1993, applications increased by the same percent that they decreased between 1988 and 1989, that would be an increase of 2,100 × 20% = 420. So in 1993 College W will receive 2,100 + 420 = 2,520 applications.

**4** **50**—In a pie chart, the whole pie represents a total quantity, while each slice represents a part or percent of that whole. So finding out how many students received a grade of B on the test is a percent problem: The percent of students who received a B, times the total number of students who took the exam, equals the number of students who received a B.

The "B" slice is identified as $x\%$, so you need to solve for $x$. All the slices together must equal 100% of the pie, so 20% + 26% + 19% + 10% + $x\%$ = 100%, 75% + $x\%$ = 100%, $x\%$ = 25%. So 25%, or $\dfrac{1}{4}$, times the total number of students who took the exam will give you the answer you need. You aren't given the total number of students, but you are told that 180 students passed the exam. Since only 10% failed the test, 90% passed it. So 180 = 90%, or $\dfrac{9}{10}$ of the total number of students, $180 \times \dfrac{10}{9}$ = the total number of students = 200. Now you can solve the problem: $\dfrac{1}{4} \times 200 = 50$, so 50 students received a grade of B.

**5** **C**—The amount of tourism revenue generated in a certain year is represented as the vertical distance from the bottom of the graph to the line above that year. The key along the vertical axis tells you that the income is measured in millions of dollars. Looking at the graph you can see that the greatest change in revenue occurs between 1989 and 1990, when it jumps from $17.5 million to $27.5 million, for an increase of $10 million.

**6** **B**—Revenue dropped from 20 million dollars in 1988 to 17.5 million dollars in 1989. This is a decrease of 2.5 million dollars. To find what percent decrease this is, use the formula:

$$\text{Percent } = \frac{\text{part}}{\text{whole}}$$
$$= \frac{2.5}{20}$$
$$= 0.125$$

To convert this decimal to a percent, multiply by 100%:

$0.125 \times 100\% = 12.5\%$, answer choice (B).

**7** **D**—On this bar graph, the number of students choosing a particular major is represented as the vertical distance from the bottom of the graph to the top of the bar above that major. Find the number of majors in Physical Sciences by reading off the graph; 450 juniors are majoring in Physical Sciences. Next find the total number of students by adding all the bars. That is 350 in Health Professions, plus 500 in Liberal Arts, plus 450 in Physical Sciences, plus 200 in other majors for a total of 1500 juniors.

The ratio of juniors majoring in Physical Sciences, to all juniors is then $\frac{450}{1500} = \frac{3}{10}$, or 3:10.

**8** **B**—Looking at the pie chart, you'll see that the slice labeled Driver's Education accounts for about a quarter of the whole pie. Since the entire pie represents 240 students, $\frac{1}{4} \times 240 = 60$, which is less than 100 in Column B.

**9** **C**—You need to find the amount of money the school contributed to the drama society and subtract from that the amount of money the school contributed to the community service organization. Since the bars in this graph are drawn vertically, the height of each shows its value. The bar for the drama society is $7,000, while the bar for the community service organization is $4,000: $7,000 − $4,000 = $3,000.

**10** **D**—Looking at the bar for the newspaper, you'll see that the newspaper received $6,000 from the school. If this represents 80% or $\frac{4}{5}$ of its total budget, $\frac{4}{5} \times$ newspaper's total budget = $6,000, so the newspaper's total budget = $\frac{5}{4} \times \$6,000 = \$7,500$.

# BASIC ALGEBRA—PRACTICE SET 8

Algebra constitutes approximately one-third of SAT Math questions. Most of these are basic algebra questions, which test the following skills (for help and a handy reference, refer to our SAT Math in a Nutshell section):

52. Evaluating an Expression
53. Adding and Subtracting Monomials
54. Adding and Subtracting Polynomials
55. Multiplying Monomials
56. Multiplying Binomials—FOIL
57. Multiplying Other Polynomials
58. Factoring Out a Common Divisor
59. Factoring the Difference of Squares
60. Factoring the Square of a Binomial
61. Factoring Other Polynomials—FOIL in Reverse
62. Simplifying an Algebraic Fraction
63. Solving a Linear Equation
64. Solving "In Terms Of"

## PRACTICE SET

### BASIC

**1** If $x = -3$, what is the value of the expression $x^2 + 3x + 3$?

(A)  $-21$
(B)  $-15$
(C)  $-6$
(D)  $3$
(E)  $21$     Ⓐ Ⓑ Ⓒ Ⓓ Ⓔ

**2** Let $<<x>> = 2x - 1$ for all positive integers. If $<<x>> = 15$, then $x =$

(A)  6
(B)  7
(C)  8
(D)  15
(E)  16     Ⓐ Ⓑ Ⓒ Ⓓ Ⓔ

**3** $5z^2 - 5z + 4 - z(3z - 4) =$

(A)  $2z^2 - z + 4$
(B)  $2z^2 - 9z + 4$
(C)  $5z^2 - 8z + 8$
(D)  $5z^2 - 8z$
(E)  $2z^2 - 5z$     Ⓐ Ⓑ Ⓒ Ⓓ Ⓔ

**4** If $a = 2$, $b = -1$, and $c = 1$, which of the following must be true?

  I.  $a + b + c = 2$
  II.  $2a + bc = 4$
  III.  $4a - b + c = 8$

(A)  I only
(B)  III only
(C)  I and II only
(D)  I and III only
(E)  I, II, and III     Ⓐ Ⓑ Ⓒ Ⓓ Ⓔ

**5** If $y \neq z$, then $\dfrac{xy - zx}{z - y} =$

(A)  $x$
(B)  $1$
(C)  $0$
(D)  $-1$
(E)  $-x$     Ⓐ Ⓑ Ⓒ Ⓓ Ⓔ

**6** For any number $w$, let $\# w \#$ be defined by the equation $\# w \# = -[w^2(w - 1)]$. What is the value of $\# -1 \#$?

(A)  $-2$
(B)  $-1$
(C)  $0$
(D)  $1$
(E)  $2$     Ⓐ Ⓑ Ⓒ Ⓓ Ⓔ

Column A | Column B

$$14x + 45 = 200$$

7    $x$              10

Ⓐ Ⓑ Ⓒ Ⓓ Ⓔ

---

8    $a(a + 1)$      $a(a - 1)$

Ⓐ Ⓑ Ⓒ Ⓓ Ⓔ

---

9   If $a = -1$ and $b = -2$, then $2a^2 - 2ab + b^2 =$

Ⓐ Ⓑ Ⓒ Ⓓ Ⓔ

---

10   If $\dfrac{3}{a} = \dfrac{5}{4}$, what is the value of $a$ ?

11   If $q \times 34 \times 36 \times 38 = 17 \times 18 \times 19$, then $q =$

---

## MEDIUM

12   Which of the following is equivalent to $3x^2 + 18x + 27$?

    (A)   $3(x^2 + 6x + 3)$
    (B)   $3(x + 3)(x + 6)$
    (C)   $3(x + 3)(x + 3)$
    (D)   $3x(x + 6 + 9)$
    (E)   $3x^2 + x(18 + 27)$      Ⓐ Ⓑ Ⓒ Ⓓ Ⓔ

---

13   $(a^2 + b)^2 - (a^2 - b)^2 =$

    (A)   $-4a^2b$
    (B)   $0$
    (C)   $(2ab)^2$
    (D)   $4a^2b$
    (E)   $b^2$      Ⓐ Ⓑ Ⓒ Ⓓ Ⓔ

---

14   If $z \neq 0$, $x = \dfrac{4}{z}$, and $yz = 8$, then $\dfrac{x}{y} =$

    (A)   0.5
    (B)   1
    (C)   2
    (D)   16
    (E)   32      Ⓐ Ⓑ Ⓒ Ⓓ Ⓔ

---

15   If $abc \neq 0$, then $\dfrac{a^2bc + ab^2c + abc^2}{abc} =$

    (A)   $a + b + c$
    (B)   $a + b + cabc$
    (C)   $a^3b^3c^3$
    (D)   $3abc$
    (E)   $2abc$      Ⓐ Ⓑ Ⓒ Ⓓ Ⓔ

---

16   If $x \blacklozenge y = (x - y)^2$ for all integers, which of the following must be true?

    I.   $x \blacklozenge y = y \blacklozenge x$
    II.   $x \blacklozenge y = x \blacklozenge (-y)$
    III.   $x \blacklozenge (-y) = (-x) \blacklozenge y$

    (A)   I only
    (B)   III only
    (C)   I and II
    (D)   I and III
    (E)   II and III      Ⓐ Ⓑ Ⓒ Ⓓ Ⓔ

---

Column A | Column B

$$x > 0$$

17   $\dfrac{x + 40}{60}$           $\dfrac{x + 20}{30}$

Ⓐ Ⓑ Ⓒ Ⓓ Ⓔ

---

$$3a + 3b + 3c = 18$$

18   The average          3
     (arithmetic mean)
     of $a$, $b$, and $c$

Ⓐ Ⓑ Ⓒ Ⓓ Ⓔ

---

$$y < 0$$

19   $10(y - 1)$          $10(1 - y)$

Ⓐ Ⓑ Ⓒ Ⓓ Ⓔ

Column A　　　　　　Column B

For all $r$ and $s$, let

$$r \blacksquare s = \frac{r+s}{r-s}.$$

**20** $(8 \blacksquare 4) \blacksquare 2$　　　　　$8 \blacksquare (4 \blacksquare 2)$

Ⓐ Ⓑ Ⓒ Ⓓ Ⓔ

---

**21** $(a + b)(c - d) + (a - b)(c - d)$　　　$2a(c - d)$

Ⓐ Ⓑ Ⓒ Ⓓ Ⓔ

---

**22** If the product of 4, 5, and $q$ is equal to the product of 5, $p$, and 2, and $pq \neq 0$, what is the value of $\dfrac{p}{q}$?

---

**23** If $x = 2$ and $y = 3$, then $\dfrac{xy}{\dfrac{1}{x} + \dfrac{1}{y}} =$

---

## HARD

---

**24** The expression $\dfrac{3}{x-1} - 6$ will equal 0 when $x$ equals which of the following?

(A)　$-3$

(B)　$-\dfrac{2}{3}$

(C)　$\dfrac{1}{2}$

(D)　$\dfrac{3}{2}$

(E)　$3$　　　　　Ⓐ Ⓑ Ⓒ Ⓓ Ⓔ

---

**25** If $x > 1$ and $\dfrac{a}{b} = 1 - \dfrac{1}{x}$, then $\dfrac{b}{a} =$

(A)　$x$

(B)　$x - 1$

(C)　$\dfrac{x-1}{x}$

(D)　$\dfrac{x}{x-1}$

(E)　$\dfrac{1}{x}$　　　Ⓐ Ⓑ Ⓒ Ⓓ Ⓔ

---

**26** If the numerical values of $(m + n)^2$ and $(m - n)^2$ are equal, then which of the following must be true?

　　I.　$m + n = 0$
　　II.　$m - n = 0$
　　III.　$mn = 0$

(A)　I only
(B)　II only
(C)　III only
(D)　I and II only
(E)　I, II, and III　　　Ⓐ Ⓑ Ⓒ Ⓓ Ⓔ

---

Column A　　　　　　Column B

$$xy \neq 0$$

$$\frac{x}{y} = \frac{y}{x}$$

**27**　　$x$　　　　　　　$y$

Ⓐ Ⓑ Ⓒ Ⓓ Ⓔ

---

**28**　　$4n + 4$　　　　$5n$

Ⓐ Ⓑ Ⓒ Ⓓ Ⓔ

Column A          Column B

$x \neq -2$

29  $\dfrac{3x^2+12x+12}{(x+2)^2}$          3

Ⓐ Ⓑ Ⓒ Ⓓ Ⓔ

---

$y > 0$

30  $\dfrac{(y-1)(y+1)}{y^2}$          $\dfrac{(y-1)(y+2)}{y^2}$

Ⓐ Ⓑ Ⓒ Ⓓ Ⓔ

---

31  If $xy = 8$ and $x^2 + y^2 = 16$, then $(x + y)^2 =$

| SCORECARD | |
|---|---|
| Number of Questions Right: | |
| Number of Questions Wrong: | |
| Number of Questions Omitted: | |
| Number of Correct Guesses: | |
| Number of Wrong Guesses: | |
| Time Used: | |

## ANSWERS AND EXPLANATIONS

### BASIC

**1** **D**—You want to find the value of the expression when $x$ is $-3$, so plug in $-3$ for each $x$:
$$x^2 + 3x + 3 = (-3)^2 + 3(-3) + 3 = 9 + (-9) + 3 = 3$$

**2** **C**—To solve for $x$, replace $<<x>>$ with the equivalent expression $2x - 1$ and set it equal to 15:
$$<<x>> = 15$$
$$2x - 1 = 15$$
$$2x = 16$$
$$x = 8.$$

**3** **A**—Before you can carry out any other operations, you have to remove the parentheses. That's what "P" stands for in PEMDAS, an acronym for the order of operations in a mathematical expression: **P**arentheses, **E**xponents, **M**ultiplication, **D**ivision, **A**ddition, **S**ubtraction (see the SAT Math in a Nutshell section). Here you can use the distributive law:
$$z(3z - 4) = z \times 3z - z \times 4$$
$$= 3z^2 - 4z$$
But there's more to do—you're *subtracting* this whole expression from $5z^2 - 5z + 4$. Since subtraction is the inverse operation of addition, you must change the signs of $3z^2 - 4z$.
$$5z^2 - 5z + 4 - (3z^2 - 4z)$$
$$= 5z^2 - 5z + 4 - 3z^2 + 4z$$
Finally, combining like terms gives us:
$$5z^2 - 5z + 4 - 3z^2 + 4z$$
$$= (5z^2 - 3z^2) + (-5z + 4z) + 4$$
$$= 2z^2 - z + 4$$

**4** **A**—Substitute $a = 2$, $b = -1$, and $c = 1$ into the statements.
Statement I: $a + b + c = 2 + (-1) + 1$
$$= 2$$
Statement I is true, so eliminate choice (B).
Statement II: $2a + bc = 2(2) + (-1)(1)$
$$= 4 - 1$$
$$= 3$$
Statement II is false, so eliminate choices (C) and (E).
Statement III: $4a - b + c = 4(2) - (-1) + 1$
$$= 8 + 1 + 1$$
$$= 10$$
Statement III is false and the correct answer is choice (A).

**5** **E**—Whenever you are asked to simplify a fraction that involves binomials, your first thought should be: Factor! Since $x$ is in both terms of the numerator, we can factor out $x$ and get
$$xy - zx = x(y - z)$$
Performing this operation on the original fraction, you find that
$$\frac{xy - zx}{z - y} = \frac{x(y - z)}{z - y}$$
Rewriting $(z - y)$ as $-1(y - z)$, you get:
$$= \frac{x(y - x)}{-1(y - x)}$$
Now cancel $y - z$ from the top and bottom:
$$\frac{x}{-1} = -x$$

*Note:* There is a reason that you are told that $y \neq z$; otherwise you could have zero in the denominator, and the expression could be undefined.

**6** **E**—Plug $(-1)$ into the expression $-[w^2(w - 1)]$ and simplify:
$$-[(-1)^2((-1) - 1)]$$
Negative 1, squared, equals positive 1, so this equals:
$$-[1(-1 - 1)]$$
$$= -[1(-2)]$$
$$= -(-2) = 2$$

**7** **A** – Feel free to solve the equation, but it's faster to see whether $x$ is 10. Substituting 10 for $x$, we find that it doesn't work; $14(10) + 45 = 185$. So 10 must be too small. Therefore, $x$ is larger than 10, and Column A is larger.

**8** **D**—Multiplying out both columns, you find $a^2 + a$ in Column A and $a^2 - a$ in Column B. Subtracting $a^2$ from both sides leaves $a$ in Column A and $-a$ in Column B. Don't be fooled into thinking that $a$ is larger than $-a$ by assuming $a$ is positive and $-a$ is negative. That's true only if $a$ is positive: If $a$ is a negative number, for instance $-4$, then $-a$ would be $-(-4)$, or 4, which is greater than $a$. You need more information to make the comparison.

**9** **2**—Plug in $-1$ for each $a$ and $-2$ for each $b$:
$$2a^2 - 2ab + b^2 = 2(-1)^2 - 2(-1)(-2) + (-2)^2$$
$$= 2 - 4 + 4$$
$$= 2.$$

**10** **2.4 or 12/5**—Cross multiply, and then divide both sides by 5:

$$\frac{3}{a} = \frac{5}{4}$$

$$3 \times 4 = 5a$$

$$12 = 5a$$

$$a = \frac{12}{5} \text{ or } 2.4$$

**11** **1/8 or .125**—Don't multiply anything out! With such a bizarre-looking expression, there's usually a shortcut. Notice that each of the numbers on the right side is a factor of a number on the left side. So divide each side of the equation by $34 \times 36 \times 38$ to isolate $q$:

$$q = \frac{17 \times 18 \times 19}{34 \times 36 \times 38}$$

$$q = \frac{17}{34} \times \frac{18}{36} \times \frac{19}{38}$$

$$q = \frac{1}{2} \times \frac{1}{2} \times \frac{1}{2}$$

$$= \frac{1}{8} \text{ or } .125$$

## MEDIUM

**12** **C**—First factor out the 3 common to all terms:
$$3x^2 + 18x + 27 = 3(x^2 + 6x + 9)$$

This is not an answer choice, so you must factor the polynomial.

$x^2 + 6x + 9$ is of the form $a^2 + 2ab + b^2$, with $a = x$ and $b = 3$.

So, $x^2 + 6x + 9 = (x + 3)^2$ or $(x + 3)(x + 3)$.

Therefore, $3x^2 + 18x + 27 = 3(x + 3)(x + 3)$.

An alternative method would be to multiply out the answer choices, and see which matches $3x^2 + 18x + 27$.

Choice (A): $3(x^2 + 6x + 3) = 3x^2 + 18x + 9$. Reject.

Choice (B): $3(x + 3)(x + 6) = 3(x^2 + 6x + 3x + 18)$. Using FOIL:

$$= 3(x^2 + 9x + 18)$$
$$= 3x^2 + 27x + 3(18). \text{ Reject.}$$

Choice (C): $3(x + 3)(x + 3) = 3(x^2 + 3x + 3x + 9)$. Using FOIL:

$$= 3(x^2 + 6x + 9)$$
$$= 3x^2 + 18x + 27. \text{ Correct.}$$

**13** **D**—Multiply out each part of the expression using FOIL.

$$(a^2 + b)^2 = (a^2 + b)(a^2 + b)$$
$$= a^4 + a^2b + ba^2 + b^2$$
$$= a^4 + 2a^2 b + b^2$$
$$(a^2 - b)^2 = (a^2 - b)(a^2 - b)$$
$$= (a^2)^2 + a^2(-b) + (-b)a^2 + (-b)^2$$
$$= a^4 - 2a^2b + b^2$$

So, $(a^2 + b)^2 - (a^2 - b)^2$
$$= (a^4 + 2a^2b + b^2) - (a^4 - 2a^2b + b^2)$$
$$= a^4 + 2a^2b + b^2 - a^4 + 2a^2b - b^2$$
$$= 2a^2b + 2a^2b$$
$$= 4a^2b$$

**14** **A**—Rearrange the first equation:
$$x = \frac{4}{z}.$$

Multiply both sides by $z$:

$$xz = 4.$$

So $xz = 4$ and $yz = 8$. That is:

$$\frac{xz}{yz} = \frac{4}{8}.$$

$$\frac{x}{y} = \frac{4}{8} = \frac{1}{2}$$

**15** **A**—The expression has three terms in the numerator, and a single term, $abc$, in the denominator. Since the three terms in the numerator each have abc as a factor, abc can be factored out from both numerator and denominator, and the expression can be reduced to a simpler form.

$$\frac{a^2bc + b(abc) + abc^2}{abc}$$

$$= \frac{a(abc) + b(abc) + c(abc)}{abc}$$

$$= \frac{(a + b + c)(abc)}{abc}$$

$$= a + b + c$$

**16** **D**—Consider each statement separately. Statement I claims $(x - y)^2 = (y - x)^2$. For any two integers, $y - x$ is the same as $-(x - y)$. So the statement claims that the squares of two integers with the same absolute value, but different signs equal each other. This is true, and can be shown by picking numbers. Therefore statement I must be true. Statement II claims $(x - y)^2 = [x - (-y)]^2$, which equals $(x + y)^2$. Clearly $x - y$ can have a totally different value from $x + y$, so statement II doesn't have to be true. (You can pick numbers to show this). Statement III claims $[x - (-y)]^2 = (-x - y)^2$. That is $(x + y)^2 = [-(x + y)]^2$. The expression being squared in the right-hand side is the negative of the expression being squared on the left-hand side. As before, squaring two numbers with identical absolute values produces the same result. So statement III must be true. That makes choice (D) the right answer.

**17** **B**—Since fractions make problems more difficult (especially fractions that include variables), try to get rid of the denominators in these fractions. You can do that by multiplying both columns by the least common multiple of the denominators: 60. You get $x + 40$ in Column A and $2(x + 20)$ in Column B. Distributing $2(x + 20)$ in Column B, you get $2x + 40$. Subtracting 40 from both columns, you are left with $x$ in Column A and $2x$ in Column B. Since $x$ is greater than 0, $2x$ must be greater than $x$, and Column B is greater.

**18** **B**—You can't find the value of any of the three variables alone, but you can find their average, since average is based on the sum of the terms and the number of terms. Dividing both sides of the equation by 3, you get:

$$3a + 3b + 3c = 18$$
$$3(a + b + c) = 18$$
$$a + b + c = 6.$$

The sum of the terms is 6, and there are three terms, so their average is $\frac{6}{3}$, or 2, making Column B greater.

**19** **B**—Dividing both columns by 10, we get $(y - 1)$ in Column A and $(1 - y)$ in Column B. Since $y$ is less than 0, $(y - 1)$ is a negative number minus 1, which gives a negative result. So Column A is negative. On the other hand, $(1 - y)$ is 1 minus a negative number, which will give us a positive result. So Column B is positive. Since a positive number is always greater than a negative number, Column B is larger.

**20** **A**—The trap here is thinking the columns are equal. In fact, the operation in parentheses must be done first, and that makes a big difference.
In Column A:
$(8 \blacksquare 4) \blacksquare 2$
$= \left(\dfrac{8+4}{8-4}\right) \blacksquare 2$
$= \left(\dfrac{12}{4}\right) \blacksquare 2$
$= 3 \blacksquare 2$

$= \left(\dfrac{3+2}{3-2}\right)$
$= \dfrac{5}{1} = 5$
In Column B:
$8 \blacksquare (4 \blacksquare 2)$
$= 8 \blacksquare \left(\dfrac{4+2}{4-2}\right)$
$= 8 \blacksquare \left(\dfrac{6}{2}\right)$
$= 8 \blacksquare 3$
$= \dfrac{8+3}{8-3}$
$= \dfrac{11}{5}$

This is smaller than 5, so Column A is greater.

**21** **C**—Since $c - d$ is a factor of both expressions being added in Column A, factor it out using the distributive law:
$(a + b)(c - d) + (a - b)(c - d)$
$= (c - d)[(a + b) + (a - b)]$
$= (c - d)(a + b + a - b)$
$= (c - d)(2a)$, or $2a(c - d)$.

**22** **2**—You're told that $4 \times 5 \times q = 5 \times p \times 2$. The number 5 is a common factor so you can cancel it from each side. You are left with $4q = 2p$ or $2q = p$. Dividing both sides by $q$ in order to get the quotient $\frac{p}{q}$ on one side, you find $\frac{p}{q} = 2$.

**23** **36/5 or 7.2**—Plug in the given values:
$$\dfrac{xy}{\dfrac{1}{x}+\dfrac{1}{y}} = \dfrac{2\times3}{\dfrac{1}{2}+\dfrac{1}{3}}$$
$$= \dfrac{6}{\dfrac{3}{6}+\dfrac{2}{6}}$$
$$= \dfrac{6}{\dfrac{5}{6}}$$
$$= 6\times\dfrac{6}{5}$$
$$= \dfrac{36}{5}\text{ or }7.2$$

## HARD

**24** **D**—You are asked to find $x$ when $\dfrac{3}{x-1} - 6 = 0$.

Clear the denominator by multiplying both sides by $x - 1$.

$$\frac{3}{x-1}(x-1) - 6(x-1) = 0(x-1)$$
$$3 - 6(x-1) = 0$$
$$3 - 6x + 6 = 0$$
$$9 - 6x = 0$$
$$9 - 6x + 6x = 0 + 6x$$
$$9 = 6x$$
$$\frac{9}{6} = \frac{6x}{6}$$
$$\frac{3}{2} = x$$

So answer choice (D) is correct. You can check your answer by plugging $\dfrac{3}{2}$ into the original equation.

**25** **D**—Since $\dfrac{b}{a}$ is the reciprocal of $\dfrac{a}{b}$, $\dfrac{b}{a}$ must be the reciprocal of $1 - \dfrac{1}{x}$ as well. Combine the terms in $1 - \dfrac{1}{x}$ and then find its reciprocal.

$$\frac{a}{b} = 1 - \frac{1}{x} = \frac{x}{x} - \frac{1}{x} = \frac{x-1}{x}$$

Therefore, $\dfrac{b}{a} = \dfrac{x}{x-1}$.

**26** **C**—You want to know which of the options must be true, given that $(m+n)^2 = (m-n)^2$.
First, expand the expressions.
$(m+n)^2 = m^2 + 2mn + n^2$
$(m-n)^2 = m^2 - 2mn + n^2$
Since these two expressions are equal, write:
$m^2 + 2mn + n^2 = m^2 - 2mn + n^2$
You have $m^2$ and $n^2$ on each side of the equal sign. Subtract these from both sides to leave:
$2mn = -2mn$
$mn = -mn$
Zero is the only number for which this is true, so $mn = 0$.
This shows statement III is certainly correct so eliminate choices (A), (B), and (D), but what about I and II?

If $mn = 0$, then either $m = 0$ or $n = 0$ (or both). But if $m$ and $n$ aren't both zero, $m + n$ and $m - n$ will not be 0. So I and II need not be true, and III is the only correct statement.

**27** **D**—Like many QCs that consist entirely of variables, the trick here is to avoid making assumptions and looking only at obvious possibilities. One of these is that $x$ and $y$ must be equal. But to show that's not the only possibility, you can pick numbers.
Say $x = 2$, $y = 2$, then $\dfrac{x}{y} = \dfrac{y}{x}$. In this case, Column A = Column B.
Say $x = 2$, $y = -2$, then $\dfrac{x}{y} = \dfrac{y}{x}$, but Column A is greater than Column B.
Without more information, it's impossible to find a consistent relationship between $x$ and $y$, so the correct answer choice is (D).

**28** **D**—Subtracting $4n$ from both columns, Column A is 4 and Column B is $n$. Since there are no conditions on the variable $n$, it can equal anything. It could be less than, greater than, or equal to 4. Therefore, choice (D) is correct.

**29** **C**—First expand the denominator, using FOIL: $(x+2)^2 = (x+2)(x+2) = x^2 + 2x + 2x + 4 = x^2 + 4x + 4$. Comparing this to the numerator, you see that each term in the numerator is 3 times a corresponding term in the denominator, so the total value of the numerator must be 3 times that of the denominator. That means the fraction equals 3, and the columns are equal.

**30** **A**—Since the square of any nonzero number is positive, $y^2$ must be positive, so multiply both columns by $y^2$. You're left with $(y-1)(y+1)$ in Column A and $(y-2)(y+2)$ in Column B. You should recognize these as differences of squares (if not, review your factoring material). Expand the columns, using the difference of squares:
Column A: $(y-1)(y+1) = y^2 - 1$
Column B: $(y-2)(y+2) = y^2 - 4$
Whatever the value of $y^2$, 1 less than $y^2$ (Column A) must be greater than 4 less than $y^2$ (Column B).

**31** **32**—First, multiply out $(x+y)^2$ using the FOIL method: $(x+y)^2 = x^2 + 2xy + y^2$.
Regroup the terms:
$= (x^2 + y^2) + 2(xy)$
Plug in the given values:
$= 16 + 2(8) = 32$.

A handful of algebra questions, mostly hard ones, test these more advanced skills (see the SAT Math in a Nutshell section near the back of the book):

66. Solving a Quadratic Equation
67. Solving a System of Equations
68. Solving an Inequality

## PRACTICE SET

### BASIC

**1** If $a < b$ and $b < c$, which of the following must be true?

(A) $b + c < 2a$
(B) $a + b < c$
(C) $a - b < b - c$
(D) $a + b < 2c$
(E) $a + c < 2b$   Ⓐ Ⓑ Ⓒ Ⓓ Ⓔ

**2** If $13 + a = 25 + b$, then $b - a =$

(A) 38
(B) 12
(C) 8
(D) −12
(E) −38   Ⓐ Ⓑ Ⓒ Ⓓ Ⓔ

**3** If $m > 1$ and $mn - 3 = 3 - n$, then $n =$

(A) 6

(B) $\dfrac{6}{m+1}$

(C) $\dfrac{6}{m-1}$

(D) $\dfrac{6}{1-m}$

(E) $-\dfrac{6}{m+1}$   Ⓐ Ⓑ Ⓒ Ⓓ Ⓔ

**4** If $r \neq -s$ and $a = \dfrac{r-s}{r+s}$, then $a + 1 =$

(A) $\dfrac{2r}{r+s}$

(B) $\dfrac{r-s+1}{r+s}$

(C) $\dfrac{2r-2s}{r+s}$

(D) $\dfrac{2s}{r+s}$

(E) $\dfrac{1-r+s}{r+s}$   Ⓐ Ⓑ Ⓒ Ⓓ Ⓔ

**5** If $a > b > c$, which of the following cannot be true?

(A) $b + c < a$
(B) $2a > b + c$
(C) $2c > a + b$
(D) $ab > bc$
(E) $a + b > 2b + c$   Ⓐ Ⓑ Ⓒ Ⓓ Ⓔ

| Column A | Column B |
|---|---|
| $14 < x < 16$ | |
| $15 < y < 17$ | |

**6**   $y$ | $x$

Ⓐ Ⓑ Ⓒ Ⓓ Ⓔ

**7** If $3m < 48$ and $2m > 24$, what is a possible value for $m$?

**8** If $y^2 + cy - 35 = 0$ and −7 is one solution of the equation, what is the value of $c$?

# SAT MATH PRACTICE

## MEDIUM

**9** If $a + b = 6$, $b + c = -3$, and $a + c = 5$, what is the value of $a + b + c$ ?

**10** If $a < b < c < 0$, which of the following expressions is the greatest?

(A)  $\dfrac{a}{b}$

(B)  $\dfrac{b}{c}$

(C)  $\dfrac{c}{a}$

(D)  $\dfrac{a}{c}$

(E)  It cannot be determined from the information given.

  Ⓐ Ⓑ Ⓒ Ⓓ Ⓔ

**11** If $y \neq 1$ and $x = \dfrac{1}{y+1}$ then, in terms of $x$, $y =$

(A)  $x - 1$

(B)  $\dfrac{1}{x} + 1$

(C)  $\dfrac{1}{x+1}$

(D)  $\dfrac{1}{x} - 1$

(E)  $\dfrac{1}{x-1}$    Ⓐ Ⓑ Ⓒ Ⓓ Ⓔ

**12** Let $\boxed{x} = \dfrac{x^2+1}{2}$ and $\widehat{y} = \dfrac{3y}{2}$, for all integers $x$ and $y$. If $m = \widehat{2}$, $\boxed{m}$ is equal to which of the following?

(A)  $\dfrac{13}{8}$

(B)  $\dfrac{5}{2}$

(C)  $\dfrac{15}{4}$

(D)  $5$

(E)  $\dfrac{37}{2}$    Ⓐ Ⓑ Ⓒ Ⓓ Ⓔ

**13** If $6a = 2b = 3c$, what is the value of $9a + 5b$, in terms of $c$ ?

(A)  $10c$
(B)  $12c$
(C)  $15c$
(D)  $18c$
(E)  $24c$    Ⓐ Ⓑ Ⓒ Ⓓ Ⓔ

**14** If $x \neq -y$ and $\dfrac{x^2 - y^2}{x+y} = 13$, then $x - y =$

(A)  $\sqrt{13}$
(B)  $7$
(C)  $13$
(D)  $169$
(E)  It cannot be determined from the information given.

  Ⓐ Ⓑ Ⓒ Ⓓ Ⓔ

| Column A | Column B |
|---|---|
| $\dfrac{2x}{3} = \dfrac{2y}{5} = \dfrac{2z}{7}$ | |
| $z > 0$ | |

**15**    $x + y$                 $z$

  Ⓐ Ⓑ Ⓒ Ⓓ Ⓔ

$$3a + 2b = 9$$
$$a - b = -2$$

**16**    $3a$                 $2b$

  Ⓐ Ⓑ Ⓒ Ⓓ Ⓔ

**17** If $-4 < m < 6$ and $-3 < n < 5$, then what is the greatest possible value of $n - m$ that will fit in the grid (four grid-in spaces)?

**18** If $2x + y = -8$ and $-4x + 2y = 16$, what is the value of $y$ ?

**KAPLAN**

## HARD

19  If $x^2 - 9 < 0$, which of the following is true?

(A)  $x < -3$
(B)  $x > 3$
(C)  $x > 9$
(D)  $x < -3$ or $x > 3$
(E)  $-3 < x < 3$

Ⓐ Ⓑ Ⓒ Ⓓ Ⓔ

20  If $x^2 - 2x - 15 = (x + r)(x + s)$ for all values of $x$, one possible value for $r - s$ is

(A)  8
(B)  2
(C)  −2
(D)  −3
(E)  −5

Ⓐ Ⓑ Ⓒ Ⓓ Ⓔ

21  If $n > 4$, which of the following is equivalent to $\dfrac{n - 4\sqrt{n} + 4}{\sqrt{n} - 2}$ ?

(A)  $\sqrt{n}$

(B)  $2\sqrt{n}$

(C)  $\sqrt{n} + 2$

(D)  $\sqrt{n} - 2$

(E)  $n + \sqrt{n}$

Ⓐ Ⓑ Ⓒ Ⓓ Ⓔ

| Column A | Column B |
|----------|----------|
| $0 < h < 1$ | |

22  $(h - 1)^2$ $\qquad$ $(h + 1)^2$

Ⓐ Ⓑ Ⓒ Ⓓ Ⓔ

$$5x - 2y = 13$$
$$3x + 5y = 14$$

23  $x$ $\qquad\qquad\qquad$ $y$

Ⓐ Ⓑ Ⓒ Ⓓ Ⓔ

For all $x$ and $y$ such that $x \neq y$,

$$\text{let } x \text{ \# } y = \frac{x + y}{x - y}$$

$$p > 0 > q$$

24  $p \text{ \# } q$ $\qquad\qquad\qquad$ $q \text{ \# } p$

Ⓐ Ⓑ Ⓒ Ⓓ Ⓔ

25  If $x$ can be expressed as $y^2$, where $y$ is a positive integer, then let $* x * = \dfrac{y^3}{2}$. For example, since $9 = 3^2$, $* 9 * = \dfrac{3^3}{2} = \dfrac{27}{2} = 13.5$. If $* m *$ $= 4$, what is the value of $* 4m *$?

| SCORECARD | |
|-----------|--|
| Number of Questions Right: | |
| Number of Questions Wrong: | |
| Number of Questions Omitted: | |
| Number of Correct Guesses: | |
| Number of Wrong Guesses: | |
| Time Used: | |

## ANSWERS AND EXPLANATIONS

### BASIC

**1** **D**—We're given two inequalities here: $a < b$ and $b < c$, which we can combine into one, $a < b < c$. We need to go through the answer choices to see which must be true.

Choice (A): $b + c < 2a$. Since $c$ is greater than $a$ and $b$ is greater than $a$, the sum of $b$ and $c$ must be *greater* than twice $a$. For instance, if $a = 1$, $b = 2$, and $c = 3$, then $b + c = 5$ and $2a = 2$, so $b + c > 2a$. Choice (A) is never true.

Choice (B): $a + b < c$. This may or may not be true, depending on the actual values of $a$, $b$, and $c$. If $a = 1$, $b = 2$, and $c = 4$, then $a + b < c$. However, if $a = 2$, $b = 3$, $c = 4$, then $a + b > c$. So choice (B) is also no good.

Choice (C): $a - b < b - c$. This choice is easier to evaluate if we simplify it by adding $(b + c)$ to both sides.
$$a - b + (b + c) < b - c + (b + c)$$
$$c + a < 2b$$
Like choice (B), this can be true, but can also be false, depending on the values of $a$, $b$, and $c$. If $a = -1$, $b = 2$, and $c = 3$, then $c + a < 2b$. But if $a = 1$, $b = 2$, and $c = 4$, then $c + a > 2b$. Choice (C) is no good.

Choice (D): $a + b < 2c$. We know that $a < c$ and $b < c$. If we add these inequalities we'll get $a + b < c + c$, or $a + b < 2c$. This statement is always true, so it must be the correct answer.

At this point on the real exam, you should proceed to the next problem. Just for discussion, however:

Choice (E): $a + c < 2b$. This is the same inequality as choice (C). That was no good, so this isn't either.

**2** **D**—You can't find the value of either variable alone, but you don't need to. Rearranging the equation, you get:
$$13 + a = 25 + b$$
$$13 = 25 + b - a$$
$$13 - 25 = b - a$$
$$b - a = -12$$

**3** **B**—We need to isolate $n$ on one side of the equation, and whatever's left on the other side will be an expression for $n$ in terms of $m$.
$$mn - 3 = 3 - n$$
First, get all the $n$s on one side.
$$n + mn - 3 = 3 - n + n$$
$$mn + n - 3 = 3$$
$$mn + n = 6$$
Then isolate $n$ by factoring and dividing.

$$n(m + 1) = 6$$
$$\frac{n(m+1)}{m+1} = \frac{6}{m+1}$$
$$n = \frac{6}{m+1}$$

**4** **A**—Since $a = \frac{r-s}{r+s}$, then $a + 1 = \frac{r-s}{r+s} + 1$. To simplify this expression, you make $r + s$ the common denominator:
$$\frac{r-s}{r+s} + 1$$
$$= \frac{r-s}{r+s} + \frac{r+s}{r+s}$$
$$= \frac{r-s+r+s}{r+s}$$
$$= \frac{2r}{r+s}$$

**5** **C**—We are told $a > b > c$, and asked which of the answer choices *cannot* be true. If we can find just one set of values $a$, $b$, and $c$, where $a > b > c$, that makes the answer choice true, then that answer choice can be eliminated.

Choice (A): $b + c < a$. This inequality can be true if $a$ is sufficiently large relative to $b$ and $c$. For example, if $a = 10$, $b = 3$, and $c = 2$, $a > b > c$ still holds, and $b + c < a$. No good.

Choice (B): $2a > b + c$. This is always true because $a$ is greater than either $b$ or $c$. So $a + a = 2a$ must be greater than $b + c$. For instance, $2(4) > 3 + 2$.

Choice (C): $2c > a + b$. This inequality can never be true. The sum of two smaller numbers ($c$s) can never be greater than the sum of two larger numbers ($a$ and $b$). This is the correct answer.

You would stop here if this were the real exam. But let's go over choices (D) and (E) for the sake of discussion.

Choice (D): $ab > bc$. This will be true when the numbers are all positive. Try $a = 4$, $b = 3$, and $c = 2$.

Choice (E): $a + b > 2b + c$. Again, this can be true if $a$ is large relative to $b$ and $c$. Try $a = 10$, $b = 2$, and $c = 1$.

**6** **D**—Don't assume that $x$ and $y$ must be in the middle of their respective ranges. That's possible, but not necessarily the case. Remember fractions and decimals. There's nothing here to indicate that $x$ and $y$ are both integers. For example, $x$ could equal 15.5 and $y$ could equal 15.2, making Column B larger. On the other hand, $y$ could be 16.5 while $x$ could be 14.5. Thus Column A would be larger. Therefore, choice (D) is correct.

**7**   **$12 < m < 16$**—If $3m < 48$, then $m < \dfrac{48}{3}$ or $m < 16$. And if $2m > 24$, then $m > \dfrac{24}{2}$ or $m > 12$. Thus, $m$ has any value between 12 and 16, or $12 < m < 16$.

**8**   **2**—Since –7 is a solution to the given equation, plug it in for $y$ to find the value of $c$ :
$$(-7)^2 + c(-7) - 35 = 0$$
$$49 - 7c - 35 = 0$$
$$14 - 7c = 0$$
$$14 = 7c$$
$$2 = c$$

## MEDIUM

**9**   **4**—The easiest way to solve is to realize that all three equations can simply be added together:
$$a + b = 6$$
$$b + c = -3$$
$$a + c = 5$$
$$\overline{\phantom{xxxxxxxxxxxxxxxx}}$$
$$2a + 2b + 2c = 8$$
$$2(a + b + c) = 8$$
$$a + b + c = 4$$

**10**   **D**—Since the quotient of two negatives is always positive and all the variables are negative, all these expressions are positive. To maximize the value of this quotient, we need a numerator with the largest possible absolute value and a denominator with the smallest possible absolute value. This means the negative numerator farthest from zero and the negative denominator closest to zero. Choice (D), $\dfrac{a}{c}$, fits the bill perfectly.

You can also pick numbers for $a$, $b$, and $c$ to verify this relationship. If you try –1 for $c$, –2 for $b$, and –3 for $a$, you'll find that $\dfrac{a}{c}$ is the largest fraction.

**11**   **D**—To solve the question you must get $y$ alone on one side of the equation. Since $x = \dfrac{x}{1}$, you can invert both sides of the equation:
$$x = \frac{1}{y+1}$$
$$\frac{1}{x} = \frac{y+1}{1} = y + 1$$
$$\frac{1}{x} - 1 = y$$

**12**   **D**—We're given *two* new symbols, and we need to complete several steps. The trick is figuring out where to start. We are asked to find $\boxed{m}$. In order to do this, we must first find the value of $m$. Since $m$ is equal to $\textcircled{2}$, we can find $m$ by finding the value of $\textcircled{2}$, and we can find $\textcircled{2}$ by substituting 2 for $y$ in the equation given for $\textcircled{y}$. The equation becomes:
$$\textcircled{2} = \frac{3(2)}{2}$$
$$\textcircled{2} = 3$$
Since $m = \textcircled{2}$, $m$ also equal 3, and $\boxed{m} = \boxed{3}$.
We find $\boxed{3}$ by substituting 3 for $x$ in the equation given for $\boxed{x}$ :
$$\boxed{3} = \frac{3^2 + 1}{2}$$
$$= \frac{9 + 1}{2}$$
$$= \frac{10}{2}$$
$$= 5$$
So $\boxed{m} = 5$

**13** **B**—You can think of the given information as two separate equations: $6a = 3c$, and $2b = 3c$. Perhaps the easiest way to proceed is to get values for $a$ and $b$ and then multiply. If:

$$6a = 3c$$

then $a = \dfrac{3c}{6} = \dfrac{c}{2}$

So $9a = \dfrac{9c}{2}$

Likewise, if:

$$2b = 3c$$

then $b = \dfrac{3c}{2}$.

So $5b = 5\left(\dfrac{3c}{2}\right) = \dfrac{15c}{2}$.

$$9a + 5b = \dfrac{9c}{2} + \dfrac{15c}{2} = \dfrac{24c}{2} = 12c$$

**14** **C**—There are a few common quadratic expressions that occasionally appear on the SAT. If you learn to recognize them, a problem like this is easy. Any expression in the form $a^2 - b^2$, which is referred to as the difference of two squares, can be factored into $(a + b)(a - b)$.

The numerator of the given fraction is in this form, so you can rewrite the fraction as $\dfrac{(x + y)(x - y)}{x + y}$.

Cancel a factor of $(x + y)$ from numerator and denominator, leaving $x - y$. So $x - y = 13$.

**15** **A**—One way to solve this problem is to pick numbers. Just make sure that anything you pick satisfies the requirements of the problem. You might try picking $x = 3$, $y = 5$, and $z = 7$, since in the equation these numbers would cancel with their denominators, leaving the equations $2 = 2 = 2$. Therefore, you know that these values satisfy the equations. In addition, if $z = 7$, then it is positive, so you have satisfied the other requirement as well. Then the sum of $x$ and $y$, in Column A, is $3 + 5$, or 8. This is larger than $z$, so in this case Column A is larger. In fact, any other numbers you pick that fit the initial information will have Column A larger. To see why, restate the initial equations.

Start by dividing all the equations through by 2, and multiply all the terms through by $3 \times 5 \times 7$, to eliminate all the fractions. This leaves:

$$35x = 21y = 15z$$

Now let's put everything in terms of $x$:

$$x = x$$
$$y = \frac{35}{21}x = \frac{5}{3}x$$
$$z = \frac{35}{15}x = \frac{7}{3}x$$

In Column A, the sum of $x$ and $y$ is $x + \dfrac{5}{3}x = \dfrac{8}{3}x$.

In Column B, the value of $z$ is $\dfrac{7}{3}x$.

Since $z$ is positive, $x$ and $y$ must also be positive. (If one of them is negative, that would make all of them negative.)

Therefore $x$ is positive, and $\dfrac{8}{3}x > \dfrac{7}{3}x$. Column A is larger.

**16** **B**—Method 1: First get one variable in terms of the other:
$$a - b = -2$$
$$a = b - 2$$
Plug this value for $a$ into the first equation:
$$3(b - 2) + 2b = 9$$
$$3b - 6 + 2b = 9$$
$$5b - 6 = 9$$
$$5b = 15$$
$$b = 3$$
Now plug $b = 3$ into either original equation to solve for $a$:
$$a - 3 = -2$$
$$a = 1.$$
Since $3a = 3$, and $2b = 6$, Column B is greater.

Method 2: Multiply the second equation by 2, and then add the equations to cancel out the $b$s:
$$a - b = -2$$
$$2a - 2b = -4$$

$$3a + 2b = 9$$
$$+\ 2a - 2b = -4$$
$$\overline{\phantom{+\ }5a = 5}$$
$$a = 1.$$
Plug in this value for $a$ into the second equation, and the result is once again that $b = 3$, making Column B greater than Column A.

**17** 8.99—Since inequalities deal with a range of values, you need to determine which parts of the range will yield the maximum value. The maximum value of $n - m <$ (the upper bound of $n$ – the lower bound of $m$): $n - m < 5 - (-4)$, or $n - m < 9$. Therefore, the greatest value for $n - m$ that will fit in the grid is 8.99.

**18** **0**—To solve for $y$, make the $x$ terms drop out. The first equation involves $2x$, while the second involves $-4x$, so multiply both sides of the first equation by 2.
$$2(2x + y) = 2(-8)$$
$$4x + 2y = -16$$
Adding the corresponding sides of this equation and the second equation together gives:
$$4x + 2y = -16$$
$$+ (-4x + 2y = 16)$$
$$\overline{\phantom{xxxxxxxxxxxxxxxxxx}}$$
$$4x + 2y - 4x + 2y = -16 + 16$$
$$4y = 0$$
$$y = 0$$
An alternative method is to solve the first equation for $x$ in terms of $y$ and then substitute this expression into the second equation.
$$2x + y = -8$$
$$2x = -8 - y$$
$$x = \frac{-8 - y}{2}$$

Now replace $x$ in the other equation with $\frac{-8 - y}{2}$, and a single equation in terms of $y$ remains. This equation can be solved for a numerical value of $y$.
$$-4x + 2y = 16$$
$$-4\left(\frac{-8 - y}{2}\right) + 2y = 16$$
$$-2(-8 - y) + 2y = 16$$
$$16 + 2y + 2y = 16$$
$$16 + 4y = 16$$
$$4y = 0$$
$$y = 0$$

**HARD**

**19** **E**—Rearrange $x^2 - 9 < 0$ to get $x^2 < 9$. We're looking for all the values of $x$ that would fit this inequality. We need to consider both *positive and negative* values of $x$. Remember that $3^2 = 9$ and also that $(-3)^2 = 9$.

If $x$ is positive, and $x^2 < 9$, we can simply say that $x < 3$. But what if $x$ is negative? $x$ can take on only values whose square is less than 9. In other words, $x$ cannot be less than or equal to $-3$. (Think of smaller numbers like $-4$ or $-5$; their squares are greater than 9.) So if $x$ is negative, $x > -3$. $x$ can also be 0. Therefore, $-3 < x < 3$.

If you had trouble solving algebraically, you could have tried each answer choice:

Choice (A): Say $x = -4$.
$(-4)^2 - 9 = 16 - 9 = 7$. No good.
Choice (B): Say $x = 4$.
$4^2 - 9 = 16 - 9 = 7$. No good.
Choice (C): Since 4 was too big, anything greater than 9 is too big. No good.
Choice (D): Combination of (A) and (B), which were both wrong. No good.
Clearly, choice (E) must be correct.

**20** **A**—Factor the quadratic expression into a pair of binomials, using FOIL in reverse.
The product of the Last terms in the binomials = $rs = -15$.
The sum of the Outer and Inner terms = $rx + sx = -2x$, $r + s = -2$.
With a little trial and error it becomes clear that $r = -5$ and $s = 3$, or $r = 3$ and $s = -5$.
The problem asks for one possible value for $r - s$. Since you don't know which number is $r$ and which is $s$, $r - s$ could be $(-5) - 3$, or $3 - (-5)$. $-5 - 3 = -8$, which is not among the answer choices. But $3 - (-5) = 3 + 5 = 8$, which is choice (A).

**21** **D**—We must try to get rid of the denominator by factoring it out of the numerator. $n - 4\sqrt{n} + 4$ is a difficult expression to work with. It may be easier if we let $t = \sqrt{n}$. Keep in mind then that $t^2 = (\sqrt{n})(\sqrt{n}) = n$.
Then $n - 4\sqrt{n} + 4 = t^2 - 4t + 4$
Using FOIL in reverse, $t^2 - 4t + 4 = (t - 2)(t - 2) = (\sqrt{n} - 2)(\sqrt{n} - 2)$.
So $\frac{n - 4\sqrt{n} + 4}{\sqrt{n} - 2} = \frac{(\sqrt{n} - 2)(\sqrt{n} - 2)}{(\sqrt{n} - 2)} = \sqrt{n} - 2$.

Or pick a number for $n$ and try each answer choice. Whichever method you use, choice (D) is correct.

**22** **B**—Expand each column by FOIL:
$$(h - 1)^2 = h^2 - 2h + 1$$
$$(h + 1)^2 = h^2 + 2h + 1.$$
Subtracting $h^2 + 1$ from both columns leaves us with $-2h$ in Column A and $2h$ in Column B. Since $h$ is positive, Column B is greater than Column A.

**23** **A**—The fastest way to solve is to add the equations. In order to make one variable cancel out when you add them, you must multiply both equations so the coefficient of one variable matches. Make the $y$s cancel:

$$5x - 2y = 13, \text{ so}$$
$$25x - 10y = 65$$

and

$$3x + 5y = 14, \text{ so}$$
$$6x + 10y = 28.$$

Now you can add the equations:

$$25x - 10y = 65$$
$$\underline{+\ 6x + 10y = 28}$$
$$31x = 93$$
$$x = 3.$$

Plugging back into one of the original equations:

$$3x + 5y = 14 \text{ becomes}$$
$$3(3) + 5y = 14$$
$$5y = 14 - 9$$
$$y = 1.$$

**24** **D**—With symbolism problems like this, it sometimes helps to put the definition of the symbol into words. For this symbol, we can say: "$x$ # $y$ means that you take the sum of the two numbers, and divide that by the difference of the two numbers."

One good way to do this problem is to pick some values. We know that $p$ is positive and $q$ is negative. Suppose $p$ is 1 and $q$ is –1. First, let's figure out what $p$ # $q$ is. We start by taking the sum of the numbers, or $1 + (-1) = 0$. That's the numerator of our fraction, and we don't need to go any further. Whatever their difference is, since the numerator is 0, the whole fraction must equal 0. (We know that the difference can't be 0 also, since $p \neq q$). That's $p$ # $q$; now what about $q$ # $p$? That's going to have the same numerator as $p$ # $q$: 0. The only thing that changes when you reverse the order of the numbers is the denominator of the fraction. So $q$ # $p$ has a numerator of 0, and that fraction must equal 0 as well.

We've found one case where the columns are equal. To see whether the columns are always equal, let's try another set of values. If $p = 1$ and $q = -2$, then the sum of the numbers is $1 + (-2)$ or –1. That's the numerator of our fraction in each column. For the

denominator of $p$ # $q$ we need $p - q$ or $1 - (-2) = 1 + 2 = 3$. Then the value of $p$ # $q$ is $-\dfrac{1}{3}$. The denominator of $q$ # $p$ is $q - p$ or $-2 - 1 = -3$. So the value of $q$ # $p$ is $\dfrac{-1}{-3}$ or $\dfrac{1}{3}$. In this case, the columns are different; therefore, the answer is (D).

**25** **32**—To answer the question you must find the value of $m$.

$$\ast\ m\ \ast\ = 4$$
$$\frac{\left(\sqrt{m}\right)^3}{2} = 4$$
$$\left(\sqrt{m}\right)^3 = 8$$
$$\sqrt{m} = 2$$
$$m = 4$$

So: $\ast 4 \ast = \ast 4(4) \ast = \ast 16 \ast$

$$= \frac{\left(\sqrt{16}\right)^3}{2}$$
$$= \frac{4^3}{2}$$
$$= \frac{64}{2} = 32.$$

**KAPLAN**

Word problems are very common on the SAT. Word problems can involve just about any Math concept—fractions, averages, rates, triangles, whatever—but fundamentally, word problems test the following skill (detailed in the SAT in a Nutshell section near the end of this book):

    65.    Translating from English into Algebra

## PRACTICE SET

### BASIC

**1** Before the market opens on Monday, a stock is priced at $25. If its price decreases $4 on Monday, increases $6 on Tuesday, and then decreases $2 on Wednesday, what is the final price of the stock on Wednesday?

  (A)  $12
  (B)  $21
  (C)  $25
  (D)  $29
  (E)  $37      Ⓐ Ⓑ Ⓒ Ⓓ Ⓔ

**2** If three times $x$ is equal to $x$ decreased by 2, then $x$ is

  (A)  −2
  (B)  −1
  (C)  $-\dfrac{2}{3}$
  (D)  1
  (E)  $\dfrac{3}{2}$      Ⓐ Ⓑ Ⓒ Ⓓ Ⓔ

**3** Greg's weekly salary is $70 less than Joan's, which is $50 more than Sue's. If Sue earns $280 per week, how much does Greg earn per week?

  (A)  $160
  (B)  $260
  (C)  $280
  (D)  $300
  (E)  $400      Ⓐ Ⓑ Ⓒ Ⓓ Ⓔ

**4** If the sum of $a$, $b$, and $c$ is twice the sum of $a$ minus $b$ and $a$ minus $c$, then $a =$

  (A)  $b + c$
  (B)  $3b + 3c$
  (C)  $3b - c$
  (D)  $2b + 3c$
  (E)  $-b - c$      Ⓐ Ⓑ Ⓒ Ⓓ Ⓔ

**5** During a certain week, a post office sold $280 worth of 14-cent stamps. How many of these stamps did they sell?

  (A)      20
  (B)    2,000
  (C)    3,900
  (D)   20,000
  (E)   39,200      Ⓐ Ⓑ Ⓒ Ⓓ Ⓔ

**6** Diane painted $\dfrac{1}{3}$ of her room with $2\dfrac{1}{2}$ cans of paint. How many more cans of paint will she need to finish painting her room?

  (A)  5
  (B)  $7\dfrac{1}{2}$
  (C)  10
  (D)  $12\dfrac{1}{2}$
  (E)  15      Ⓐ Ⓑ Ⓒ Ⓓ Ⓔ

**7** Liza took $5n$ photographs on a certain trip. If she gives $n$ photographs to each of her 3 friends, how many photographs will she have left?

  (A)  $2n$
  (B)  $3n$
  (C)  $4n - 3$
  (D)  $4n$
  (E)  $4n + 3$      Ⓐ Ⓑ Ⓒ Ⓓ Ⓔ

8   Ed has 100 dollars more than Robert. After Ed
    spends 20 dollars on groceries, Ed has 5 times
    as much money as Robert. How much money
    does Robert have?

    (A)   $20
    (B)   $30
    (C)   $40
    (D)   $50
    (E)   $120          Ⓐ Ⓑ Ⓒ Ⓓ Ⓔ

9   The average of 5 numbers is 13. If the average
    of 4 of these numbers is 10, what is the fifth
    number?

10  An office has 27 employees. If there are 7 more
    women than men in the office, how many
    employees are women?

## MEDIUM

11  Between 1950 and 1960 the population of
    Country A increased by 3.5 million people. If
    the amount of increase between 1960 and 1970
    was 1.75 million more than the increase from
    1950 to 1960, what was the total amount of
    increase in population in Country A between
    1950 and 1970?
    (A)   1.75 million
    (B)   3.5 million
    (C)   5.25 million
    (D)   7 million
    (E)   8.75 million       Ⓐ Ⓑ Ⓒ Ⓓ Ⓔ

12  On a scaled map, a distance of 10 centimeters
    represents 5 kilometers. If a street is 750 meters
    long, what is its length on the map, in centime-
    ters? (1 kilometer = 1,000 meters)

13  In a certain baseball league, each team plays
    160 games. After playing half of their games,
    Team A has won 60 games and Team B has won
    49 games. If Team A wins half of its remaining
    games, how many of its remaining games must
    Team B win to have the same number of wins
    as Team A at the end of the season?

14  A painter charges $12 an hour, while his son
    charges $6 an hour. If the father and his son
    worked the same amount of time together on a
    job, how many hours did each of them work if
    the combined charge for their labor was $108?

    (A)   6
    (B)   8
    (C)   9
    (D)   12
    (E)   18          Ⓐ Ⓑ Ⓒ Ⓓ Ⓔ

15  A man has an estate worth $15 million that he
    will either divide equally among his 10 chil-
    dren or among his 10 children and 5 stepchil-
    dren. How much more will each of his children
    inherit if his 5 stepchildren are excluded?

    (A)   $500,000
    (B)   $1,000,000
    (C)   $1,500,000
    (D)   $2,500,000
    (E)   $5,000,000      Ⓐ Ⓑ Ⓒ Ⓓ Ⓔ

16  An hour-long test has 60 problems. If a student
    completes 30 problems in 20 minutes, how
    many seconds does he have on average for
    completing each of the remaining problems?

17  At a clothing company, each blouse requires 1
    yard of material, four shirts require 2 yards of
    material, and one blouse and 2 dresses require
    4 yards of material. How many yards of mater-
    ial are needed to make 1 blouse, 1 shirt, and 1
    dress?

18  If the product of 3 and $x$ is equal to 2 less than
    $y$, which of the following must be true?

    (A)   $6x - y - 2 = 0$
    (B)   $6x - 6 = 0$
    (C)   $3x - y - 2 = 0$
    (D)   $3x + y - 2 = 0$
    (E)   $3x - y + 2 = 0$      Ⓐ Ⓑ Ⓒ Ⓓ Ⓔ

19  If a man earns $200 for his first 40 hours of work in a week and is then paid $1\frac{1}{2}$ times his regular hourly rate for any additional hours, how many hours must he work to make $230 in a week?

(A)  4
(B)  5
(C)  6
(D)  44
(E)  45

Ⓐ Ⓑ Ⓒ Ⓓ Ⓔ

20  In a typical month, $\frac{1}{2}$ of the UFO sightings in a certain state are attributable to airplanes and $\frac{1}{3}$ of the remaining sightings are attributable to weather balloons. If there were 108 UFO sightings during one typical month, how many would be attributable to weather balloons?

(A)  18
(B)  24
(C)  36
(D)  54
(E)  72

Ⓐ Ⓑ Ⓒ Ⓓ Ⓔ

21  Ms. Smith drove a total of 700 miles on a business trip. If her car averaged 35 miles per gallon of gasoline and gasoline cost an average of $1.25 per gallon, how much did she spend on gasoline for this trip?

(A)  $17.50
(B)  $25.00
(C)  $35.00
(D)  $70.00
(E)  $250.00

Ⓐ Ⓑ Ⓒ Ⓓ Ⓔ

22  Gheri is $n$ years old. Carl is 6 years younger than Gheri and 2 years older than Jean. What is the sum of the ages of all three?

(A)  $3n + 16$
(B)  $3n + 4$
(C)  $3n - 4$
(D)  $3n - 8$
(E)  $3n - 14$

Ⓐ Ⓑ Ⓒ Ⓓ Ⓔ

23  During a drought the amount of water in a pond was reduced by a third. If the amount of water in the pond was 48,000 gallons immediately after the drought, how many thousands of gallons of water were lost during the drought?

(A)  6,000
(B)  12,000
(C)  18,000
(D)  24,000
(E)  30,000

Ⓐ Ⓑ Ⓒ Ⓓ Ⓔ

## HARD

24  There is enough candy in a bag to give 12 pieces of candy to each of 20 children, with no candy left over. If 5 children do not want any candy, how many pieces of candy can be given to each of the others?

(A)  12
(B)  15
(C)  16
(D)  18
(E)  20

Ⓐ Ⓑ Ⓒ Ⓓ Ⓔ

25  Chris has twice as many baseball cards as Lee. If Chris gives Lee 10 of his baseball cards, he will have half as many as Lee. How many baseball cards do Chris and Lee have together?

(A)  10
(B)  20
(C)  30
(D)  40
(E)  60

Ⓐ Ⓑ Ⓒ Ⓓ Ⓔ

**26** The total fare for 2 adults and 3 children on an excursion boat is $14. If each child's fare is one half of each adult's fare, what is the adult fare?

- (A) $2.00
- (B) $3.00
- (C) $3.50
- (D) $4.00
- (E) $4.50  Ⓐ Ⓑ Ⓒ Ⓓ Ⓔ

**27** Doris spent $\frac{2}{3}$ of her savings on a used car, and she spent $\frac{1}{4}$ of her remaining savings on a new carpet. If the carpet cost her $250, how much were Doris's original savings?

- (A) $1,000
- (B) $1,200
- (C) $1,500
- (D) $2,000
- (E) $3,000  Ⓐ Ⓑ Ⓒ Ⓓ Ⓔ

**28** If John gives Allen 5 dollars and Allen gives Frank 2 dollars, the 3 boys will have the same amount of money. How much more money does John have than Allen?

- (A) $3
- (B) $5
- (C) $6
- (D) $7
- (E) $8  Ⓐ Ⓑ Ⓒ Ⓓ Ⓔ

**29** Ida owes her parents $x$ dollars. Last month she paid $\frac{1}{6}$ of the amount owed. This month she paid them $\frac{1}{6}$ of the remaining amount plus $20.00. In terms of $x$, how much money does she still owe?

- (A) $\dfrac{x-20}{6}$

- (B) $\dfrac{5}{6}x - 20$

- (C) $\dfrac{5x-20}{6}$

- (D) $\dfrac{25}{36}x - 20$

- (E) $\dfrac{25x-20}{36}$  Ⓐ Ⓑ Ⓒ Ⓓ Ⓔ

**30** John can shovel a certain driveway in 50 minutes. If Mary can shovel the same driveway in 20 minutes, how long will it take them, to the nearest minute, to shovel the driveway if they work together?

- (A) 12
- (B) 13
- (C) 14
- (D) 16
- (E) 18  Ⓐ Ⓑ Ⓒ Ⓓ Ⓔ

**31** In a group of 60 workers, the average (arithmetic mean) salary is $80 a day per worker. If some of the workers earn $75 a day and all the rest earn $100 a day, how many workers earn $75 a day?

**32** A street vendor sells two types of newspapers, one for 25 cents and the other for 40 cents. If she sold 100 newspapers for $28.00, how many newspapers did she sell at 25 cents?

- (A) 80
- (B) 60
- (C) 50
- (D) 40
- (E) 20  Ⓐ Ⓑ Ⓒ Ⓓ Ⓔ

33 A grocer has $c$ pounds of coffee that he wants to divide equally among $s$ sacks. If $n$ more sacks are to be used, then each sack would hold how many fewer pounds of coffee?

(A) $\dfrac{c}{s+n}$

(B) $\dfrac{c}{s+cn}$

(C) $\dfrac{c}{s^2+sn}$

(D) $\dfrac{c}{s^2+sn}$

(E) $\dfrac{cn}{s^2+sn}$     Ⓐ Ⓑ Ⓒ Ⓓ Ⓔ

| SCORECARD | |
| --- | --- |
| Number of Questions Right: | |
| Number of Questions Wrong: | |
| Number of Questions Omitted: | |
| Number of Correct Guesses: | |
| Number of Wrong Guesses: | |
| Time Used: | |

## ANSWERS AND EXPLANATIONS

### BASIC

**1** **C**—Translate directly into math. A price decrease makes the price smaller, so we subtract. A price increase makes the price greater, so we add. For the final price we get

$25 – $4 + $6 – $2 = $25 + $0 = $25

So the final price is $25.

**2** **B**—Translate piece by piece: "three times $x$" = $3x$, "$x$ decreased by 2" = $x – 2$.

So $3x = x – 2$

Solve for $x$:

$3x – x = – 2$

$2x = –2$

$x = –1$

**3** **B**—Sue makes $280. If Joan makes $50 more than this, then Joan must make $280 + $50 or $330. Greg makes $70 less than this amount, or $330 – $70, or $260.

**4** **A**—Translate piece by piece:

"the sum of $a$, $b$, and $c$" = $a + b + c$

"twice the sum of $a$ minus $b$ and $a$ minus $c$" = $2[(a – b) + (a – c)]$

So $a + b + c = 2[(a – b) + (a – c)]$

Solve for $a$:

$a + b + c = 2a – 2b + 2a – 2c$

$a + b + c = 4a – 2b – 2c$

$b + c + 2b + 2c = 4a – a$

$3b + 3c = 3a$

$b + c = a$

**5** **B**—To calculate the number of 14-cent stamps sold by the post office, divide the total amount of money spent on these stamps by the cost of each stamp. This means dividing $280 by 14¢. Since the units are not the same, we convert 14¢ to dollars to get .14 dollars, so that we are dividing dollars by dollars. We get 280 ÷ .14 = 2,000. So 2,000, 14-cent stamps were sold.

**6** **A**—Diane has painted $\frac{1}{3}$ of her room with $2\frac{1}{2}$ cans of paint. To complete the remaining $\frac{2}{3}$ of her room, twice as much paint will be needed. So

$2 \times 2\frac{1}{2} = 5$ more cans are needed.

**7** **A**—Liza originally has $5n$ photographs. If she gives $n$ photos to each of her 3 friends, she gives away $3 \times n$, or $3n$, photos. She is left with $5n – 3n$, or $2n$, photos.

**8** **A**—Translate to get two equations. Let $E$ be the amount Ed has and $R$ be the amount Robert has.

"Ed has $100 more than Robert" becomes $E = R + 100$.

"Ed spends $20" means he'll end up with $20 less, or $E – 20$.

"5 times as much as Robert" becomes $5R$. So $E – 20 = 5R$.

Substitute $R + 100$ for $E$ in the second equation and solve for $R$:

$E – 20 = 5R$

$(R + 100) – 20 = 5R$

$R + 80 = 5R$

$80 = 4R$

$20 = R$

So Robert has $20.

**9** **25**—Average $= \dfrac{\text{sum of the terms}}{\text{number of terms}}$, so 13 = the sum of the 5 numbers ÷ 5.

That means the sum is $5 \times 13$, or 65. If four of these numbers have an average of 10, their sum must be $4 \times 10$, or 40. The fifth number must make up the difference between 40 and 65, which is 25.

**10** **17**—What 2 numbers 7 apart add up to 27? With trial and error you should be able to find them pretty quickly: 10 and 17. So there must be 17 women working at the office.

Alternatively, set up two equations each with two unknowns. There are 27 employees at the office total, all either men or women, so $m$ (the number of men) + $w$ (the number of women) = 27. There are 7 more women than men, so: $m + 7 = w$, or $m = w – 7$.

Substitute $w – 7$ for $m$ into the first equation:

$(w – 7) + w = 27$

$2w – 7 = 27$

$2w = 34$

$w = 17$

There are 17 women in the office. (In problems like these, check at the end to make sure you answered the right question. It would have been easy here to misread the question and solve for the number of men.)

## MEDIUM

**11** **E**—In Country *A*, the amount of population increase between 1960 and 1970 was 1.75 million more than the amount of increase between 1950 and 1960, or 1.75 million more than 3.5 million. So the increase between 1960 and 1970 must have been 1.75 + 3.5 million, or 5.25 million. The total growth in population over the two decades equals 3.5 million (the amount of growth between 1950 and 1960), plus 5.25 million (the amount of growth between 1960 and 1970), for a total increase of 8.75 million.

**12** **1.5 or 3/2**—Start by converting kilometers to meters. Since a meter is smaller than a kilometer, we must multiply. We are told that a length of 10 centimeters on the map represents 5 kilometers, or 5,000 meters; therefore, 1 centimeter must represent $\frac{1}{10}$ as much, or 500 meters. We want to know how many centimeters would represent 750 meters. We could set up a proportion here, but it's quicker to use common sense. We have a distance of $1\frac{1}{2}$ times 500 meters ($750 = 1\frac{1}{2} \times 500$), so we need a map distance of $1\frac{1}{2}$ times 1 centimeter, or 1.5 centimeters.

**13** **51**—Since the teams have played half their games, there are 80 games left. If Team *A* wins half its remaining games, that's another 40 games, for a total of 60 + 40, or 100, games. Team *B* has won 49 games so far, so in order to tie Team *A*, it must win another 100 – 49, or 51, games.

**14** **A**—When the painter and his son work together, they charge the sum of their hourly rates, $12 + $6, or $18, per hour. Their bill equals the product of this combined rate and the number of hours they work. Therefore $108 must equal $18 per hour times the number of hours they worked. We need to divide $108 by $18 per hour to find the number of hours. $108 ÷ $18 = 6.

**15** **A**—The amount each of the children stands to gain equals the difference between what he or she will make if the stepchildren are excluded and what he or she will make if they're included. If the stepchildren are excluded, the children will inherit $15 million divided by 10 (the number of children), or $1.5 million each. If the stepchildren are included, they'll inherit $15 million divided by 15 (the number of children and stepchildren combined) or $1 million each. The difference is $1.5 million – $1 million, or $500,000.

**16** **80**—The student has done 30 of the 60 problems, and has used up 20 of the 60 minutes. Therefore, he has 60 – 30, or 30 problems left, to be done in 60 – 20, or 40 minutes. We find his average time per problem by dividing the time by the number of problems.

$$\text{Time per problem} = \frac{40 \text{ minutes}}{30 \text{ problems}}$$

$$= \frac{4}{3} \text{ minutes per problem}$$

Each minute has 60 seconds. So we multiply by 60 to find the number of seconds.

$$\frac{4}{3} \text{ minutes} \times 60 \frac{\text{seconds}}{\text{minute}} = 80 \text{ seconds}$$

**17** **3**—We need to keep track of the amount of material that it takes to make each of the different items of clothing. Each blouse requires 1 yard of material. Four shirts require 2 yards of material; therefore, each shirt requires $\frac{2}{4}$, or $\frac{1}{2}$ yard. One blouse and 2 dresses require a total of 4 yards. One of these yards goes to the blouse, leaving 3 yards for the 2 dresses, so a single dress requires $\frac{3}{2}$, or $1\frac{1}{2}$, yards of material. Now let's find how much we need for the assortment we want: 1 blouse, 1 shirt, 1 dress. One blouse takes 1 yard. One shirt takes $\frac{1}{2}$ yard. And the dress takes $1\frac{1}{2}$ yards. So the amount of material needed is $1 + \frac{1}{2} + 1\frac{1}{2}$ yards, or 3 yards.

**18** **E**—Translate into math, remembering that "2 less than $y$" means $y - 2$, not $2 - y$.

"The product of 3 and $x$" means $3x$. So we have the equation $3x = y - 2$.

Since this doesn't match any of the answer choices, we have to determine which of the answer choices corresponds to it. Since all the answer choices are equations in which the right side is zero, let's move all the terms in our equation to the left side. We get $3x - y + 2 = 0$, which is choice (E).

**19** **D**—To learn the man's overtime rate of pay we have to figure out his regular rate of pay. Divide the amount of money made, $200, by the time it took to make it, 40 hours. $200 ÷ 40$ hours = $5 per hour. That is his normal rate. The man is paid time and a half for overtime, so when working more than 40 hours, he makes $\frac{3}{2} \times \$5$ per hour = $7.50 per hour.

Now we can figure out how long it takes the man to make $230. It takes him 40 hours to make the first $200. The last $30 are made at the overtime rate. Since it takes the man 1 hour to make $7.50 at this rate, we can figure out the number of extra hours by dividing $30 by $7.50 per hour. $30 ÷ $7.50 per hour = 4 hours. The total time needed is 40 hours plus 4 hours, or 44 hours.

**20** **A**—We need to find a fraction of a fraction. The total number of UFO sightings is 108. Of these, $\frac{1}{2}$ turn out to be airplanes: $\frac{1}{2} \times 108 = 54$. If $\frac{1}{2}$ are airplanes, $\frac{1}{2}$ are not, so 54 sightings remain that are not airplanes. Of these 54, $\frac{1}{3}$ are weather balloons. We multiply $\frac{1}{3} \times 54$ to find the number of weather balloons, which is 18.

**21** **B**—If Ms. Smith's car averages 35 miles per gallon, then she can go 35 miles on 1 gallon. To go 700 miles, she will need $700 ÷ 35$, or 20, gallons of gasoline. The average price of gasoline was $1.25 per gallon, so she spent $20 \times \$1.25$, or $25, for the gasoline on her trip.

**22** **E**—Gheri is $n$ years old. Carl is 6 years younger than Gheri, or $n - 6$ years old. Jean is 2 years younger than Carl, or $n - 6 - 2 = n - 8$ years old. The sum of their ages is then $n + (n - 6) + (n - 8) = 3n - 14$ years.

This problem could also be solved by picking numbers. Let's say that Gheri is 20 years old (so $n = 20$). Carl is 6 years younger, or 14, and Jean is 2 years younger still, or 12. The sum of their ages is $20 + 14 + 12 = 46$. Now we plug $n = 20$ into each answer choice and see which one, or ones, have a value of 46. A little quick math will show you that only choice (E) works.

**23** **D**—One-third of the original volume of water in the pond was lost during the drought. The amount of water that remains must be two-thirds of the original amount, that is, twice as much as was lost. So the one-third that was lost is equal to half of what was left. That is, the amount of water lost = $\frac{48,000}{2} = 24,000$ gallons of water.

Or, set up an equation in which $W$ represents how much water was originally in the pond:

$$W - \frac{1}{3}W = 48{,}000$$

$$\frac{2}{3}W = 48{,}000$$

$$W = 72{,}000$$

The amount lost was $\frac{1}{3}$ of the original amount, or $\frac{1}{3}$ of $W$, which is $\frac{1}{3}(72{,}000) = 24{,}000$.

## HARD

**24** **C**—Find the total number of pieces of candy in the bag, then divide by the number of children who will be sharing them. There's enough candy to give 12 pieces to each of 20 children, so there are $12 \times 20$, or 240, pieces of candy total. Five children do not want candy, so there remain $20 - 5$, or 15, children to share the 240 pieces of candy. Each will get $240 \div 15$, or 16, pieces of candy.

**25** **C**—Let $C$ represent the number of baseball cards Chris has and $L$ represent the number of baseball cards Lee has. Since Chris has twice as many baseball cards as Lee, we can write
$C = 2L$.
If Chris gives Lee 10 baseball cards, then he will have 10 fewer, or $C - 10$, and Lee will have 10 more, or $L + 10$. In this case Chris would end up with half as many as Lee, so

$$C - 10 = \frac{1}{2}(L + 10).$$

We have two equations with two variables. Solve for $C$ and $L$. Substitute the first expression for $C$—that is, $C = 2L$—into the second equation and solve for $L$.

$$2L - 10 = \frac{1}{2}(L + 10)$$
$$4L - 20 = L + 10$$
$$3L = 30$$
$$L = 10$$

**26** **D**—If each adult's fare is twice as much as each child's fare, then 2 adult fares cost as much as

4 child fares. This, added to the 3 children's fares, gives us a total of $4 + 3$, or 7, children's fares. This equals \$14. If 7 children's fares cost \$14, then the cost of each child's fare is $\frac{14}{7}$, or \$2. Adult fares cost twice as much, or \$4.

If you get stumped on a problem like this, you can try backsolving, plugging in each answer choice to see which one gives the correct total cost of \$14. (For an example of backsolving, see the next solution.)

**27** **E**—The \$250 that Doris spent on the carpet is one quarter of the one-third of Doris's savings that's left over after she buys the car, or $\frac{1}{4} \times \frac{1}{3} = \frac{1}{12}$ of her original savings. Therefore, her original savings must have been $12 \times \$250$ or \$3,000.

You can also work backward and try plugging in the answer choices on this one. As usual, we'll start with choice (C).

Choice (C): If Doris originally had \$1,500, then spent $\frac{2}{3}$ of that on the car, she was left with $\frac{1}{3} \times$ \$1,500, or \$500. The amount spent on the carpet was $\frac{1}{4}$ of this, and $\frac{1}{4} \times \$500 = \$125$, not \$250. So this choice is too small, and we move to the next, larger choice.

Choice (D): $\frac{1}{3} \times \$2,000$ is about \$667. And $\frac{1}{4}$ of that is somewhere between \$150 and \$200. Still too small.

So choice (E)—the only remaining choice that is larger—must be correct. You could check it out, although it's not necessary.

**28** E—Let the amount of John's money = $J$ and let the amount of Allen's money = $A$. John gives $5 to Allen so now he has $J - 5$ and Allen has $A + 5$. Allen gives $2 to Frank so now he has $2 less, or $A + 5 - 2 = A + 3$. They all have the same amount of money now, so

$A + 3 = J - 5$

or

$A + 8 = J$

Since Allen needs $8 to have the same as John, John has $8 more.

**29** D—The best way to solve this problem is to pick a number for $x$. Choose a number that is divisible by 6: Let $x = 180$. Last month she paid $\frac{1}{6} \times \$180$, or $30. So she still owes $180 - \$30$, or $150. This month she paid them ($\frac{1}{6} \times \$150$) + $20 = \$25 + \$20$, or $45. So she still owes $150 - \$45$, or $105. Now try each of the answer choices to eliminate any answer choice that does not equal 105 when $x = 180$.

Choice (A): $[180 - 20] \div 6 = 160 \div 6 = 26.67$. Discard.

Choice (B): $(5 \div 6)(180) - 20 = 150 - 20 = 130$. Discard.

Choice (C): $[(5)(180) - 20] \div 6 = 880 \div 6 = 146.67$. Discard.

Choice (D): $(25 \div 36)(180) - 20 = 125 - 20 = 105$. Possibly correct.

Choice (E): $[(25)(180) - 20] \div 36 = 4480 \div 36 = 124.44$. Discard.

Since choice (D) was only one that yielded 105 when $x = 180$, it is the correct answer.

**30** C—John can shovel the whole driveway in 50 minutes, so each minute he does $\frac{1}{50}$ of the driveway. Mary can shovel the whole driveway in 20 minutes; in each minute, she does $\frac{1}{20}$ of the driveway. In one minute they do $\frac{1}{50} + \frac{1}{20} = \frac{2}{100} + \frac{5}{100} = \frac{7}{100}$.

If they do $\frac{7}{100}$ of the driveway in one minute, they do the entire driveway in $\frac{100}{7}$ minutes. (If you do $\frac{1}{2}$ of a job in 1 minute, you do the whole job in the reciprocal of $\frac{1}{2}$, or 2, minutes.) So all that remains is to round off $\frac{100}{7}$ to the nearest integer. Since $\frac{100}{7} = 14\frac{2}{7}$, $\frac{100}{7}$ is approximately 14. It takes about 14 minutes for both of them to shovel the driveway.

**31** 48—If the average salary of the 60 workers is $80, the total amount received by the workers is $60 \times \$80$ or $4,800. This equals the total income from the $75 workers plus the total income from the $100 workers. Let $x$ represent the number of $75 workers.

Since we know there are 60 workers altogether, and everyone earns either $75 or $100, then $60 - x$ must earn $100. We can set up an equation for the total amount received by the workers by multiplying the rate times the number of workers receiving that rate and adding:

$75x + 100(60 - x) = 4,800$

Solve this equation to find $x$, the number of workers earning $75.

$$75x + 6,000 - 100x = 4,800$$
$$-25x = -1,200$$
$$25x = 1,200$$
$$x = 48$$

There were 48 workers earning $75.

**32** **A**—Call the number of 25-cent newspapers $x$, and the number of 40-cent newspapers $y$. Since she sold 100 newspapers in total, $x + y = 100$. Also, the total cost of these newspapers was \$28.00, or 2,800 cents. So $25x + 40y = 2,800$. We want to find $x$, the number of 25-cent newspapers sold. From the first equation, $y = 100 - x$. Substitute this value for $y$ into the second equation, and solve for $x$.

$$25x + 40y = 2,800$$
$$25x + 40(100 - x) = 2,800$$
$$25x + 4,000 - 40x = 2,800$$
$$25x - 40x = 2,800 - 4,000$$
$$-15x = -1,200$$
$$x = -1,200 \div (-15)$$
$$x = 80$$

So she sold 80 newspapers at 25 cents each.

**33** **E**—Pick numbers for all 3 variables so you can easily determine the relationship among them:

Let $c = 20$ pounds of coffee.

Let $s = 4$ sacks.

Let $n = 6$ additional sacks.

Since the grocer originally wanted to divide $c$ pounds of coffee into $s$ sacks, there would have been $\dfrac{c}{s}$ pounds per sack, or 20 pounds of coffee ÷ 4 sacks = 5 pounds per sack. But now the coffee is to be divided equally among $s + n$ sacks, or 20 pounds of coffee ÷ (4 + 6) sacks = $\dfrac{20}{10}$, or 2 pounds per sack. Therefore, the difference between the original number of pounds per sack and the new number of pounds per sack is 5 − 2, or 3 pounds per sack. So now, try each of the answer choices to eliminate any choice that does not equal 3 when $c = 20$, $s = 4$, and $n = 6$:

Choice (A): $\dfrac{c}{s + n} = 20 \div [4 + 6] = 20 \div 10 = 2$. Discard.

Choice (B): $\dfrac{c}{s + cn} = 20 \div [4 + (20)(6)] = 20 \div 124 = 5 \div 31$. Discard.

Choice (C): $\dfrac{c}{s^2 + sn} = 20 \div [(4^2 + (4)(6)] = 20 \div 40 = 1 \div 2$. Discard.

Choice (D): $\dfrac{cn}{s + n} = (20)(6) \div [4 + 6] = 120 \div 10 = 12$. Discard.

Choice (E): $\dfrac{cn}{s^2 + sn} = (20)(6) \div [4^2 + (4)(6)] = 120 \div 40 = 3$. Correct.

Since (E) was the only one that yielded 3, it is the correct answer.

Some problems in this category test your logical reasoning ability more than your knowledge of traditional Math. Also included are questions that involve the following skills (see SAT in a Nutshell section):

45.  Counting the Possibilities
46.  Probability

## PRACTICE SET

### BASIC

1   Team $X$ and Team $Y$ have a tug of war. From their starting positions Team $X$ pulls Team $Y$ forward 3 meters, and Team $X$ is then pulled forward 5 meters. Team $Y$ then pulls Team $X$ forward 2 meters. If the first team to be pulled forward 10 meters loses, how many more meters must Team $Y$ pull Team $X$ forward to win?

(A)   0
(B)   4
(C)   6
(D)   8
(E)   14          Ⓐ Ⓑ Ⓒ Ⓓ Ⓔ

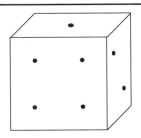

2   On the face of a regular die, the dots are arranged in such a way that the total number of dots on any 2 opposite faces is 7. If the figure above shows a regular die, what is the total number of dots on the faces that are not shown?

(A)   7
(B)   9
(C)   12
(D)   13
(E)   14          Ⓐ Ⓑ Ⓒ Ⓓ Ⓔ

3   Out of 40 sandwiches, 19 are turkey, 9 are bologna, and the rest are tuna fish. If one sandwich is randomly picked, what is the probability of picking a tuna fish sandwich?

4   Achmed finds that by wearing different combinations of the jackets, shirts, and pairs of trousers that he owns, he can make up 90 different outfits. If he owns 5 jackets and 3 pairs of trousers, how many shirts does he own?

(A)   3
(B)   6
(C)   12
(D)   18
(E)   30          Ⓐ Ⓑ Ⓒ Ⓓ Ⓔ

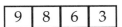

5   The figure above shows an example of a 4-digit identification code used by a certain bank for its customers. If the digits in the code must appear in descending numerical order and no digit can be used more than once, what is the difference between the largest and the smallest possible codes?

(A)   6,666
(B)   5,555
(C)   5,432
(D)   4,444
(E)   1,110          Ⓐ Ⓑ Ⓒ Ⓓ Ⓔ

6. Bill purchased an item and received no change. Before the purchase, he had only a $5 bill, two $10 bills, and a $20 dollar bill. How many distinct possibilities were there for the total amount of his purchase?

(A) 3
(B) 4
(C) 6
(D) 9
(E) 10        Ⓐ Ⓑ Ⓒ Ⓓ Ⓔ

7. A box contains 5 right-handed gloves and 6 left-handed gloves. If Sabina randomly removes 1 glove from the box, how many times must she remove a glove in order to be certain to get a right-handed glove?

(A) 5
(B) 6
(C) 7
(D) 10
(E) 11        Ⓐ Ⓑ Ⓒ Ⓓ Ⓔ

## MEDIUM

8. A vault holds only 8-ounce tablets of gold and 5-ounce tablets of silver. If there are 130 ounces of gold and silver total, what is the greatest amount of gold that can be in the vault, in ounces?

(A) 40
(B) 80
(C) 120
(D) 128
(E) 130        Ⓐ Ⓑ Ⓒ Ⓓ Ⓔ

9. Five light bulbs that are either on or off are lined up in a row. A certain code uses different combinations of lights turned on to represent different words. If exactly 2 lights must be turned on to represent a word, how many different words can be formed using the 5 light bulbs?

10. Robert purchased $2,000 worth of U.S. savings bonds. If bonds are sold in $50 or $100 denominations only, which of the following CANNOT be the number of U.S. savings bonds that Robert purchased?

(A) 20
(B) 27
(C) 30
(D) 40
(E) 50        Ⓐ Ⓑ Ⓒ Ⓓ Ⓔ

11. At a parade, balloons are given out in the order of blue, red, red, yellow, yellow, yellow, blue, red, red, yellow, yellow, yellow, etcetera. If this pattern continues, how many red balloons will have been given out when a total of 70 balloons have been distributed?

(A) 18
(B) 22
(C) 24
(D) 26
(E) 35        Ⓐ Ⓑ Ⓒ Ⓓ Ⓔ

12. Twelve index cards, numbered 3 through 14, are placed in an empty box. If one card is randomly drawn from the box, what is the probability that a prime number will be on the card?

(A) $\dfrac{1}{4}$

(B) $\dfrac{1}{3}$

(C) $\dfrac{5}{12}$

(D) $\dfrac{1}{2}$

(E) $\dfrac{5}{7}$        Ⓐ Ⓑ Ⓒ Ⓓ Ⓔ

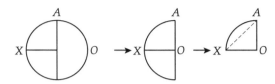

13 In the figure above, a circular sheet of paper is folded along diameter *AB,* and then along radius *OX.* If the folded paper is then cut along dotted line *AX* and unfolded, which of the following could result?

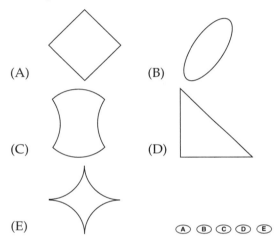

(A)

(B)

(C)

(D)

(E)  Ⓐ Ⓑ Ⓒ Ⓓ Ⓔ

14 A class of 40 students is to be divided into smaller groups. If each group is to contain 3, 4, or 5 people, what is the largest number of groups possible?

(A)   8
(B)   10
(C)   12
(D)   13
(E)   14        Ⓐ Ⓑ Ⓒ Ⓓ Ⓔ

$$A = \{0, 1, -3, 6, -8\}$$
$$B = \{-1, 2, -4, 7\}$$

15 If *a* is a number that is randomly selected from set *A,* and *b* is a number that is randomly selected from set *B,* what is the probability that $ab < 0$?

(A)  $\dfrac{1}{4}$

(B)  $\dfrac{1}{3}$

(C)  $\dfrac{2}{5}$

(D)  $\dfrac{4}{9}$

(E)  $\dfrac{1}{2}$        Ⓐ Ⓑ Ⓒ Ⓓ Ⓔ

16 A vending machine dispenses gumballs in a regularly repeating cycle of 10 different colors. If a quarter buys 3 gumballs, what is the minimum amount of money that must be spent before 3 gumballs of the same color are dispensed?

(A)   $1.00
(B)   $1.75
(C)   $2.00
(D)   $2.25
(E)   $2.50        Ⓐ Ⓑ Ⓒ Ⓓ Ⓔ

## HARD

17 During a season in a certain basketball league, every team plays every other team in the league 10 times. If there are ten teams in the league, how many games are played in the league in one season?

(A)      45
(B)      90
(C)     450
(D)     900
(E)   1,000        Ⓐ Ⓑ Ⓒ Ⓓ Ⓔ

18 Henry and Eleanor are waiting in line for a movie. If Henry is fourth in line, and there are $n$ people ahead of Eleanor, where $n > 4$, how many people are between Henry and Eleanor?

(A) $n - 5$
(B) $n - 4$
(C) $n - 3$
(D) $n + 3$
(E) $n + 4$

Ⓐ Ⓑ Ⓒ Ⓓ Ⓔ

19 If three coins are tossed simultaneously, what is the probability of getting exactly 2 tails?

20 The largest number in a series of consecutive even integers is $w$. If the number of integers is $p$, what is the smallest number in terms of $w$ and $p$ ?

(A) $w - 2p$
(B) $w - p + 1$
(C) $w - 2(p - 1)$
(D) $p - 6 + w$
(E) $w - \dfrac{p}{2}$

Ⓐ Ⓑ Ⓒ Ⓓ Ⓔ

21 A picket fence is composed of $x$ pickets, each of which is $\dfrac{1}{2}$ inch wide. If there are six inches of space between each pair of pickets, which of the following represents the length of the fence, in feet? (1 foot = 12 inches.)

(A) $\dfrac{13}{2}x$

(B) $\dfrac{13}{2}x - 6$

(C) $\dfrac{13}{24}x$

(D) $\dfrac{13x + 1}{24}$

(E) $\dfrac{13x - 12}{24}$

Ⓐ Ⓑ Ⓒ Ⓓ Ⓔ

22 There are 7 people on committee $A$ and 8 people on committee $B$. If three people serve on both committees, how many people serve on only one of the committees?

23 At a certain factory $\dfrac{5}{8}$ of the workers are married and $\dfrac{3}{4}$ are at least 40 years old. If $\dfrac{1}{4}$ of the married workers are younger than 40, what fraction of the workers who are at least 40 are not married?

24 Poplar trees are planted on both sides of a straight street for a length of $\dfrac{3}{8}$ of a kilometer. Each tree is planted in a plot that is 1 meter wide, and there are 16 meters of space between adjacent plots on the same side of the street. What is the maximum number of poplars lining the street? (1 kilometer = 1,000 meters.)

(A) 36
(B) 40
(C) 42
(D) 44
(E) 46

Ⓐ Ⓑ Ⓒ Ⓓ Ⓔ

Column A         Column B

Two coins are to be selected simultaneously and at random from a jar containing 3 pennies, 5 nickels, and 2 dimes.

25   The probability that the coins will have a combined value of 10 cents      The probability that the coins will have a combined value of 11 cents

Ⓐ Ⓑ Ⓒ Ⓓ Ⓔ

| SCORECARD | |
| --- | --- |
| Number of Questions Right: | |
| Number of Questions Wrong: | |
| Number of Questions Omitted: | |
| Number of Correct Guesses: | |
| Number of Wrong Guesses: | |
| Time Used: | |

## ANSWERS AND EXPLANATIONS

### BASIC

**1** **C**—Find out how much Team $X$ has moved so far. Team $X$ pulled Team $Y$ forward 3 meters, so $X$ moved backward 3 meters. Then Team $X$ was pulled forward 5 meters and then a further 2 meters. In total, then, Team $X$ has moved forward $(-3) + 5 + 2 = 4$ meters. Team $X$ must be pulled forward a further 6 meters to be pulled 10 meters forward.

**2** **E**—A die has six faces, and the number of dots on opposite faces sum to 7. Since we can see the faces corresponding to 1, 2, and 4 dots in the picture, the ones we cannot see must contain 6, 5, and 3 dots respectively. Since $6 + 5 + 3 = 14$, there are 14 dots hidden from view.

**3** **3/10, or .3**—First find the number of tuna fish sandwiches. Out of the 40 sandwiches, 19 are turkey and 9 are bologna, so the remaining 40—19 – 9, or 12 are tuna fish. So the probability of picking out a tuna fish sandwich is 12 out of 40, or $\frac{12}{40}$, or $\frac{3}{10}$.

**4** **B**—He owns 3 pairs of trousers and 5 jackets. For every pair of trousers, he can wear 5 different jackets, giving 5 different combinations for each pair of trousers, or $3 \times 5 = 15$ different combinations of trousers and jackets. With each of these combinations he can wear any of his different shirts. The different combinations of shirts, jackets, and trousers is (number of shirts) $\times$ 15. We are told this equals 90, so number of shirts = $\frac{90}{15} = 6$.

**5** **A**—We need the difference between the largest and smallest possible codes. A digit cannot be repeated, and the digits must appear in descending numerical order. The largest such code will have the largest digit, 9, in the thousands place, followed by the next largest digits, 8, 7, and 6, in the next three places, so 9,876 is the largest possible number. For the smallest, start with the smallest digit, 0, and put it in the ones place. Working up from there—we end up with 3,210 as the smallest possible code. The difference between the largest and smallest codes is $9,876 - 3,210 = 6,666$.

**6** **D**—Bill had a five, two tens, and a twenty, for a total of $45. Since he didn't receive any change after purchasing an item, he must have paid exactly the amount of the purchase. He didn't have to spend all his money, though, so the cost wasn't necessarily $45. We know that all of Bill's bills are in amounts that are divisible by five, so the purchase price must also be divisible by five. The smallest denomination that Bill has is a five-dollar bill. So we can start with $5, and then count up all the possible distinct combinations of these bills. These are $5 ($5 bill), $10 ($10 bill), $15 ($5 + $10 bills), $20 ($20 bill), $25 ($5 + $20 bills), $30 ($10 + $20 bills), $35 ($5 + $10 + $20 bills), $40 ($10 + $10 + $20 bills), and $45 (all 4 bills). So, in fact, all prices that are multiples of $5 between $5 and $45 are possible; there are 9 in all.

**7** **C**—Sabina cannot be certain that she will pick a right-handed glove until all of the left-handed gloves have been removed. Suppose she's not having much luck and she keeps picking left-handed gloves. After she's picked all 6 left-handed gloves, the seventh glove that she picks must be right-handed. So she must pick out 7 gloves in order to be certain she'll have a right-handed glove.

### MEDIUM

**8** **C**—The vault has a total of 130 ounces of gold and silver. Not all of the 130 ounces can be gold, since 130 is not a multiple of 8. There must be some silver in there as well. The largest multiple of 8 less than 130 is $16 \times 8$ or 128, but this can't be the amount of gold either, since this leaves only $130 - 128$, or 2 ounces for the silver, and each silver tablet weighs 5 ounces. The next smallest multiple of 8 is $15 \times 8$ or 120. That leaves us with $130 - 120$, or 10 ounces of silver, and since $2 \times 5 = 10$, this amount works. There are 15 tablets of gold, for a total of 120 ounces, and 2 tablets of silver, for a total of 10 ounces. So 120 ounces is the greatest possible amount of gold.

**KAPLAN**

**9** **10**—In a combinations problem, the key is to count the possibilities in an organized way. Let's call the 5 light bulbs *A, B, C, D,* and *E*. If bulb *A* is turned on, we can also turn on *B,* or *C,* or *D,* or *E*. That's 4 pairs. Now we count starting with bulb *B,* but we have to skip *A,* because we already counted the *A-B* combination. So we have *B* and *C, B* and *D,* and *B* and *E*—three more combinations. Next, we have *C* and *D,* and *C* and *E*. Finally we have *D* and *E*. This adds up to 10 possible pairs of lights turned on at the same time.

**10** **E**—This is best solved intuitively. The maximum number of bonds that can be bought is when all the bonds are in $50 denominations. Since Robert bought $2,000 worth of bonds, the maximum number of bonds he could buy is $\frac{2,000}{50}$ = 40 bonds. Answer choice (E) is 50, which is too much. If he bought any $100 bonds he would spend even more money. So it is impossible to buy $2,000 worth of bonds by purchasing 50, $100, or $50 bonds.

**11** **C**—This balloon distribution is an unending series of cycles. Each cycle is 1 blue, 2 red, and 3 yellow, so each cycle contains 6 balloons, 2 of which are red. In 70 balloons, there are $\frac{70}{6} = 11\frac{4}{6}$ cycles; that is, 11 complete cycles and then the first 4 balloons in the next cycle. Since each cycle has 2 red balloons, you will have distributed 2 × 11, or 22, red balloons by the 66th. After the 66th balloon, you go through the beginning of a new cycle, so the 67th balloon is blue, the 68th and 69th red, and the 70th yellow. This adds 2 more red balloons, for a total of 24 in the first 70.

**12** **C**—Since probability equals the number of desired events divided by the number of possible events, we need to find out how many of the cards have prime numbers on them: 4, 6, 8, 9, 10, 12, and 14 are all divisible by smaller numbers, so they're not prime. That leaves 3, 5, 7, 11, and 13 as the primes from 3 to 14, inclusive. So 5 of the 12 cards have prime numbers on them. That means 5 of the 12 possible outcomes fit the description, so the probability is $\frac{5}{12}$, answer choice (C).

**13** **A**—Label a point *Y* directly across the circle from point *X* to keep track of what's happening to the circle as we fold it.

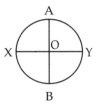

The first fold, along diameter *AB,* brings *Y* right on top of *X*.

The second fold, along radius *OX,* brings *B* right on top of *A*.

With the first fold, we have two semicircular pieces of paper, one on top of the other, folded along *AB*. If we were to cut the line *AX* after the first fold, we would also cut the top piece from *A* to *Y*. With the second fold, there are four quarter-circles. Cutting through the top piece from *A* to *X,* we would also cut through the second piece from *A* to *Y,* the third piece from *B* to *Y,* and the fourth piece from *B* to *X*. This would leave a square with the four corners *A, X, B,* and *Y* and the center *O* after the paper was unfolded:

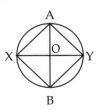

**14** **D**—We will get the maximum number of groups by making each group as small as possible. Each group must have at least 3 people in it, so divide 40 by 3 to find the number of 3-person groups:

$\frac{40}{3}$ = 13 with a remainder of 1.

So we have 13 groups with 1 person left over. Since each group must have at least 3 people, we must throw the extra lonely student in with one of the other groups. So we have 12 groups with 3 students each, and 1 group with 4 students, for a maximum total of 13 groups.

**15** **C**—First of all, how many pairs can come from the two sets? Each of the 5 numbers in set $A$ can be paired with 4 different numbers from set $B$. So there are $4 \times 5$, or 20, possible pairs. Now in order for $ab$ to be less than 0, or negative, one of the variables must be positive and the other negative. So we need to find the number of possible pairs of numbers that would include 1 positive number and 1 negative number.

Consider the possible pairs. First of all, any number paired off with 0 from set $A$ will have a product of 0. Since we need pairs with a product less than 0, these four pairs are out. Of the 4 pairs with 1 from set $A$, two will be negative: $1 \times (-1)$ and $1 \times (-4)$. Likewise, two of the pairs possible with $-3$ will be negative: $(-3) \times 2$ and $(-3) \times 7$, and the same is true for 6 and $-8$. So the number of pairs with a negative product is $2 + 2 + 2 + 2$, or 8.

The probability of getting a pair of numbers with a negative product is therefore 8 out of 20, or $\frac{8}{20}$, which can be reduced to $\frac{2}{5}$.

**16** **B**—Since the vending machine dispenses gumballs in a regular cycle of 10 colors, there are exactly 9 other gumballs dispensed between each pair of gumballs of the same color. For example, gumballs 1 and 11 must be the same color, as must gumballs 2 and 12, 42 and 52, etcetera. To get 3 gumballs all of the same color, you get the first gumball, then 9 of another color before another the same color as the first, then nine of another color before the third of the same color as the first. That's a total of $1 + 9 + 1 + 9 + 1 = 21$ gumballs to get three matching ones.

Since each quarter buys 3 gumballs, and you need 21 gumballs in all, you have to spend $\frac{21}{3}$ = 7 quarters to get three matching gumballs. $7 \times \$0.25 = \$1.75$.

### HARD

**17** **C**—In our 10-team league, each team plays the other 9 teams 10 times each. $9 \times 10 = 90$, so each team plays 90 games. Since there are 10 different teams, and $10 \times 90 = 900$, a total of 900 games are played by the 10 teams. But this counts each game twice, since it counts when Team $A$ plays Team $B$ as one game and when Team $B$ plays Team $A$ as another game. But they're the same game. So, we must halve the total to take into account the fact that two teams play each game: $\frac{900}{2}$ = 450. So 450 games are played in total.

**18** **B**—**Method I:** *Common sense.*
There are $n$ people ahead of Eleanor in line. One of them is Henry. Three more of them are in front of Henry (since Henry is fourth in line). So that makes 4 people who are not behind Henry. All the rest, or $n - 4$, are behind Henry and in front of Eleanor, so $n - 4$ is our answer.
**Method II:** *Picking numbers.*
Say Eleanor is 6th in line. Henry is 4th in line, so there is one person between them, the person 5th in line. There are $n$ people ahead of Eleanor, and since Eleanor is 6th, $n = 5$. Substitute this in the answer choices and see which separates Henry and Eleanor by 1.
Choice (A): $n - 5 = 5 - 5 = 0$. Discard.
Choice (B): $n - 4 = 5 - 4 = 1$. Hold onto.
Choice (C): $n - 3 = 5 - 3 = 2$. Discard.
Choice (D): $n + 3 = 5 + 3 = 8$. Discard.
Choice (E): $n + 4 = 5 + 4 = 9$. Discard.
Only answer choice (B) gives a separation of 1; this must be the correct answer.

**19** **3/8, or .375**—To solve this one we must determine how many different ways the three coins could land, and then count the number of possibilities that have exactly two coins tails up. It's easiest to do this systematically on paper, using "H" for "Heads" and "T" for "Tails."

H-H-H      T-H-H
H-H-T      T-H-T
H-T-H      T-T-H
H-T-T      T-T-T

Be sure to find every combination. There are eight possible outcomes when the three coins are thrown. Only three of them have exactly two tails showing. (Remember: The combination with *three* tails up doesn't fit the description.) So the probability of getting exactly two tails is 3 out of 8, or $\frac{3}{8}$.

**20** **C**—Since we are dealing with a series of consecutive even numbers, each term is 2 more than the previous term. Let's work backward from $w$. If there were 2 numbers in the series, the first number would be the even number just before $w$, or $w - 2$. If there were 3 numbers, the first would be $w - 2 \times 2$, or $w - 4$. If there were 4 terms, the first would be $w - 2 \times 3$, or $w - 6$. To find the first term in the series, we must subtract 2 from $w$ once for each term in the series, with the exception of $w$ itself. If there are $p$ terms in the series (including $w$ itself), we must subtract $2 \times (p - 1)$ from $w$ to get the smallest term. Therefore, the smallest term is $w - 2(p - 1)$.

Alternatively, we could pick numbers. Say $w = 6$, and $p = 3$. Then we have the series 2, 4, 6. The smallest number is 2. Plug our values for $p$ and $w$ into the answer choices and eliminate any choice that does not give us an answer of 2.

Choice (A): $w - 2p = 6 - 6 = 0$. Discard.
Choice (B): $w - p + 1 = 6 - 3 + 1 = 4$. Discard.
Choice (C): $w - 2(p - 1) = 6 - 2(2) = 2$. Hold.
Choice (D): $p - 6 + w = 3 - 6 + 6 = 3$. Discard.
Choice (E): $w - \frac{p}{2} = 6 - \frac{3}{2} = \frac{9}{2}$ Discard.

Since answer choice (C) is the only one that works, it must be the right answer.

**21** **E**—The picket fence contains $x$ pickets, each of width $\frac{1}{2}$ inch. The total width of the pickets in the fence is $\frac{1}{2} \times (x)$ or $\frac{x}{2}$ inches. There are 12 inches in a foot, so $\frac{x}{2}$ inches represents $\frac{x}{24}$ feet. (Divide to get the larger unit.) Now we must find the total width between the pickets. Are there $x$ spaces between the $x$ pickets? No. Let's look at a simple example.

Suppose there are 3 pickets in the fence:

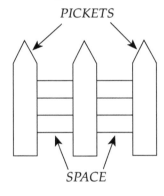

*PICKETS*

*SPACE*

Then there are 3 posts, but only two spaces between them. In general, if there are $x$ pickets in a straight fence, there are $(x - 1)$ spaces between the pickets. Since each space is 6 inches wide, the total width of the spaces is $6(x - 1)$ inches or $\frac{6(x - 1)}{12}$ feet.

Therefore, the total length of the fence in feet is
$$\text{Pickets} + \text{spaces} = \frac{x}{24} + \frac{6(x - 1)}{12} = \frac{x}{24} + \frac{12(x - 1)}{24}$$
$$= \frac{13x - 12}{24}$$

**22** **9**—Of the 7 people on committee $A$, 3 of them are also on committee $B$, leaving 7 – 3 or 4 people who are only on committee $A$. Similarly, there are 8 people on committee $B$; 3 of them are on both committees, leaving 8 – 3, or 5 people only on committee $B$. There are 4 people only on $A$, and 5 people only on $B$, making 4 + 5 or 9 people on only one committee.

**23** **3/8, or .375**—To avoid working with lots of fractions, pick a number for the number of workers in the factory, one that is divisible by all the denominators in the given ratios. Let's take 32 as the total number of workers in the factory. There are four different groups of workers; make a chart to illustrate:

|           | Under 40 | 40+ | Totals |
|-----------|----------|-----|--------|
| Married   | 5        | 15  | 20     |
| Unmarried |          | 9   |        |
| Totals    |          | 24  | 32     |

The four groups of workers are (1) married and under 40, (2) married and 40 or older, (3) unmarried and under 40, and (4) unmarried and 40 or older. The chart also includes numbers for totals, so let's start by filling in as many spaces as we can. The grand total of workers is 32. We're told $\frac{5}{8}$ are married so $\frac{5}{8} \times 32$, or 20, workers are married. Put 20 in the "total married" slot. We're also told that $\frac{3}{4}$ of the workers are at least 40, so put $\frac{3}{4} \times 32$, or 24 in the "40+" slot. Now, we're told that $\frac{1}{4}$ of the married workers are under 40. That means $\frac{1}{4} \times 20$, or 5,

workers are married and under 40, so put a 5 in that space. Since there are 20 total who are married and 5 of them are under 40, 15 must be 40 or older, so put a 15 in that space. Since the total number of workers 40 or older is 24, and the number of those who are married is 15, there must be 9 who are not married and 40 or older (24 – 15 = 9). The fraction of workers 40 or older who are not married is $\frac{9}{24}$, or $\frac{3}{8}$.

**24** **E**—Each plot contains one poplar, and each plot is 1 meter in width. There are 16 meters between every two adjacent plots. Starting at the first poplar, there is 1 meter for the plot, plus 16 meters of space before the next plot, for a total of 17 meters. The second plot then takes up 1 meter, plus 16 meters of space between that plot and the third plot, or 17 more meters. So we need 17 meters for each plot and the space before the next plot.

The street is $\frac{3}{8}$ kilometer long. We change this to meters by multiplying $\frac{3}{8}$ by 1,000—the number of meters in a kilometer. The street is 375 meters long. Each plot and the space before the next plot take up 17 meters, so we divide 17 into 375 to find the number of plots and spaces we can fit in: $\frac{375}{17}$ gives us 22 with 1 left over. This is the number of plots followed by a space. But there is no need for a space after the last plot—there is only a space between pairs of plots; since there's no plot after the last one, there's no need to have a space there. So 374 meters contain 22 plots and the spaces between them, and then there is 1 more plot in the last meter of space, for a total of 23 poplars on each side. Since there are poplars on both sides of the street, we can fit 46 poplars in all.

**25** **A**—Probability is the number of desired outcomes divided by the number of possible outcomes. Since in both columns the number of possible outcomes is the same, just compare the number of desired outcomes. The column with the greater number of desired outcomes has the greater probability of occurring.

In Column A, the only way 2 of these coins will add up to 10 cents is if both coins are nickels. How many pairs are there that are made up of 2 nickels? Well, there are 5 nickels. The first nickel could be paired with each of the 4 other nickels, so that's 4 pairs. The second nickel could be paired with any of the remaining 3 nickels, so that's 3 more pairs. (We've already counted the second nickel paired off with the first nickel, so that isn't counted again.) Likewise, the third nickel can be paired off with the 2 nickels remaining. Finally, the fourth nickel can be paired with the fifth. So we can make $4 + 3 + 2 + 1$, or 10 different pairs of nickels. So 10 out of all the possible pairs will have a combined value of 10 cents.

In Column B, we're looking for pairs that have a combined value of 11 cents. This can only occur if we pair up a dime and a penny. How many pairs can we make using the 3 pennies and 2 dimes? Well, each of the 3 pennies can be paired with 2 different dimes, so there are 6 completely different pairs that can be made using the pennies and dimes. That means only 6 out of all possible pairs will have a combined value of 11 cents. So the probability of drawing 10 cents is greater, making choice (A) correct.

Lines and angles are the subjects of some of the more basic SAT geometry questions. These two basic concepts, covered in detail in the SAT Math in a Nutshell section, also apply to some of the advanced questions.

73.    Intersecting Lines
74.    Parallel Lines and Transversals

## PRACTICE SET

### BASIC

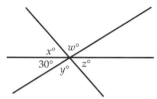

**1**  In the figure above, $w + x + y + z =$

   (A)    330
   (B)    300
   (C)    270
   (D)    240
   (E)    210     Ⓐ Ⓑ Ⓒ Ⓓ Ⓔ

**2**  In the figure above, what is the value of $x + y$?

   (A)    30
   (B)    60
   (C)    90
   (D)    110
   (E)    It cannot be determined from the
        information given.
                   Ⓐ Ⓑ Ⓒ Ⓓ Ⓔ

**3**  If $Y$ is the midpoint of line segment $XZ$, then which of the following is true?

   (A)    $XY < YZ$

   (B)    $YZ < XY$

   (C)    $XZ < YZ$

   (D)    $\frac{1}{2} XZ = 2XY$

   (E)    $2YZ = XZ$     Ⓐ Ⓑ Ⓒ Ⓓ Ⓔ

<u>Column A</u>        <u>Column B</u>

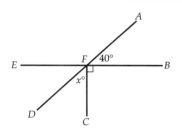

$EB \perp FC$

$AD$ and $EB$ intersect at point $F$.

**4**     $x$                40
                           Ⓐ Ⓑ Ⓒ Ⓓ Ⓔ

Note: Figure not drawn to scale.

$AC > BD$

**5**    $AB$             $CD$
                       Ⓐ Ⓑ Ⓒ Ⓓ Ⓔ

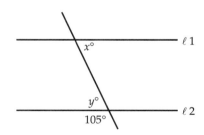

**6**  In the figure above, if $\ell_1 \parallel \ell_2$, then what is the value of $x + y$ ?

# SAT MATH PRACTICE

## MEDIUM

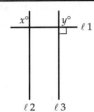

**7** In the figure above, if $x = y$, which of the following MUST be true?

    I. $\ell_2 \parallel \ell_3$
    II. $\ell_1 \perp \ell_2$
    III. Any line that intersects $\ell_1$ also intersects $\ell_2$.

    (A)  I only
    (B)  II only
    (C)  III only
    (D)  I and II only
    (E)  I, II, and III    Ⓐ Ⓑ Ⓒ Ⓓ Ⓔ

<u>Column A</u>            <u>Column B</u>

The length of segment $PQ$ is $2b$.

**8**    $a + 4$                  $b$

                             Ⓐ Ⓑ Ⓒ Ⓓ Ⓔ

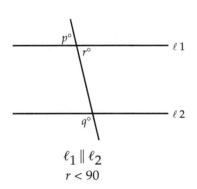

$\ell_1 \parallel \ell_2$
$r < 90$

**9**     $p$                       $q$

                             Ⓐ Ⓑ Ⓒ Ⓓ Ⓔ

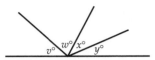

Note: Figure not drawn to scale.

**10** In the figure above, $v = 2w$, $w = 2x$, and $x = \dfrac{y}{3}$. What is the value of $y$ ?

    (A)  18
    (B)  36
    (C)  45
    (D)  54
    (E)  60              Ⓐ Ⓑ Ⓒ Ⓓ Ⓔ

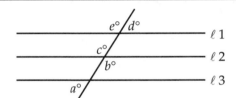

**11** In the figure above, $\ell_1 \parallel \ell_2$ and $\ell_2 \parallel \ell_3$. What is the value of $a + b + c + d + e$ ?

    (A)  180
    (B)  270
    (C)  360
    (D)  450
    (E)  It cannot be determined from the information given.

                             Ⓐ Ⓑ Ⓒ Ⓓ Ⓔ

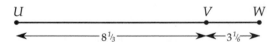

**12** In the figure above, if $X$ (not shown) is the midpoint of $UV$ and if $Y$ (not shown) is the midpoint of $VW$, what is the length of $XY$ ?

**KAPLAN**

**HARD**

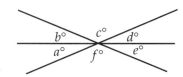

**13** Which of the following must be true of the angles marked in the figure above?
  I. $a + b = d + e$
  II. $b + e = c + f$
  III. $a + c + e = b + d + f$
  (A)  I only
  (B)  I and II only
  (C)  I and III only
  (D)  II and III only
  (E)  I, II, and III   Ⓐ Ⓑ Ⓒ Ⓓ Ⓔ

**14** In the diagram above, $AD = BE = 6$ and $CD = 3(BC)$. If $AE = 8$, then $BC =$
  (A)  6
  (B)  4
  (C)  3
  (D)  2
  (E)  1   Ⓐ Ⓑ Ⓒ Ⓓ Ⓔ

Column A                Column B

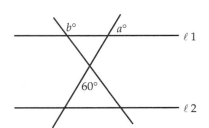

Note: Figure not drawn to scale.

$$\ell_1 \parallel \ell_2$$

**15**    $b - a$                      60

Ⓐ Ⓑ Ⓒ Ⓓ Ⓔ

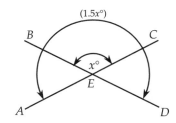

**16** In the figure above, what is the degree measure of $\angle AEB$ ?

| SCORECARD | |
|---|---|
| Number of Questions Right: | |
| Number of Questions Wrong: | |
| Number of Questions Omitted: | |
| Number of Correct Guesses: | |
| Number of Wrong Guesses: | |
| Time Used: | |

## ANSWERS AND EXPLANATIONS

### BASIC

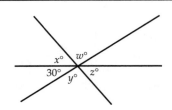

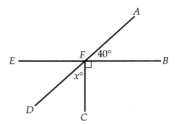

**1** | **B**—In the diagram, the unmarked angle and the 30° angle are vertical angles; therefore, the unmarked angle must also measure 30°. The sum of the measures of the angles around a point is 360°, so we can set up the following equation:

$$30 + x + w + 30 + z + y = 360$$

Rearranging the terms on the left side of the equation gives:

$$w + x + y + z + 60 = 360$$
$$w + x + y + z = 360 - 60 = 300$$

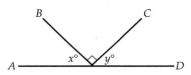

**2** | **C**—There's no way to find either $x$ or $y$ alone, but their sum is a different story. Since $AD$ is a straight line, the angle marked $x°$, the angle marked $y°$, and the right angle together make up a straight angle, which measures 180°. So:

$$x + y + 90 = 180$$
$$x + y = 180 - 90 = 90$$

**3** | **E**—Draw line segment $XZ$ with $Y$ as its midpoint:

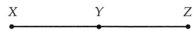

Since $Y$ is the midpoint of $XZ$, $XY = YZ$. Therefore, choices (A) and (B) are false and can be eliminated. Choice (C) is false because the length of the whole segment cannot be less than a part of the segment. Choice (D) is false because $2XY = XZ$. So choice (E) is correct because twice the length of half of the segment equals the whole segment.

**4** | **A**—$\angle AFD$ is a straight angle. The angle marked 40°, the right angle, and the angle marked $x°$ together form $\angle AFD$; therefore, they must add up to 180°.

$$x + 90 + 40 = 180$$
$$x + 130 = 180$$
$$x = 50$$

So Column A is greater than Column B, and choice (A) is correct.

**5** | **A**—Redraw the diagram, exaggerating the difference in length between $AC$ and $BD$:

You can clearly see that $AB$ is greater than $CD$.

You could also use an algebraic approach. You're given that $AC > BD$. Line segment $AC$ is made up of line segments $AB$ and $BC$. Therefore, $AC = AB + BC$. Line segment $BD$ is made up of line segments $BC$ and $CD$. Therefore, $BD = BC + CD$. Now you can plug in for $AC$ and $BD$ in the original inequality:

$$AC > BD$$
$$AB + BC > BC + CD$$

Subtract $BC$ from both sides of the inequality:

$$AB > CD$$

Again, Column A is greater than Column B.

**6** | **150**—The angles represented by $y°$ and 105° are supplementary because they form a straight line. Therefore, $y + 105 = 180$, and $y = 75$. Since $\ell_1 \parallel \ell_2$, angles $y$ and $x$ have equal measures because they are alternate interior angles. Therefore, $x = 75$.

So $x + y = 75 + 75$, or 150.

## MEDIUM

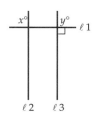

**7** **D**—From the diagram, we see that the angle marked $y°$ is supplementary to a right angle. This means that $y$ must be $180 - 90$, or 90. We are told that $x$ equals $y$, so $x$ must also be 90. This means that both $\ell_2$ and $\ell_3$ are perpendicular to $\ell_1$; therefore, they must be parallel to each other. This means that, statements I and II are true. But statement III is not necessarily true. For instance, $\ell_3$ intersects $\ell_1$, but never meets $\ell_2$.

**8** **A**—You're given that $PQ = 2b$. But $PQ$ is also made up of line segments with lengths $a$ and 8, so $PQ = a + 8$. Therefore, $a + 8 = 2b$. So solve for $b$ in terms of $a$: $a + 8 = 2b$.

$$\frac{a + 8}{2} = b$$

$$\frac{a}{2} + 4 = b$$

Column B is $\frac{a}{2}$ + 4. Subtracting 4 from both columns leaves $a$ in Column A and $\frac{a}{2}$ in Column B. Since $a$ represents a distance, it must be positive. So $a$ must be greater than $\frac{a}{2}$, and Column A is greater than Column B.

**9** **B**—Since $r < 90$, $p$ must also be less than 90 because $r$ and $p$ are measures of vertical angles. Since $\ell_1 \parallel \ell_2$ angles $p$ and $q$ must be supplementary to each other. Therefore, $p + q = 180$. Since $p < 90$, $q$ must be greater than 90 in order to make the equation true. So Column B is greater than Column A, and choice (B) is correct.

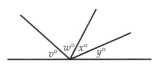

**10** **D**—The sum $v + w + x + y$ must equal 180 since the angles with these measures together form a straight line. Since the question asks for the value of $y$, define all variables in terms of $y$. If $w = 2x$ and $x = \frac{y}{3}$, then $w = \frac{2y}{3}$. Similarly, $v = 2w$, so $v = 2\left(\frac{2y}{3}\right)$ or $\frac{4y}{3}$.

Substitute the angles in terms of $y$ into the equation:
$$v + w + x + y = 180$$
$$\frac{4y}{3} + \frac{2y}{3} + \frac{y}{3} + y = 180$$
$$\frac{7y}{3} + y = 180$$
$$\frac{10y}{3} = 180$$
$$y = \frac{3}{10} \times 180 = 3 \times 18 = 54$$

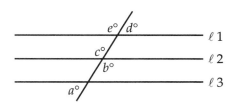

**11** **E**—We're given that $\ell_1$, $\ell_2$, and $\ell_3$ are all parallel to one another. Remember, when parallel lines are cut by a transversal, all acute angles formed by the transversal are equal, all obtuse angles are equal, and any acute angle is supplementary to any obtuse angle. We can get 2 pairs of supplementary angles from the 5 marked angles:

$$\underbrace{a + b}_{180} + \underbrace{c + d}_{180} + e$$

We're left with $360 + e$. Since we don't know the value of $e$, we cannot find the sum. So choice (E) is correct.

**12** **23/4, or 5.75**—If $X$ and $Y$ are the midpoints of $UV$ and $VW$, respectively, then the length of $XY$ equals half the length of the whole line segment $UW$.

$$UW = 8\frac{1}{3} + 3\frac{1}{6} = 8\frac{2}{6} + 3\frac{1}{6} = 11\frac{1}{2} \text{, or } \frac{23}{2}.$$

So the length of $XY = \frac{1}{2} \times \frac{23}{2} = \frac{23}{4}$, or 5.75 in decimal form.

### HARD

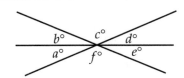

**13** **C**—We have three pairs of vertical angles around the point of intersection: $a$ and $d$, $b$ and $e$, and $c$ and $f$. Therefore, $a = d$, $b = e$, and $c = f$. Let's look at the three statements one at a time.

I: $a + b = d + e$. Since $a = d$ and $b = e$, this is true. Eliminate choice (D).

II: $b + e = c + f$. We know that $b = e$ and $c = f$, but we don't how the pairs relate to each other. Statement II does not have to be true. Eliminate choices (B) and (E).

III: $a + c + e = b + d + f$. This is true, since $a = d$, $c = f$, and $b = e$. That is, we can match each angle on one side of the equation with a different angle on the other side. Statement III must be true.

Statements I and III must be true. So choice (C) is correct.

**14** **E**—Since $AE$ is a line segment, all the lengths are additive, so $AE = AD + DE$. We're told that $AD = 6$ and $AE = 8$. So $DE = AE - AD = 8 - 6 = 2$. We're also told that $BE = 6$. So $BD = BE - DE = 6 - 2 = 4$. We have the length of $BD$, but still need the length of $BC$. Since $CD = 3(BC)$, the situation looks like this:

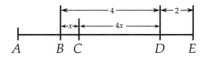

Here $x$ stands for the length of $BC$. Since $BD = 4$, we can write:

$$x + 3x = 4$$
$$4x = 4$$
$$x = 1$$

So BC = 1, answer choice (E).

**15** **C**—Since $\ell_1 \parallel \ell_2$, you can determine which angles are equal to each other and then label the diagram accordingly:

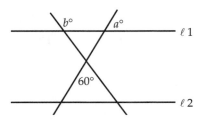

The two triangles contain $a°$, $c°$, and 60°. Therefore, $a + c + 60 = 180$, and $a + c = 120$. You can see from the diagram that angles $b$ and $c$ are supplementary because they form a straight line. Therefore, $b + c = 180$. Since you need to find the value of $b - a$, subtract the first equation from the second:

$$b + c = 180$$
$$-[a + c = 120]$$
$$b - a = 60$$

So the two columns are equal, and choice (C) is correct.

**16** **36**—The angle measuring $(1.5x)°$ is made up of $\angle AEB$, $\angle BEC$, and $\angle CED$. That is, $\angle AEB + \angle BEC + \angle CED = (1.5x)°$. We can rearrange this to get an expression for $\angle AEB$, the angle we want. We get:

$$\angle AEB = 1.5x° - \angle BEC - \angle CED$$

Since $\angle BEC = x°$, substitute $x°$ for $\angle BEC$:

$$\angle AEB = 1.5x° - x° - \angle CED$$
$$= 0.5x° - \angle CED$$

Also, $\angle AEB$ and $\angle CED$ are vertical angles, so $\angle AEB = \angle CED$. Let's put this into our equation:

$$\angle AEB = 0.5x° - \angle AEB$$
$$2\angle AEB = 0.5x°$$
$$\angle AEB = 0.25x°$$
$$= \frac{1}{4}x°$$

Now we need to find out what $x$ is to get a value for $\angle AEB$. Since $\angle AED$ and $\angle BEC$ are also vertical angles, $\angle AED = \angle BEC$, or $\angle AED = x°$. Marking this in on our diagram, we see that the sum of all the angles around point $E$ is $1.5x° + x° = 2.5x°$, which equals $360°$.

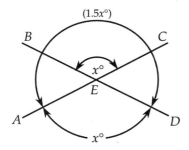

Therefore $2.5x = 360$, or $x = 144$.

Since the measure of $\angle AEB$ is $\dfrac{1}{4}x°$, we get

$\angle AEB = \dfrac{1}{4}(144°) = 36°$ .

Triangles appear on the SAT as often as all other geometric figures combined. This is a big and important category, testing all of the following skills (which are all summarized in our SAT Math in a Nutshell section):

75. Interior Angles of a Triangle
76. Exterior Angles of a Triangle
77. Similar Triangles
78. Area of a Triangle
79. Triangle Inequality Theorem
80. Isosceles Triangles
81. Equilateral Triangles
82. Pythagorean Theorem
83. The 3-4-5 Triangle
84. The 5-12-13 Triangle
85. The 30-60-90 Triangle
86. The 45-45-90 Triangle

Note: It's not necessary to memorize any formulas because they're printed in the test booklet.

## PRACTICE SET

### BASIC

**1** In the figure above, $x =$

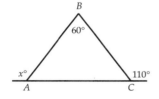

**2** In the figure above, $x = 2z$ and $y = 3z$. What is the value of $z$ ?

(A) 24
(B) 30
(C) 36
(D) 54
(E) 60

Ⓐ Ⓑ Ⓒ Ⓓ Ⓔ

**3** In the figure above, what is $x$ in terms of $y$ ?

(A) $150 - y$
(B) $150 + y$
(C) $80 + y$
(D) $30 + y$
(E) $30 - y$

Ⓐ Ⓑ Ⓒ Ⓓ Ⓔ

**4** The angles of a triangle are in the ratio of 2:3:4. What is the degree measure of the largest angle?

(A) 40
(B) 80
(C) 90
(D) 120
(E) 150

Ⓐ Ⓑ Ⓒ Ⓓ Ⓔ

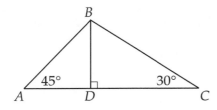

**5** In the figure above, if $AB = 2$, what is the length of $BC$ ?

(A) $\sqrt{2}$
(B) $2$
(C) $2\sqrt{2}$
(D) $3$
(E) $\sqrt{6}$

ⓐ ⓑ ⓒ ⓓ ⓔ

Column A      Column B

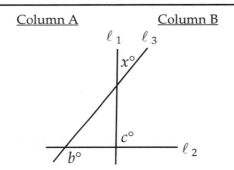

**6**    $x$              $b + c - 180$

ⓐ ⓑ ⓒ ⓓ ⓔ

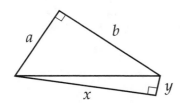

**7**    $a^2 + b^2$            $x^2 + y^2$

ⓐ ⓑ ⓒ ⓓ ⓔ

Column A      Column B

In right $\Delta XYZ$, the length of leg $XY$ is 6 and the length of the hypotenuse $XZ$ is 8.

**8**   Length of $YZ$        10

ⓐ ⓑ ⓒ ⓓ ⓔ

In $\Delta PQR$, $PQ = 4$ and $PR = 7$.

**9**     $QR$             11

ⓐ ⓑ ⓒ ⓓ ⓔ

In right $\Delta ABC$, $\angle B = 90°$, $AC = 13$, and $AB = 5$.

**10**   The number of       The number of
square units in         units in the
the area of $\Delta ABC$    perimeter of $\Delta ABC$

ⓐ ⓑ ⓒ ⓓ ⓔ

**11** If the perimeter of isosceles triangle $ABC$ is 20 and the length of side $AC$ is 8, what is one possible value for the length of side $BC$ ?

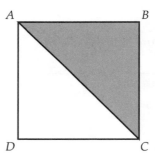

**12** In square $ABCD$ shown above, if $AC = 5$, what is the area of the shaded region?

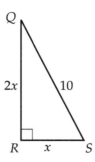

**13** In the figure above, what is the area of right △QRS ?

(A) $4\sqrt{5}$

(B) 10

(C) $8\sqrt{5}$

(D) 20

(E) 40

Ⓐ Ⓑ Ⓒ Ⓓ Ⓔ

## MEDIUM

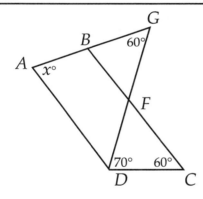

**14** In the figure above, if AD ∥ BC, then x =

(A) 20

(B) 30

(C) 50

(D) 60

(E) 70

Ⓐ Ⓑ Ⓒ Ⓓ Ⓔ

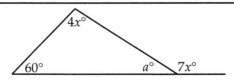

Note: Figure not drawn to scale.

**15** What is the value of *a* in the figure above?

Column A          Column B

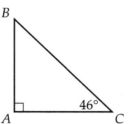

Note: Figure not drawn to scale.

**16**     AB                    AC

Ⓐ Ⓑ Ⓒ Ⓓ Ⓔ

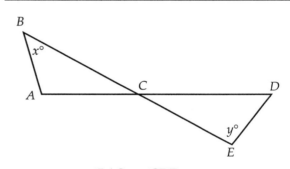

∠BAC > ∠CDE

**17**     x                    y

Ⓐ Ⓑ Ⓒ Ⓓ Ⓔ

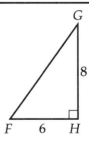

**18** The area of △ FGH          48

Ⓐ Ⓑ Ⓒ Ⓓ Ⓔ

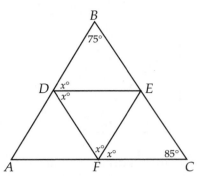

Note: Figure not drawn to scale.

19  In the figure above, what is the measure of ∠BED ?

(A)  40°
(B)  55°
(C)  65°
(D)  80°
(E)  It cannot be determined from the
     information given.

Ⓐ Ⓑ Ⓒ Ⓓ Ⓔ

20  What is the length of the hypotenuse of an
isosceles right triangle with an area of 32?

(A)  4
(B)  $4\sqrt{2}$
(C)  8
(D)  $8\sqrt{2}$
(E)  $\sqrt{3}$

Ⓐ Ⓑ Ⓒ Ⓓ Ⓔ

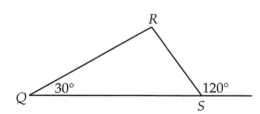

21  In △QRS shown above, if QS = 6, RS =

(A)  12
(B)  $6\sqrt{3}$
(C)  6
(D)  $3\sqrt{3}$
(E)  3

Ⓐ Ⓑ Ⓒ Ⓓ Ⓔ

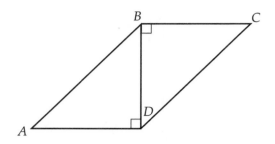

Note: Figure not drawn to scale.

22  If AD = 2CD and BD = BC = 6, what is the
length of AB ?

(A)  $6\sqrt{2}$
(B)  9
(C)  12
(D)  $12\sqrt{2}$
(E)  18

Ⓐ Ⓑ Ⓒ Ⓓ Ⓔ

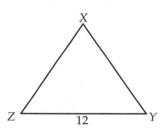

23  If ∠XYZ = ∠XZY and the area of △XYZ is 48,
what is the perimeter of the figure above?

**KAPLAN**

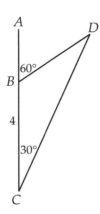

**24** In the figure above, if ∠ *DBA* has measure 60°, ∠ *DCB* has measure 30°, and *BC* = 4, what is the length of *BD* ?

(A) $\sqrt{2}$

(B) 4

(C) $4\sqrt{2}$

(D) $4\sqrt{3}$

(E) 8 Ⓐ Ⓑ Ⓒ Ⓓ Ⓔ

---

Column A      Column B

Δ*P* has its vertices at the points (0, 0), (6, 0), and (6, 5).

Δ*Q* has its vertices at the points (0, 0), (6, 0), and (6, –5).

**25** Area of Δ*P*      Area of Δ*Q*

Ⓐ Ⓑ Ⓒ Ⓓ Ⓔ

## HARD

**26** The length of each side of a certain triangle is an even number. If no two of the sides have the same length, what is the smallest perimeter the triangle could have?

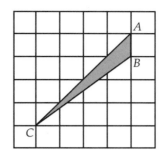

**27** The figure above consists of 36 squares, each with a side of 1. What is the area of Δ*ABC* ?

---

Column A      Column B

The lengths of the legs of right triangle *PQR* are *x* and *y*.

The lengths of the legs of right triangle *RST* are 2*x* and 2*y*.

**28** Twice the area      The area of Δ*RST*
of Δ*PQR*

Ⓐ Ⓑ Ⓒ Ⓓ Ⓔ

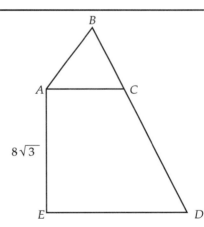

**29** In the figure above, if the perimeter of equilateral Δ*ABC* is 24, and *AC* ∥ *ED*, what is the perimeter of *ABDE* ?

(A) $12(3 + \sqrt{3})$

(B) $8(6 + \sqrt{3})$

(C) $4(17 + 7\sqrt{3})$

(D) $72\sqrt{3}$

(E) $8(3 + 11\sqrt{3})$ Ⓐ Ⓑ Ⓒ Ⓓ Ⓔ

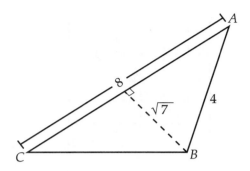

Note: Figure not drawn to scale.

**30** In the above figure, what is the length of *BC* ?

(A)  $4\sqrt{2}$

(B)  $4\sqrt{3}$

(C)  $4\sqrt{5}$

(D)  $\sqrt{74}$

(E)  $4\sqrt{7}$          Ⓐ Ⓑ Ⓒ Ⓓ Ⓔ

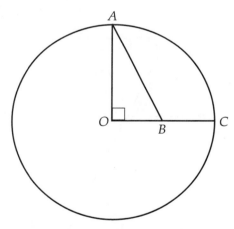

**31** In the figure above, circle *O* has a circumference of $12\pi$. If *AB* = 8, what is the length of *BC* ?

(A)  $2\sqrt{7}$

(B)  $2(3 - \sqrt{7})$

(C)  $2(6 - \sqrt{7})$

(D)  $4\sqrt{5}$

(E)  $2(3 - 2\sqrt{5})$          Ⓐ Ⓑ Ⓒ Ⓓ Ⓔ

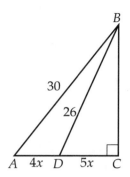

**32** What is the length of *BC* in the figure above?

(A)  10
(B)  16
(C)  18
(D)  20
(E)  24          Ⓐ Ⓑ Ⓒ Ⓓ Ⓔ

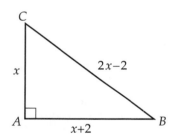

**33** In right triangle *ABC* above, *x* =

(A)  6
(B)  8
(C)  $6\sqrt{2}$
(D)  10
(E)  13          Ⓐ Ⓑ Ⓒ Ⓓ Ⓔ

**KAPLAN**

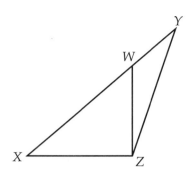

Note: Figure not drawn to scale.

34 In the figure above, the ratio of the area of
△WXZ to the area of △WYZ is 7:2. If XY = 21,
what is the length of segment WY ?

| SCORECARD | |
|---|---|
| Number of Questions Right: | |
| Number of Questions Wrong: | |
| Number of Questions Omitted: | |
| Number of Correct Guesses: | |
| Number of Wrong Guesses: | |
| Time Used: | |

## ANSWERS AND EXPLANATIONS

**BASIC**

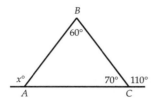

**1** **130**—The angle with measure $x°$ is an exterior angle of the triangle; therefore it must equal the sum of the two remote interior angles: $\angle ABC$ and $\angle BCA$. $\angle ABC$ has a measure of 60°. Since $\angle BCA$ is supplementary to the angle marked 110°, its measure must be $180° - 110°$, or 70°. Therefore, $x = 60 + 70$, or 130.

**2** **C**—Since the angle marked $x°$ and the angle marked $y°$ together form a straight angle, their measures must sum to 180°.

Substitute in $2z$ for $x$ and $3z$ for $y$, and solve for $z$.
$$x + y = 180$$
$$2z + 3z = 180$$
$$5z = 180$$
$$z = \frac{1}{5} \times 180 = 36$$

**3** **A**—Once again, we are dealing with the sum of the interior angles in a triangle. We can write:
$$x + y + 30 = 180$$
$$x + y = 180 - 30$$
$$x + y = 150$$
Subtracting $y$ from each side, we find that
$$x = 150 - y.$$

**4** **B**—The measures of the three interior angles are in the ratio of 2:3:4, and they must add up to 180°. So the three angles must have degree measures that are $2x$, $3x$, and $4x$. Find $x$:
$$2x + 3x + 4x = 180$$
$$9x = 180$$
$$x = 20$$
The largest angle has measure $4x$, or $4(20)$, which is 80.

**5** **C**—$\triangle ABD$ has one angle of 90° and another of 45°. Therefore, it is an isosceles right triangle, with sides in the ratio $1:1:\sqrt{2}$. Since the hypotenuse is 2, the length of the legs must be $\frac{2}{\sqrt{2}} = \sqrt{2}$. $\triangle BCD$ has an angle of 30° and another of 90°. Therefore it is a 30°-60°-90° right triangle, with sides in the ratio $1:\sqrt{3}:2$. Since $BD$, the shorter leg, has a length of $\sqrt{2}$, the length of the hypotenuse must be twice this, or $2\sqrt{2}$.

**6** **C**—The three lines form a triangle. One interior angle of the small triangle is supplementary to $b$, so its measure is $180 - b$. Another interior angle is supplementary to $c$, so its measure is $180 - c$. The angle marked $x$ is vertical to the other interior angle of the triangle. The sum of the angles of a triangle is 180, so you can relate the variables $x$, $b$, and $c$ in an equation: $x + (180 - b) + (180 - c) = 180$. Isolating $x$, we get $x = b + c - 180$.

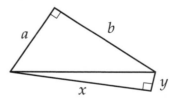

**7** **C**—These are right triangles, with the same hypotenuse. By the Pythagorean theorem, $a^2 + b^2 = (\text{hypotenuse})^2$. Similarly, $x^2 + y^2 = (\text{hypotenuse})^2$. So $a^2 + b^2 = x^2 + y^2$ and the columns are equal.

**8** **B**—Don't assume this is a 3–4–5 right triangle! In this case the two sides in the ratio of 3:4 are a leg and the *hypotenuse*. The hypotenuse in a right triangle is always the longest side. Therefore, the length of the unknown leg $YZ$ in Column A must be less than 8. So it must also be less than 10 in Column B.

**9** **B**—The key to solving this problem is knowing properties of triangles. The sum of the lengths of any two sides of a triangle is greater than the length of the third side. Since $PQ$ plus $PR$ equals $4 + 7$, or 11, the third side, $QR$, must be less than 11. So Column B is greater than Column A.

**10** **C**—Sketch this triangle:

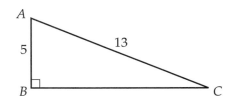

You should recognize that this is a 5-12-13 special right triangle. So $BC = 12$. If you didn't realize that, you could have found $BC$ using the Pythagorean theorem. Since the area of a triangle equals $\frac{1}{2} \times$ base $\times$ height, the area of $\triangle ABC = \frac{1}{2} \times 5 \times 12$, or Column A is 30. The perimeter of $\triangle ABC = 5 + 12 + 13 = 30$, so Column B is also 30.

**11** **4, 6, or 8**—There are three possible ways to draw isosceles triangle $ABC$ with a perimeter of 20 and $AC$ with a length of 8:

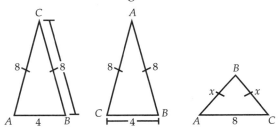

In the first case, $AC$ and $BC$ are the two equal sides in the isosceles triangle. Therefore, the length of $BC$ is 8.

In the second case, $AC$ and $AB$ are the two equal sides. Therefore, the length of $BC$ is $20 - 8 - 8$, or 4.

In the third case, $BC$ and $AB$ are the two equal sides. Let $x$ represent the length of $BC$ and $AB$. You know that the perimeter is 20, so $AC + BC + AB = 20$, or $8 + x + x = 20$. Solving for $x$, you find that $x = 6$. Therefore, the length of $BC$ in this case is 6.

You're asked to find only one possible value for $BC$, so you can give 4, 6, or 8 and still be correct.

**12** **25/4, or 6.25**—Since $ABCD$ is a square, diagonal $AC$ divides it into two isosceles right triangles, one of which is shaded $\triangle ABC$. In an isosceles or 45–45–90 right triangle, the hypotenuse is equal to the length of a leg times $\sqrt{2}$. So leg $\times \sqrt{2} = AC$

$$\text{leg} \times \sqrt{2} = 5$$
$$\text{leg} = \frac{5}{\sqrt{2}}$$

The area of a triangle is $\frac{1}{2}$ (base $\times$ height):

$$\begin{aligned} \text{area} &= \frac{1}{2} \left( \frac{5}{\sqrt{2}} \times \frac{5}{\sqrt{2}} \right) \\ &= \frac{1}{2} \left( \frac{25}{\sqrt{2} \times \sqrt{2}} \right) \\ &= \frac{1}{2} \times \frac{25}{2} \\ &= \frac{25}{4} \end{aligned}$$

**13** **D**—The area of a triangle is $\frac{1}{2}$ (base $\times$ height). Since $QRS$ is a right triangle, use the Pythagorean theorem—the sum of the squares of the two legs equals the square of the hypotenuse—to solve for each of these lengths:

$$x^2 + (2x)^2 = 10^2$$
$$x^2 + 4x^2 = 100$$
$$5x^2 = 100$$
$$x^2 = 20$$
$$x = \sqrt{20} = \sqrt{4} \times \sqrt{5} = 2\sqrt{5}$$

So the base is $2\sqrt{5}$ and the height is

$$2 \times 2\sqrt{5} = 4\sqrt{5}.$$

$$\begin{aligned} \text{Area} &= \frac{1}{2} \left( 2\sqrt{5} \right)\left( 4\sqrt{5} \right) \\ &= \frac{1}{2} (2 \times 4)\left( \sqrt{5} \times \sqrt{5} \right) \\ &= \frac{1}{2} \times 8 \times 5 \\ &= 20 \end{aligned}$$

**MEDIUM**

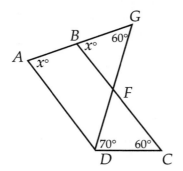

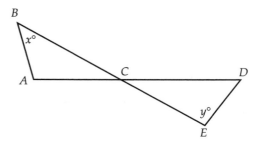

**14** **E**—Since *BC* is parallel to *AD*, ∠*GBF* must have the same degree measure as *x* (two parallel lines cut by transversal *AG*). Finding *x*, then, is the same as finding the measure of ∠*GBF*.

Let's look at Δ*BFG* and Δ*DCF*. The two interior angles of these two triangles at point *F* must have the same degree measure, since they are a pair of vertical angles. In addition, each triangle has a 60° angle. Since we have two triangles with two pairs of equal angles, the third pair of angles must be equal, too, because the sum of all three angles in any triangle is 180°. The third angle in Δ*DCF* has measure 70°; therefore,
∠*GBF* = *x*° = 70°.

**15** **40**—The exterior angle of a triangle equals the sum of the two remote interior angles, so $7x = 4x + 60$, or $3x = 60$, or $x = 20$. The angle marked *a*° and that marked $7x°$ are supplementary, so $a + 7x = 180$, or $a + 7(20) = 180$, or $a = 40$.

Alternatively, you may have seen that the angle marked *a*° and that marked $7x°$ were supplementary, which means that $a = 180 - 7x$. Since the sum of the interior angles of a triangle is 180°, $60 + 4x + (180 - 7x) = 180$. That is $4x - 7x = 180 - 60 - 180$, or $-3x = -60$, or $x = 20$. If $x = 20$, and $a = 180 - 7x$, then $a = 180 - 7(20) = 40$.

**16** **A**—The key to solving this problem is knowing that in any triangle, the greater an angle, the greater the length of the side opposite that angle. Since triangle *ABC* is a right triangle, and angle *C* = 46°, then angle *B* = 180° − 90° − 46°, or 44°. So angle *C* is greater than angle *B*. Therefore, side *AB* opposite angle *C* is greater than side *AC* opposite angle *B*. So Column A is greater than Column B.

**17** **B**—Redraw the diagram, exaggerating the difference between ∠*BAC* and ∠*CDE*: From this we can conclude that $y > x$.

Alternatively, you know that the sum of the angles of a triangle is 180°. So the sum of the interior angles in both triangles is 180°. So $x + ∠BAC + ∠BCA = 180 = y + ∠CDE + ∠DCE$. Both triangles share a pair of vertical angles at *C*, so ∠*BCA* = ∠*DCE*, so they cancel out of the equation, leaving $x + ∠BAC = y + ∠CDE$. Also, ∠*BAC* > ∠*CDE*. So *y* must be greater than *x* to balance out the equation. So choice (B) is correct.

**18** **B**—The area of a triangle = $\frac{1}{2}$ × base × height.

In Δ*FGH*, we can consider *FH* as the base and *GH* as the height. It's given that $FH = 6$ and $GH = 8$. So the area of Δ*FGH* is $\frac{1}{2} × 6 × 8$, or 24. So 48 in Column B is greater than the area of Δ*FGH* in Column A.

**19** **B**—Find *x* first. The sum of the angles of quadrilateral *DBCF* is 360°. Therefore, $2x + 75 + 85 + 2x = 360$, or $4x = 200$, so $x = 50$. In Δ*DBE*, $x° + 75° + ∠BED = 180°$, $50° + 75° + ∠BED = 180°$, or ∠*BED* = 55°.

**20** **D**—The area of a right triangle is $\frac{1}{2}(\text{leg}_1 × \text{leg}_2)$

Since an isosceles right triangle has legs of the same length, this equals $\frac{1}{2}$ (leg)². So $\frac{1}{2}$ (leg)² = 32, (leg)² = 64, and leg = $\sqrt{64}$ = 8. Therefore, the triangle has legs of length 8. In an isosceles right triangle, the ratio of either leg to the hypotenuse is 1: $\sqrt{2}$ , so here the hypotenuse must be 8 $\sqrt{2}$ in length.

**21** **E**—∠QSR is 60° because it is supplementary to the exterior 120° angle. Therefore, ∠QRS is 90° because the sum of the measures of the angles of a triangle equals 180. So ΔQRS is a 30-60-90 right triangle, with side lengths in a ratio of 1: $\sqrt{3}$ :2. Since QS is 6, and it is the side opposite the 90° angle (i.e., it is the hypotenuse), it is twice the length of RS, the side opposite the 30° angle. Therefore, RS = 3.

**22** **E**—Since BD = BC, ΔBCD is an isosceles right triangle. So the legs and the hypotenuse are in the ratio 1:1: $\sqrt{2}$ . Since the legs have length 6, CD has length 6 $\sqrt{2}$ . Since AD = 2CD, AD = 12 $\sqrt{2}$ . By the Pythagorean theorem:

$$AB^2 = BD^2 + AD^2$$
$$= 6^2 + (12\sqrt{2})^2$$
$$= 36 + 288$$
$$= 324$$

So AB = $\sqrt{324}$ = 18.

**23** **32**—Since ∠XYZ = ∠XZY, the sides opposite those angles are equal. Thus XY = XZ, so ΔXYZ is isosceles. To find the missing side lengths, you can divide ΔXYZ into two congruent right triangles:

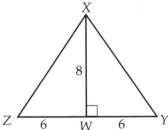

Let YZ be the base of ΔXYZ. The altitude (height) is the perpendicular line drawn from X to YZ. Since the area of a triangle equals $\frac{1}{2}$ × base × height, $\frac{1}{2}$ × 12 × XW = 48, or XW = 8. Now the altitude divides the base of ΔXYZ in half. So WY = 6. ΔXWY is a special right triangle: Its sides are in the ratio 6:8:10 (a multiple of 3:4:5). Therefore, XY = 10, so XZ = 10 as well. So the perimeter of ΔXYZ = 10 + 10 + 12 = 32.

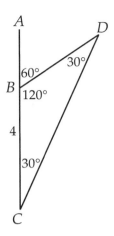

**24** **B**—If ∠DBA has a measure of 60°, ∠CBD, which is supplementary to it, must have a measure of 180 − 60, or 120°.

∠BCD has a measure of 30°; that leaves 180 − (120 + 30), or 30° for the remaining interior angle: BDC.

Since ∠BCD has the same measure as ∠BDC, ΔBCD is an isosceles triangle, and the sides opposite the equal angles will have equal lengths. Therefore, BD must have the same length as BC, 4.

**25** **C**—The area of a triangle is $\frac{1}{2}$ × base × height. Plotting each triangle, we note that both are right triangles sharing the same base.

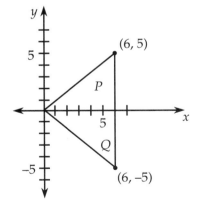

This common base runs along the x-axis and has a length of 6. The height of ΔP is parallel to the y-axis and extends from (6, 0) to (6, 5) for a length of 5. The height of ΔQ is also parallel to the y-axis, and has a length of 5. Since the base and height of each triangle are equal, their areas must be equal as well.

## HARD

**26** **18**—Let's try some numbers for the sides of the triangle. Keep in mind that the sum of any two sides of a triangle is always greater than the third side. Since we want to know the *smallest* perimeter possible, let's start with the smallest possible numbers. How about 2, 4, and 6? These are the three smallest distinct positive even numbers (we can't have negative lengths), but we can't make a triangle out of them, since the largest number is *not* less than the sum of the two smaller ones. The next two smallest combinations (2, 4, 8; and 2, 6, 8) can be crossed off for the same reason. Now try 4, 6, and 8: 4 + 6 > 8; 6 + 8 > 4; 4 + 8 > 6. So the smallest possible perimeter is 4 + 6 + 8, or 18.

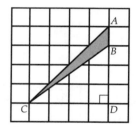

**27** **2**—(Note that we've added point *D* for clarity.) The area of a triangle is $\frac{1}{2}$ × base × height. If we treat *AB* as the base of △*ABC*, then the triangle's height is *CD*. Each square has side 1, so we can count the squares. *AB* = 1 and *CD* = 4, so the area is $\frac{1}{2} \times 1 \times 4 = 2$.

**28** **B**—The area of a triangle = $\frac{1}{2}$ × base × height. In a right triangle, the legs are the base and the height. Column A equals twice the area of triangle *PQR*: $2 \times \left( \frac{1}{2} \times x \times y \right) = xy$. Column B equals the area of △*RST*: $\frac{1}{2} \times 2x \times 2y = 2xy$. So Column B is greater than Column A.

Triangles *PQR* and *RST* are similar right triangles because each leg of △*RST* is twice the length of a corresponding leg in △*PQR*. However, this does not mean that the area of △*RST* is twice that of △*PQR*. The ratio of the areas of two similar figures is the ratio of their lengths *squared*. In this case, the area of △*RST* is 4 times that of △*PQR*.

**29** **B**—Since △*ABC* is equilateral, its sides are the same length. So the length of any one side is one-third of the perimeter. So $AC = AB = BC = \frac{24}{3} = 8$. Label the diagram accordingly. Draw a line from *C* perpendicular to *DE* at point *F* as shown below:

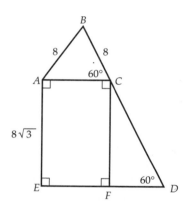

This forms rectangle *ACFE*. Side *CF* has the same length as opposite side *AE*, so it also equals $8\sqrt{3}$. Since *AC* and *ED* are parallel, ∠*FDC* has the same measure as ∠*ACB*—that is, 60°. You should recognize that △*CDF* is a 30-60-90 triangle with side lengths in a ratio of 1: $\sqrt{3}$ :2. So *FD* = 8 and *CD* = 16. So the perimeter of *ABDE* = 8 + 24 + 16 + $8\sqrt{3}$, or 48 + $8\sqrt{3}$, or 8(6 + $\sqrt{3}$).

**30** **A**—If you turn the diagram around so that side *AC* is horizontal, it is easier to notice that the perpendicular dotted-line segment from point *B* divides △*ABC* into two right triangles. Label the point where this perpendicular line meets *AC* point *D*. *BC* is the hypotenuse of right △*BDC*, and its leg

$BD$ is labeled as $\sqrt{7}$; if you knew the length of its other leg $DC$, you could use the Pythagorean theorem to find the length of $BC$. The other right triangle, $ADB$, shares leg $BD$, and its hypotenuse $AB$ is of the length 4; use the Pythagorean theorem to find the length of its other leg $AD$:

$$( \sqrt{7} )^2 + AD^2 = 4^2$$
$$7 + AD^2 = 16$$
$$AD^2 = 9$$
$$AD = 3$$

Since $AC = AD + DC$, $8 = 3 + DC$, so $DC = 5$. Now you can use the Pythagorean theorem to find $BC$:

$$( \sqrt{7} )^2 + 5^2 = BC^2$$
$$7 + 25 = BC^2$$
$$32 = BC^2$$
$$\sqrt{32} = BC$$
$$\sqrt{16} \times \sqrt{2} = BC$$
$$4\sqrt{2} = BC$$

**31** **B**—If the circumference of the circle $O$ is $12\pi$ its radius is 6. (Remember, circumference = $2\pi r$.) Radius $OC$ is made up of $OB$ and $BC$, so the length of $BC = 6 - OB$. Since $OB$ is a leg of right $\triangle AOB$, use the Pythagorean theorem to find its length. $OA$ is a radius of the circle, so it must also be 6, and you are told that $AB$ is 8, so:

$$6^2 + OB^2 = 8^2$$
$$36 + OB^2 = 64$$
$$OB^2 = 28$$
$$OB = \sqrt{28} = \sqrt{4} \times \sqrt{7} = 2\sqrt{7}$$

So $BC = 6 - 2\sqrt{7} = 2(3 - \sqrt{7} )$

**32** **E**—You can find the length of $BC$ from the Pythagorean theorem, if you know the length of either $AC$ or $DC$.

From the Pythagorean theorem: $AB^2 = AC^2 + BC^2$ and $BD^2 = DC^2 + BC^2$
So $BC^2 = AB^2 - AC^2$ and $BC^2 = BD^2 - DC^2$
So $AB^2 - AC^2 = BD^2 - DC^2$

$$30^2 - (9x)^2 = 26^2 - (5x)^2$$
$$900 - 81x^2 = 676 - 25x^2$$
$$900 - 676 = 81x^2 - 25x^2$$
$$224 = 56x^2$$
$$4 = x^2$$
$$2 = x$$

So $DC = 5 \times 2 = 10$ and $AC = 9 \times 2 = 18$.

You might recognize $\triangle ABC$ as a 3-4-5 right triangle, or $\triangle BCD$ as a 5-12-13 right triangle and so be able to calculate immediately that $BC = 24$. If not, use the Pythagorean theorem:

$$BC^2 = BD^2 - DC^2$$
$$= 26^2 - 10^2$$
$$= 576$$
$$BC = \sqrt{576} = 24$$

**33** **A**—Using the Pythagorean theorem, we know that $BC^2 = AB^2 + AC^2$.

$$(2x - 2)^2 = (x + 2)^2 + x^2$$

Expand using FOIL: $4x^2 - 8x + 4 = 2x^2 + 4x + 4$
$$4x^2 - 8x - 2x^2 - 4x = 4 - 4$$
$$2x^2 - 12x = 0$$

Factor out $2x$: $2x(x - 6) = 0$
So $x = 0$ or $x = 6$. But $CA = x$, and $CA$ is a length and therefore cannot be equal to zero. So $x = 6$.

**34** **14/3 or 4.66 or 4.67**—If you regard $WX$ as the base of $\triangle WXZ$ and $WY$ as the base of $\triangle WYZ$, you will notice that both triangles share the same altitude. We don't know its value, but since it is the same in each triangle, the ratio of the base $WX$ of $\triangle WXZ$ to the base $WY$ of $\triangle WYZ$ is 7:2. So the ratio of $WX$ to $WY$ is 7:2. Since these two segments make up $XY$, which has a length of 21:

$$7x + 2x = 21$$
$$9x = 21$$
$$x = \frac{7}{3}$$
$$WY = 2x = \frac{14}{3}.$$

The vast majority of quadrilateral questions involve squares and rectangles. Parallelograms only rarely appear, and trapezoids and rhombi turn up even less frequently. Here are the basic skills you'll need (which you'll find in the SAT Math in a Nutshell section near the end of this book):

87. Characteristics of a Rectangle
88. Area of a Rectangle
89. Characteristics of a Parallelogram
90. Area of a Parallelogram
91. Characteristics of a Square
92. Area of a Square
93. Interior Angles of a Polygon

Note: It's not necessary to memorize any formulas because they're printed in the test booklet.

## PRACTICE SET

### BASIC

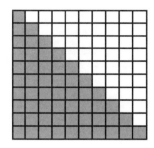

**1** If each of the small squares in the figure above has area 1, what is the area of the shaded region?

(A)  50
(B)  55
(C)  59
(D)  60
(E)  61    Ⓐ Ⓑ Ⓒ Ⓓ Ⓔ

**2** In the figure above, if the perimeter of rectangle ABCD is 56, and if the length of AD = 16, what is the area of ABCD?

| Column A | Column B |
| --- | --- |

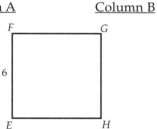

**3** Half of the number of square units in the area of square EFGH          18

Ⓐ Ⓑ Ⓒ Ⓓ Ⓔ

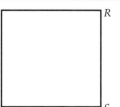

**4** In the figure above, if PQRS is a square, what is the value of a ?

(A)  $\dfrac{9}{5}$

(B)  $\dfrac{9}{2}$

(C)  5

(D)  7

(E)  9    Ⓐ Ⓑ Ⓒ Ⓓ Ⓔ

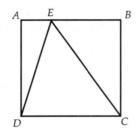

**5** What is the ratio of the area of $\triangle DEC$ to the area of square $ABCD$ in the figure above?

(A)  $\dfrac{1}{4}$

(B)  $\dfrac{1}{3}$

(C)  $\dfrac{1}{2}$

(D)  $\dfrac{2}{1}$

(E)  It cannot be determined from the information given.

Ⓐ Ⓑ Ⓒ Ⓓ Ⓔ

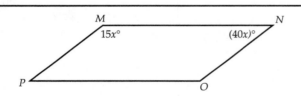

**6** In the figure above, $MNOP$ is a parallelogram. What is the value of $x$ ?

(A)  20
(B)  10
(C)  5

(D)  $\dfrac{25}{7}$

(E)  $\dfrac{5}{2}$

Ⓐ Ⓑ Ⓒ Ⓓ Ⓔ

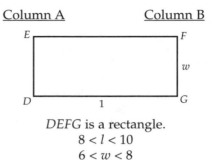

$DEFG$ is a rectangle.
$$8 < l < 10$$
$$6 < w < 8$$

**7**  The area of $DEFG$             63

Ⓐ Ⓑ Ⓒ Ⓓ Ⓔ

## MEDIUM

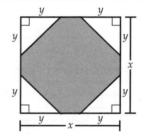

**8** In the figure above, what is the area of the shaded region?

(A)  $x^2 - y^2$
(B)  $x^2 - 2y^2$
(C)  $x^2 - 4y^2$
(D)  $(x - y)(x - y)$
(E)  $(x - 2y)(x - 2y)$     Ⓐ Ⓑ Ⓒ Ⓓ Ⓔ

**9** If the length of rectangle $A$ is one-half the length of rectangle $B$, and the width of rectangle $A$ is one-half the width of rectangle $B$, what is the ratio of the area of rectangle $A$ to the area of rectangle $B$ ?

**10** In quadrilateral $DEFG$, the degree measures of its four angles are in the ratio of 2:3:5:6. What is the difference in the degree measures between the largest and smallest angles?

(A)  135
(B)  112.5
(C)  90
(D)  67.5
(E)  45      Ⓐ Ⓑ Ⓒ Ⓓ Ⓔ

Column A    Column B

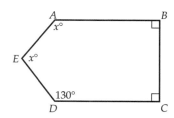

Note: Figure not drawn to scale.

11    $x$                    130

Ⓐ Ⓑ Ⓒ Ⓓ Ⓔ

---

The area of rectangle $ABCD$ is 48, and its perimeter is 28.

12    $AB - BC$              2

Ⓐ Ⓑ Ⓒ Ⓓ Ⓔ

---

13  In quadrilateral $ABCD$, $\angle A + \angle B + \angle C = 2\angle D$. What is the degree measure of $\angle D$ ?

(A)    90
(B)    120
(C)    135
(D)    270
(E)    It cannot be determined from the information given.

Ⓐ Ⓑ Ⓒ Ⓓ Ⓔ

---

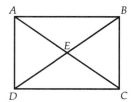

14  In the figure above, $ABCD$ is a rectangle. If the area of $\triangle AEB$ is 8, what is the area of $\triangle ACD$ ?

---

**HARD**

Column A    Column B

15  The perimeter of        The perimeter of
    a rectangle with        a rectangle with
    area 10                 area 16

Ⓐ Ⓑ Ⓒ Ⓓ Ⓔ

---

16  The perimeter of a rectangle is $6w$. If one side has length $\dfrac{w}{2}$, what is the area of the rectangle?

(A)    $\dfrac{w^2}{4}$

(B)    $\dfrac{5w^2}{4}$

(C)    $\dfrac{5w^2}{2}$

(D)    $\dfrac{11w^2}{4}$

(E)    $\dfrac{11w^2}{2}$            Ⓐ Ⓑ Ⓒ Ⓓ Ⓔ

---

17  The length of each side of square $A$ is increased by 100 percent to make square $B$. If the length of each side of square $B$ is increased by 50 percent to make square $C$, by what percent is the area of square $C$ greater than the sum of the areas of squares $A$ and $B$ ?

(A)    75%
(B)    80%
(C)    100%
(D)    150%
(E)    180%            Ⓐ Ⓑ Ⓒ Ⓓ Ⓔ

---

18  What is the greatest number of rectangles with integer side lengths and perimeter 10 that can be cut from a piece of paper with width 24 and length 60?

(A)    144
(B)    180
(C)    240
(D)    360
(E)    480            Ⓐ Ⓑ Ⓒ Ⓓ Ⓔ

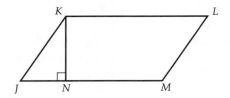

19  In the figure above, if the area of parallelogram *JKLM* is $n$, and if the length of *KN* is $n + \dfrac{1}{n}$, then the length of *JM* is

(A)  $\dfrac{1}{n}$

(B)  $\dfrac{1}{n + 1}$

(C)  $n + 1$

(D)  $\dfrac{n^2}{n + 1}$

(E)  $\dfrac{n^2}{n^2 + 1}$  Ⓐ Ⓑ Ⓒ Ⓓ Ⓔ

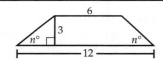

20  What is the perimeter of the quadrilateral shown above?

(A)  21

(B)  24

(C)  $24 + \sqrt{2}$

(D)  $18 + 6\sqrt{2}$

(E)  $24\sqrt{2}$  Ⓐ Ⓑ Ⓒ Ⓓ Ⓔ

| SCORECARD | |
| --- | --- |
| Number of Questions Right: | |
| Number of Questions Wrong: | |
| Number of Questions Omitted: | |
| Number of Correct Guesses: | |
| Number of Wrong Guesses: | |
| Time Used: | |

**KAPLAN**

## ANSWERS AND EXPLANATIONS

### BASIC

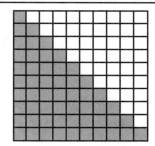

**1** **B**—The fastest way to get the total area is to count the number of shaded small squares in each row (there's a pattern here: each row has one more shaded square than the row above it), and add. This gives a total of $1 + 2 + 3 + 4 + 5 + 6 + 7 + 8 + 9 + 10$, or 55 shaded squares.

**2** **192**—To find the area of $ABCD$, you need to know the width and the length. The perimeter of a rectangle $= 2(l + w)$. Let $AD$ be the length. Since you know the length and perimeter, plug in those values into the formula and solve for $w$, the width:

$56 = 2(16 + w)$
$56 = 32 + 2w$
$24 = 2w$
$12 = w$

Since area of a rectangle $= l \times w$, the area of $ABCD = 16 \times 12$, or 192.

**3** **C**—The area of a square $=$ (length of a side)$^2$. Therefore, the area of square $EFGH = 6^2$, or 36. So half the area is $\frac{1}{2} \times 36$, or 18. Therefore the columns are equal and choice (C) is correct.

**4** **C**—Since the lengths of each side of a square are the same, $PQ = PS$. Therefore:

$3a + 2 = 2a + 7$
$a = 5$

PSo choice (C) is correct.

**5** **C**—The height of $\triangle DEC$ is the perpendicular distance from point $E$ to base $DC$, and that's the same as the length of side $AD$ or side $BC$ of the square. The base of $\triangle DEC$ is also a side of the square, so the area of $\triangle DEC$ must equal one-half the length of a side of the square times the length of a side of the square. Or, calling the length of a side $s$, the area

of $\triangle DEC$ is $\frac{1}{2}s^2$, while the area of the square is just $s^2$. Since the triangle has half the area of the square, the ratio is 1:2, or $\frac{1}{2}$.

**6** **B**—In a parallelogram, opposite angles are equal. Therefore $\angle P = (40 - x)°$ and $\angle O = 15x°$. The interior angles of any quadrilateral add up to $360°$, so:

$15x + 15x + 40 - x + 40 - x = 360$
$28x = 280$
$x = 10$

**7** **D**—Pick numbers for $l$ and $w$ that fit the given conditions. Suppose $l = 9$ and $w = 7$. Then the area of $DEFG = l \times w = 9 \times 7$, or 63. In this case, the columns are equal. However, suppose $l = 8.5$ and $w = 6.5$; then the area of $DEFG = 8.5 \times 6.5$, or 55.25. So in this case, Column B is greater than Column A. Since more than one possible relationship between the columns exists, the correct answer is choice (D).

### MEDIUM

**8** **B**—The area of the shaded region = total area minus the unshaded region. The total area of the figure equals length $\times$ width $= x \times x = x^2$.

The unshaded region is made up of 4 right isosceles triangles with base and height equal to $y$.

Since area of a triangle $= \frac{1}{2} \times$ base $\times$ height, the area of the 4 unshaded triangles $= 4(\frac{1}{2})(y)(y)$, or $2y^2$.

Therefore, the area of the shaded region equals $x^2 - 2y^2$, and choice (B) is correct.

**9** **1/4, or .25**—Watch out for the trap: The ratio of areas is *not* the same as the ratio of lengths. We can pick numbers for the length and width of rectangle $A$. Let's pick 4 for the length and 2 for the width. The area of rectangle $A$ is then $4 \times 2$, or 8. The length of rectangle $B$ is twice the length of rectangle $A : 2 \times 4 = 8$. The width of rectangle $B$ is twice the width of rectangle $A : 2 \times 2 = 4$. So the area of rectangle $B$ is $8 \times 4$, or 32. Therefore, the ratio of the area of rectangle $A$ to the area of rectangle $B$ is $\frac{8}{32}$, or $\frac{1}{4}$.

As a general rule for similar polygons, the ratio of areas is equal to the square of the ratio of lengths.

**10** **C**—The sum of the degree measures of the angles of a quadrilateral is 360. Since the angles of quadrilateral $DEFG$ are in a ratio of 2:3:5:6, you can set up an equation in which $x$ represents part of the ratio:
$$2x + 3x + 5x + 6x = 360$$
$$16x = 360$$
$$x = 22.5$$
Now find the difference in the degree measures of the largest and smallest angles:
$$6x - 2x = 4x = 4(22.5) = 90$$
So answer choice (C) is correct.

**11** **B**—What is the sum of the interior angles of a pentagon? Drawing two diagonals from a single vertex, we can divide a pentagon into three triangles.

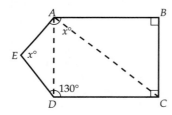

The sum of the interior angles must be three times the sum for each triangle: $3 \times 180° = 540°$. Therefore, the two angles with measure $x$ degrees, the two right angles, and the 130° angle must sum to 540°. Now we can set up an equation to solve for $x$:
$$x + x + 90 + 90 + 130 = 540$$
$$2x + 310 = 540$$
$$2x = 230$$
$$x = 115$$
So Column B is greater than Column A, and choice (B) is correct.

**12** **D**—The area of a rectangle = $l \times w$, and the perimeter of a rectangle = $2(l + w)$. You're given that the area of $ABCD = 48$ and its perimeter = 28. So the length and width of $ABCD$ must be 8 and 6. Suppose that $AB = 8$ and $BC = 6$; then $AB - BC = 2$, and the columns are equal. However, if $AB = 6$ and $BC = 8$, then $AB - BC = 6 - 8$, or $-2$, which makes

Column B greater than Column A. Since more than one possible relationship between the columns exists, choice (D) is correct.

**13** **B**—Since the sum of the interior angles of a quadrilateral is 360°, $A + B + C + D = 360$. At the same time, $A + B + C = 2D$. So we can substitute for $A + B + C$ in our first equation, to get:
$$2D + D = 360$$
$$3D = 360$$
$$D = 120$$

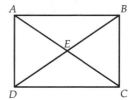

**14** **16**—The bases of $\triangle AEB$ and $\triangle ACD$ both have the same length, since $AB = CD$. We just need to find the relationship between their respective heights. $AC$ and $BD$ intersect at the center of the rectangle, which is point $E$. Therefore, the perpendicular distance from $E$ to side $AB$ is half the distance from side $CD$ to side $AB$. This means that the height of $\triangle AEB$ is half the height of $\triangle ACD$. So the area of $\triangle ACD$ is twice the area of $\triangle AEB$ : $2 \times 8 = 16$.

**HARD**

**15** **D**—There are several ways to draw both rectangles with respective areas of 10 and 16. Look at the following possibilities:

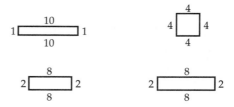

In the first case, the rectangle in Column A has a perimeter of 22, while the rectangle in Column B has a perimeter of 16. However, in the second case, the rectangle in Column A has a perimeter of 14, while the rectangle in Column B has a perimeter of 20. Since the relationship between the columns changes depending upon how the rectangles are drawn, choice (D) is the correct answer.

**16** **B**—The sum of all four sides is $6w$. The two short sides add up to $\frac{w}{2}+\frac{w}{2}$, or $w$. This leaves $6w - w$, or $5w$, for the *sum* of the other two sides. *Each* long side is $\frac{1}{2}(5w)$, or $\frac{5}{2}w$. So, Area $= \left(\frac{w}{2}\right)\left(\frac{5w}{2}\right) = \frac{5w^2}{4}$.

**17** **B**—The best way to solve this problem is to pick a value for the length of a side of square $A$. We want our numbers to be easy to work with, so let's pick 10 for the length of each side of square $A$. The length of each side of square $B$ is 100 percent greater, or twice as great as a side of square $A$. So the length of a side of square $B$ is $2 \times 10$, or 20. The length of each side of square $C$ is 50 percent greater, or $1\frac{1}{2}$ times as great as a side of square $B$. So the length of a side of square $C$ is $1\frac{1}{2} \times 20$, or 30. The area of square $A$ is $10^2$, or 100. The area of square $B$ is $20^2$, or 400. The sum of the areas of squares $A$ and $B$ is $100 + 400$, or 500. The area of square $C$ is $30^2$, or 900. The area of square $C$ is greater than the sum of the areas of squares $A$ and $B$ by $900 - 500$ or 400. By what percent is the area of square $C$ greater than the sum of the areas of squares $A$ and $B$? $\frac{400}{500} \times 100\%$, or 80%.

**18** **D**—First, if a rectangle has perimeter 10, what could its dimensions be? Perimeter $= 2l + 2w$, or $2(l + w)$. The perimeter is 10, so $2(l + w) = 10$, or $l + w = 5$. Since $l$ and $w$ must be integers, there are two possibilities: $l = 4$ and $w = 1$ ($4 + 1 = 5$), or $l = 3$ and $w = 2$ ($3 + 2 = 5$). Let's consider each possibility separately.

If $l = 4$, how many of these rectangles fit along the length of the larger rectangle? The length of the larger rectangle is 60; $60 \div 4 = 15$, so 15 smaller rectangles fit, if they are lined up with their longer sides against the longer side of the large rectangle.

The width of the smaller rectangles is 1, and the width of the large rectangle is 24. $24 \div 1 = 24$, so 24 small rectangles fit against the width of the large rectangle. The total number of small rectangles that fit inside the large rectangle is the number along the length times the number along the width, which is $15 \times 24 = 360$.

In the second case, $l = 3$ and $w = 2$. $60 \div 3 = 20$, so 20 small rectangles fit along the length; $24 \div 2 = 12$, so 12 small rectangles fit along the width. Therefore the total number of small rectangles is $20 \times 12$, or 240. We're asked for the greatest number, which we got from the first case: 360.

**19** **E**—The area of a parallelogram = base $\times$ height. You're given that the area of $JKLM = n$, and the length of the height $KN = n + \frac{1}{n}$. So plug these variables into the formula and solve for the length of $JM$ :

$$n = \left(n + \frac{1}{n}\right) \times (JM)$$

Find a common denominator for $n$ and $\frac{1}{n}$:

$$n = \left(\frac{n^2}{n} + \frac{1}{n}\right) \times (JM)$$

$$n = \left(\frac{n^2 + 1}{n}\right) \times (JM)$$

Solve for $JM$ by multiplying both sides by the reciprocal of $\frac{n^2 + 1}{n}$:

$$\left(\frac{n}{n^2 + 1}\right) \times n = \left(\frac{n}{n^2 + 1}\right) \times \left(\frac{n^2 + 1}{n}\right) \times (JM)$$

$$\frac{n^2}{n^2 + 1} = JM$$

Therefore, choice (E) is correct.

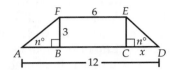

**20** **D**—We've labeled points $A$, $B$, $C$, $D$, $E$, and $F$ in the diagram above for clarity. If we drop a perpendicular line segment from point $E$ to point $C$ on side $AD$, our figure is divided into two right triangles and a rectangle in the middle. $BC$ is opposite $EF$ in rectangle $BCEF$, so $BC$ must also be 6. $\triangle ABF$ and $\triangle CDE$ are both the same shape and size, so $AB$ must be the same length as $CD$. If we call this length $x$, we can set up an equation:

$$AB + BC + CD = 12$$
$$x + 6 + x = 12$$
$$2x = 6$$
$$x = 3$$

At this point, we have lengths for $FE$, $AB$, $BC$, and $CD$ as follows:

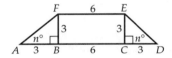

We still need the length of $AF$ and the length of $DE$ to get the perimeter.

Notice that $\triangle ABF$ and $\triangle CDE$ are both right isosceles triangles. Since the lengths of the sides of an isosceles right triangle are in a ratio of 1:1:$\sqrt{2}$, the length of $AF$ and $DE$ is $3 \times \sqrt{2}$, or $3\sqrt{2}$. (If you didn't recognize this, you could have used the Pythagorean theorem to find the lengths of $AF$ and $DE$.)

Adding together the lengths of the four sides gives us $6+12+3\sqrt{2}+3\sqrt{2}$, or $18+6\sqrt{2}$.

# CIRCLES—PRACTICE SET 15

Here's what you need to know about circles:
94. Circumference of a Circle
95. Length of an Arc
96. Area of a Circle
97. Area of a Sector

Note: It's not necessary to memorize any formulas because they're printed in the test booklet.

## PRACTICE SET

### BASIC

**1** If the area of a circle is $64\pi$, then the circumference of the circle is

(A) $8\pi$
(B) $16\pi$
(C) $32\pi$
(D) $64\pi$
(E) $128\pi$  Ⓐ Ⓑ Ⓒ Ⓓ Ⓔ

---

**2** If $d$ is the diameter of a circle, then $\pi d^2$ represents

(A) the area of the circle
(B) half the area of the circle
(C) twice the area of the circle
(D) one-fourth the area of the circle
(E) four times the area of the circle

Ⓐ Ⓑ Ⓒ Ⓓ Ⓔ

---

**3** If the minute hand of a clock moves 45 degrees, how many minutes of time have passed?

(A) 6
(B) 7.5
(C) 15
(D) 30
(E) 36.5  Ⓐ Ⓑ Ⓒ Ⓓ Ⓔ

---

| Column A | Column B |
| --- | --- |
| **4** Radius of a circle with area $50\pi$ | Diameter of a circle with area $25\pi$ |

Ⓐ Ⓑ Ⓒ Ⓓ Ⓔ

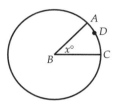

Note: Figure not drawn to scale.

**5** In the figure above, the ratio of the circumference of circle $B$ to the length of arc $ADC$ is 8:1. What is the value of $x$ ?

### MEDIUM

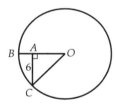

Note: Figure not drawn to scale.

**6** In the figure above, if the area of the circle with center $O$ is $100\pi$ and $CA$ has a length of 6, what is the length of $AB$ ?

(A) 2
(B) 3
(C) 4
(D) 5
(E) 6  Ⓐ Ⓑ Ⓒ Ⓓ Ⓔ

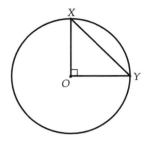

**7** In the figure above, $O$ is the center of the circle. If the area of triangle $XOY$ is 25, what is the area of the circle?

(A)  $25\pi$

(B)  $25\pi\sqrt{2}$

(C)  $50\pi$

(D)  $50\pi\sqrt{3}$

(E)  $625\pi$  Ⓐ Ⓑ Ⓒ Ⓓ Ⓔ

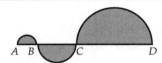

Note: Figure not drawn to scale.

**8** Each of the three shaded regions above is a semicircle. If $AB = 4$, $CD = 2BC$, and $BC = 2AB$, then the area of the entire shaded figure is

(A)  $28\pi$

(B)  $42\pi$

(C)  $84\pi$

(D)  $96\pi$

(E)  $168\pi$  Ⓐ Ⓑ Ⓒ Ⓓ Ⓔ

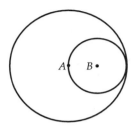

**9** In the diagram above, if the circle with center $A$ has an area of $72\pi$, what is the area of the circle with center $B$ ?

(A)  $18\pi$

(B)  $24\pi$

(C)  $30\pi$

(D)  $36\pi$

(E)  $48\pi$  Ⓐ Ⓑ Ⓒ Ⓓ Ⓔ

| Column A | Column B |
|---|---|

$P$ and $Q$ are points on a circle with center $O$.

**10**  The diameter          Twice the length
of circle $O$                  of $PQ$

Ⓐ Ⓑ Ⓒ Ⓓ Ⓔ

**HARD**

**11** If the diameter of a circle increases by 50 percent, by what percent will the area of the circle increase?

(A)  25%

(B)  50%

(C)  100%

(D)  125%

(E)  225%  Ⓐ Ⓑ Ⓒ Ⓓ Ⓔ

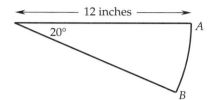

12 The figure above shows the path traced by the hand of a scale as it moves from $A$ to $B$. What is the area, in square inches, of the region passed over by the scale's hand?

(A) $2\pi$
(B) $8\pi$
(C) $12\pi$
(D) $16\pi$
(E) $144\pi$          Ⓐ Ⓑ Ⓒ Ⓓ Ⓔ

13 If an arc with a length of $12\pi$ is $\dfrac{3}{4}$ of the circumference of a circle, what is the shortest distance between the endpoints of the arc?

(A) 4
(B) $4\sqrt{2}$
(C) 8
(D) $8\sqrt{2}$
(E) 16          Ⓐ Ⓑ Ⓒ Ⓓ Ⓔ

14 The total area of the four equal circles in the figure above is $36\pi$, and the circles are all tangent to one another. What is the diameter of the small circle?

(A) $6\sqrt{2}$
(B) $6 + \sqrt{2}$
(C) $3\sqrt{2} - 3$
(D) $6\sqrt{2} - 6$
(E) $6\sqrt{2} + 6$          Ⓐ Ⓑ Ⓒ Ⓓ Ⓔ

| Column A | Column B |
| --- | --- |
| 15 The circumference of a circle with radius $2x$ | The circumference of a circle with diameter $x$ |

Ⓐ Ⓑ Ⓒ Ⓓ Ⓔ

| SCORECARD | |
| --- | --- |
| Number of Questions Right: | |
| Number of Questions Wrong: | |
| Number of Questions Omitted: | |
| Number of Correct Guesses: | |
| Number of Wrong Guesses: | |
| Time Used: | |

## ANSWERS AND EXPLANATIONS

### BASIC

**1** **B**—We need to find the radius in order to get the circumference. The area is $64\pi$, so use the area formula to get the radius:

$$\text{Area} = \pi r^2 = 64\pi$$
$$r^2 = 64$$
$$r = 8$$

The circumference, which is $2\pi r$, is $2\pi(8)$, or $16\pi$.

**2** **E**—The diameter of a circle is twice the radius, or $d = 2r$. Therefore, $\pi d^2 = \pi(2r)^2 = 4\pi r^2$, which is four times the area of the circle.

**3** **B**—The minute hand of a clock traces out a complete circle every hour. That is, it moves $360°$ every 60 minutes. Since $45°$ is $\frac{1}{8}$ of $360°$, the time it takes to move $45°$ will be $\frac{1}{8}$ of 60 minutes, that is, 7.5 minutes.

**4** **B**—Find the quantity in each column by manipulating the area formula, $\text{Area} = \pi r^2$.

In Column A: $\text{Area} = \pi r^2$
$$50\pi = \pi r^2$$
$$50 = r^2$$
$$\sqrt{50} = r$$

In Column B: $\text{Area} = \pi r^2$
$$25\pi = \pi r^2$$
$$25 = r^2$$
$$\sqrt{25} = r$$
$$5 = r$$

Since diameter $= 2r$, Column $B = 10$. This is greater than $\sqrt{50}$.

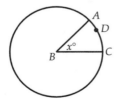

**5** **45**—We need to use the following ratio.

$$\frac{\text{length of arc}}{\text{circumference}} = \frac{\text{measure of arc's central angle}}{360°}$$

The measure of the arc's central angle is $x$

degrees, and the length of the arc is $\frac{1}{8}$ of the circumference:

$$\frac{1}{8} = \frac{x}{360}$$

$$x = 45$$

### MEDIUM

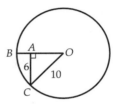

**6** **A**—Since we know the area of circle $O$, we can find the radius of the circle. And if we find the length of $OA$, then $AB$ is just the difference between $OB$ and $OA$.

Since the area of the circle is $100\pi$, the radius must be $\sqrt{100}$ or 10. Radius $OC$, line segment $CA$, and line segment $OA$ together form a right triangle, so we can use the Pythagorean Theorem to find the length of $OA$. But notice that 10 is twice 5 and 6 is twice 3, so right triangle $ACO$ has sides whose lengths are in a 3–4–5 ratio.

$OA$ must have a length of twice 4, or 8. $AB$ is the segment of radius $OB$ that's not a part of $OA$; its length equals the length of $OB$ minus the length of $OA$, or $10 - 8 = 2$.

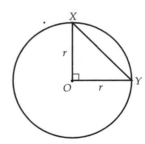

**7** **C**—Each leg of right triangle $XOY$ is also a radius of circle $O$. If we call the radius $r$, then the area of $\triangle XOY$ is $\frac{1}{2}(r)(r)$, or $\frac{r^2}{2}$. At the same time, the area of circle $O$ is $\pi r^2$. So, we can use the area of

ΔXOY to find $r^2$, and then multiply $r^2$ by π to get the area of the circle.

$$\text{Area of } \Delta XOY = \frac{r^2}{2} = 25$$

$$r^2 = 50$$

Area of circle $O = \pi r^2 = \pi(50) = 50\pi$

Note: It is unnecessary (and extra work) to find the actual value of $r$, since the value of $r^2$ is sufficient to find the area.

**8** **B**—Since you're given the diameter of the semicircle around $AB$, you should begin with the semicircle. The radius of semicircle $AB$ is $\frac{4}{2}$, or 2. The area of a semicircle is half the area of the circle, or $\frac{1}{2}\pi r^2$. So the area of semicircle $AB$ is $\frac{1}{2}\pi(2)^2$, or $2\pi$. $BC = 2AB$, so $BC = 2(4)$, or 8.

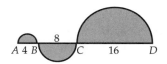

The radius of semicircle $BC$ is 4, so the area of semicircle $BC$ is $\frac{1}{2}\pi(4)^2$, or $8\pi$. $CD = 2BC$, so $CD = 2(8)$, or 16. The radius of semicircle $CD$ is 8, so the area of semicircle $CD$ is $\frac{1}{2}\pi(8)^2$, or $32\pi$. Adding the three areas together gives $2\pi + 8\pi + 32\pi$, or $42\pi$.

**9** **A**—If you draw a radius of the larger circle from $A$ to the point on the circumference where the two circles touch, you can see that the diameter of the smaller circle is equal to the radius of the larger circle. That is, the radius of circle $B$ is half the radius of the circle A. Find the radius of the larger circle:

$$\pi r^2 = 72\pi$$
$$r^2 = 72$$
$$r = \sqrt{72} = 6\sqrt{2}$$

So the radius of the smaller circle is half this, or $3\sqrt{2}$. Its area $= \pi(3\sqrt{2})^2 = 18\pi$.

**10** **D**—There are many ways to draw points $P$ and $Q$ on the circumference of circle $O$. Two possibilities follow:

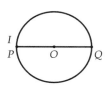 

In the first case, $PQ$ is drawn as a diameter of circle O. So, twice the length of $PQ$ in Column B is greater than the diameter of circle O in Column A.

In the second case, $P$ and $Q$ are drawn close together on the circumference of circle $O$. So twice the length of $PQ$ in Column B is less than the length of the diameter. Since the relationship between the columns changes depending upon how $P$ and $Q$ are drawn, choice (D) is the correct answer.

## HARD

**11** **D**—The fastest method is to pick a value for the diameter of the circle. Let's suppose that the diameter is 4. Then the radius is $\frac{4}{2}$, or 2, which means that the area is $\pi(2)^2$, or $4\pi$. Increasing the diameter by 50 percent means adding on half of its original length: $4 + (50\% \text{ of } 4) = 4 + 2 = 6$. So the new radius is $\frac{6}{2}$, or 3, which means that the area of the circle is now $\pi(3)^2$, or $9\pi$. The percent increase is the amount of increase, over the original area, times 100%. That's $\frac{9\pi - 4\pi}{4\pi} \times 100\% = \frac{5\pi}{4\pi} \times 100\%$, or 125%.

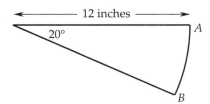

**12** **B**—If the hand turned all the way around, it would trace out a full circle. In the question, the hand moves 20°, which is $\frac{20}{360}$, or $\frac{1}{18}$ of a full circle. So the area it covers is $\frac{1}{18}$ of the area of a circle with radius 12:

$$\text{Area} = \frac{1}{18}\pi(12)^2 = \frac{144}{18}\pi = 8\pi$$

**13** D—Call the endpoints of the arc $A$ and $B$ and the center of the circle $C$. Major arc $AB$ represents $\frac{3}{4}$ of 360°, or 270°. Therefore, minor arc $AB$ is 360° − 270°, or 90°. Since $AC$ and $CB$ are both radii of the circle, $\triangle ABC$ must be an isosceles right triangle:

You can find the distance between $A$ and $B$ if you know the radius of the circle. Major arc $AB$, which takes up $\frac{3}{4}$ of the circumference, has a length of $12\pi$, so the entire circumference is $16\pi$. The circumference of any circle is $2\pi$ times the radius, so a circle with circumference $16\pi$ must have radius 8. The ratio of a leg to the hypotenuse in an isosceles right triangle is $1:\sqrt{2}$. The length of $AB$ is $\sqrt{2}$ times the length of a leg, or $8\sqrt{2}$.

**14** D—Connect the centers of the circles $O$, $P$, and $Q$ as shown. Each leg in this right triangle consists of two radii. The hypotenuse consists of two radii plus the diameter of the small circle.

You can find the radii of the large circles from the given information. Since the total area of the four large circles is $36\pi$, each large circle has area $9\pi$. Since the area of a circle is $\pi r^2$, we know that the radii of the large circles all have length 3.

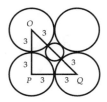

Therefore, each leg in the isosceles right triangle $OPQ$ is 6. The hypotenuse then has length $6\sqrt{2}$. (The hypotenuse of an isosceles right triangle is always $\sqrt{2}$ times a leg.) The hypotenuse is equal to two radii plus the diameter of the small circle, so $6\sqrt{2} = 2(3) + \text{diameter}$, or diameter $= 6\sqrt{2} - 6$.

**15** A—This problem is a trap. The diameter is twice the radius in any circle. Since the problem tells us about a radius and a diameter, and one is $x$ while the other is $2x$, it sounds like the two circles are identical and have the same circumference. But that's not the case. If the radius were $x$ and the diameter $2x$, the circles would be identical. But here the values are reversed. In Column A, the circle has a radius of $2x$, or a diameter of $4x$, which is four times the diameter of the circle in Column B. So the circle in Column A is a much larger circle with a greater circumference.

Multiple figures questions on the SAT usually combine different kinds of figures, so just about any geometric concept could come into play.

## PRACTICE SET

### MEDIUM

Column A　　　Column B

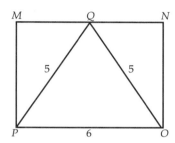

**1** The area of rectangle *MNOP*　　　20

(A) (B) (C) (D) (E)

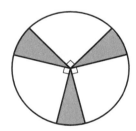

**2** In the circle above, three right angles have vertices at the center of the circle. If the radius of the circle is 8, what is the combined area of the shaded regions?

(A)　$8\pi$
(B)　$9\pi$
(C)　$12\pi$
(D)　$13\pi$
(E)　$16\pi$

(A) (B) (C) (D) (E)

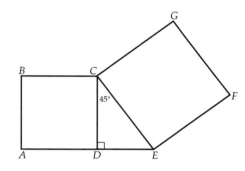

**3** In the figure above, *ABCD* and *CEFG* are squares. If the area of *CEFG* is 36, what is the area of *ABCD* ?

(A)　6
(B)　$6\sqrt{2}$
(C)　9
(D)　18
(E)　24

(A) (B) (C) (D) (E)

**4** A triangle and a circle have equal areas. If the base of the triangle and the diameter of the circle each have length 5, what is the height of the triangle?

(A)　$\dfrac{5}{2}$

(B)　$\dfrac{5}{2}\pi$

(C)　$5\pi$
(D)　$10\pi$
(E)　It cannot be determined from the information given.

(A) (B) (C) (D) (E)

**HARD**

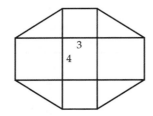

5   The figure above is composed of nine regions: four squares, four triangles, and one rectangle. If the rectangle has length 4 and width 3, what is the perimeter of the entire figure?

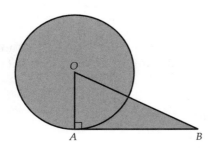

Note: Figure not drawn to scale.

6   In the figure above, if radius *OA* is 8 and the area of right triangle *OAB* is 32, what is the area of the shaded region?

(A)   $64\pi + 32$
(B)   $60\pi + 32$
(C)   $56\pi + 32$
(D)   $32\pi + 32$
(E)   $16\pi + 32$          Ⓐ Ⓑ Ⓒ Ⓓ Ⓔ

7   In the figure above, *AB* is an arc of a circle with center *O*. If the length of arc *AB* is $5\pi$ and the length of *CB* is 4, what is the sum of the areas of the shaded regions?

(A)   $25\pi - 60$
(B)   $25\pi - 48$
(C)   $25\pi - 36$
(D)   $100\pi - 48$
(E)   $100\pi - 36$          Ⓐ Ⓑ Ⓒ Ⓓ Ⓔ

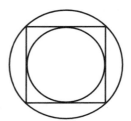

8   In the figure above, the smaller circle is inscribed in the square and the square is inscribed in the larger circle. If the length of each side of the square is *s*, what is the ratio of the area of the larger circle to the area of the smaller circle?

(A)   $2\sqrt{2}$
(B)   2
(C)   $\sqrt{2}$
(D)   $2s$
(E)   $s\sqrt{2}$          Ⓐ Ⓑ Ⓒ Ⓓ Ⓔ

| SCORECARD | |
|---|---|
| Number of Questions Right: | |
| Number of Questions Wrong: | |
| Number of Questions Omitted: | |
| Number of Correct Guesses: | |
| Number of Wrong Guesses: | |
| Time Used: | |

## Answers and Explanations

### MEDIUM

**1** **A**—Area = $\ell \times w$. We are given the length of this rectangle ($OP = 6$), but we need to find the width. Draw a perpendicular line from point $Q$ to $OP$ and label the point $R$ as shown below:

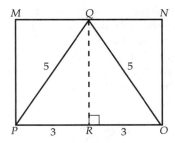

In an isosceles triangle, the altitude bisects the base, so $QR$ bisects $OP$. Therefore, $PR = \frac{1}{2}$ (6), or 3.

Hypotenuse $QP$ is 5. So $\Delta PQR$ is a 3-4-5 right triangle. Therefore, segment $QR$ must have length 4. This is equal to the height of rectangle $MNOP$, so the area of the rectangle is $\ell \times w = 6 \times 4$, or 24.

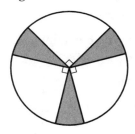

**2** **E**—The three right angles define three sectors of the circle, each with a central angle of 90°.

Together, the three sectors account for $\frac{270°}{360°}$, or $\frac{3}{4}$ of the area of the circle, leaving $\frac{1}{4}$ of the circle for the shaded regions. So the total area of the shaded regions $= \frac{1}{4} \times \pi(8)^2$, or $16\pi$.

**3** **D**—Notice that both squares share a side with right triangle $CDE$. Since square $CEFG$ has an area of 36, $CE$ has a length of $\sqrt{36}$, or 6. Since right triangle $CDE$ has a 45° angle, $CDE$ must be an isosceles right triangle. Therefore, $CD$ and $DE$ are the same length. Let's call that length $x$.

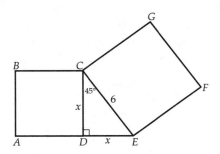

Remember, we're looking for the area of square $ABCD$, which will be $x^2$. Using the Pythagorean theorem on $\Delta CDE$, we get:

$$(\text{leg})^2 + (\text{leg})^2 = (\text{hypotenuse})^2$$
$$x^2 + x^2 = 6^2$$
$$2x^2 = 36$$
$$x^2 = 18$$

So the area is 18. (There's no need to find $x$.)

**4** **B**—The diameter of the circle is 5, so the radius is $\frac{5}{2}$ and the area is $\pi\left(\frac{5}{2}\right)^2$ or $\frac{25}{4}\pi$. This is equal to the area of the triangle. Since the base of the triangle is 5, we can solve for the height:

$$\frac{1}{2}(5)(h) = \frac{25}{4}\pi$$
$$5h = \frac{25}{4}\pi$$
$$h = \frac{5}{2}\pi$$

**HARD**

**5** **34**—The central rectangle shares a side with each of the four squares, and the four squares form the legs of the four right triangles. Two of the rectangle's sides have a length of 4, so the two squares that share these sides must also have sides of length 4. The other two sides of the rectangle have a length of 3, so the other two squares, which share these sides, must also have sides of length 3. Each triangle shares a side with a small square and a side with a large square, so the legs of each triangle have lengths of 3 and 4, respectively.

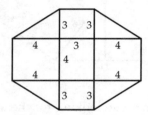

Since the legs are of length 3 and 4, the hypotenuse of each triangle must have a length of 5. The perimeter is the sum of the hypotenuses of the triangles and a side from each square:

Perimeter = 4(5) + 2(4) + 2(3)
= 20 + 8 + 6
= 34

**6** **C**—The total area of the shaded region = (the area of the circle) + (the area of the right triangle) − (the area of overlap). The area of circle O is $\pi(8)^2$, or $64\pi$. The area of right triangle $OAB$ is 32. So we just need to find the area of overlap, the area of right triangle $OAB$ inside circle O, which forms a sector of the circle. Let's see what we can find out about $\angle AOB$, the central angle of the sector.

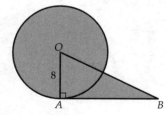

The area of right triangle $OAB$ is 32, and its height is the radius of circle O. So $\frac{1}{2}(8)(AB) = 32$, or $AB = 8$. Since $AB = OA$, $\triangle OAB$ is an isosceles right

triangle. Therefore, $\angle AOB$ has a measure of 45°. So the area of the sector is $\frac{45}{360}(64\pi)$, or $8\pi$. Now we can get the total area of the shaded region:

$64\pi + 32 - 8\pi = 56\pi + 32$

**7** **B**—The total area of the shaded regions equals the area of the quarter circle minus the area of the rectangle. Since the length of arc $AB$ (a quarter of the circumference of circle O) is $5\pi$, the whole circumference equals $4 \times 5\pi$, or $20\pi$. Thus, the radius $OE$ has length 10. (We've added point E in the diagram for clarity.) Since $OB$ also equals 10, $OC = 10 - 4$, or 6. This tells us that $\triangle OEC$ is a 6-8-10 right triangle and $EC = 8$.

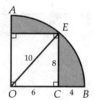

Now we know the dimensions of the rectangle, so we can find its area: area = $\ell \times w = 8 \times 6 = 48$. And the area of the quarter circle equals $\frac{1}{4}\pi(10)^2$ or $25\pi$. Finally, we can get the total area of the shaded regions:

Area of shaded regions = $\frac{1}{4} \times \pi \times (10)^2 - 48$
= $25\pi - 48$

**8** **B**—The length of each side of the square is given as $s$.

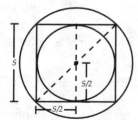

A side of the square has the same length as the diameter of the smaller circle. (You can see this more clearly if you draw the vertical diameter in the smaller circle.)

The diameter you draw will connect the upper and lower tangent points where the smaller circle and square intersect.) This means that the radius of the smaller circle is $\frac{s}{2}$, so its area is $\left(\frac{s}{2}\right)^2 \pi$, or $\frac{s^2}{4}\pi$. Now draw a diagonal of the square, and you'll see that it's the diameter of the larger circle. The diagonal breaks up the square into two isosceles right triangles, where each leg has length $s$, as we see in the diagram. So the diagonal must have length $s\sqrt{2}$. Therefore, the radius of the larger circle is $\frac{s\sqrt{2}}{2}$, so its area is $\left(\frac{s\sqrt{2}}{2}\right)^2 \pi$, or $\frac{2s^2}{4}\pi$, or $\frac{s^2}{2}\pi$. This is twice the area of the smaller circle.

In high school, you probably learned a lot more about coordinate geometry than you need to know for the SAT. About all you need to know for the SAT is the following list of facts you'll find referenced in our SAT Math in a Nutshell section:

69. Finding the Distance Between Two Points
70. Using Two Points to Find the Slope
71. Using an Equation to Find the Slope
72. Using an Equation to Find an Intercept

## PRACTICE SET

### BASIC

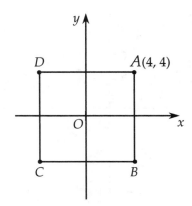

**1** In the figure above, *ABCD* is a square with center at the origin. If the coordinates of vertex *A* are (4, 4), what are the coordinates of vertex *C* ?

(A) $(-4\sqrt{2}, -4\sqrt{2})$
(B) $(-4\sqrt{2}, -4)$
(C) $(-4, -4)$
(D) $(-4, 4)$
(E) $(4, -4)$     (A) (B) (C) (D) (E)

**2** If point A has coordinates (1, 2) and point *B* has coordinates (9, 8), what is the distance between points *A* and *B* ?

(A) 10
(B) 9
(C) 8
(D) 7
(E) 6     (A) (B) (C) (D) (E)

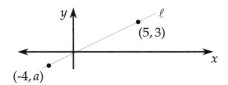

**3** In the above figure, if the slope of line $\ell$ is $\frac{4}{9}$, what is the value of *a* ?

(A) −3
(B) −2
(C) −1
(D) 1
(E) 2     (A) (B) (C) (D) (E)

**4** Points *P* and *Q* lie on the same line and have coordinates (1, 3) and (5, 8), respectively. Which of the following points lies on the same line as points *P* and *Q* ?

(A) (−4, −5)
(B) (−3, −2)
(C) (−2, −3)
(D) (−1, −4)
(E) (0, −1)     (A) (B) (C) (D) (E)

Column A          Column B                    Column A          Column B

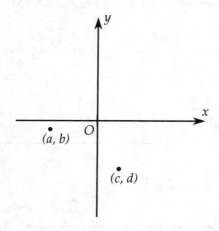

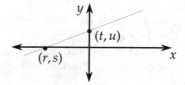

The slope of the line above is $\dfrac{1}{2}$.

| 5 | $ac$ | $bd$ |

Ⓐ Ⓑ Ⓒ Ⓓ Ⓔ

| 9 | $s$ | $t$ |

Ⓐ Ⓑ Ⓒ Ⓓ Ⓔ

---

**6** What is the slope of the line in the coordinate plane containing the points (3, 8) and (9, 10)?

### MEDIUM

**7** What is the perimeter of a triangle with vertices at the points (1, 4), (1, 7), and (4, 4)?

(A)  $3 + \sqrt{2}$
(B)  $3\sqrt{2}$
(C)  6
(D)  $6 + 3\sqrt{2}$
(E)  $9 + 3\sqrt{2}$          Ⓐ Ⓑ Ⓒ Ⓓ Ⓔ

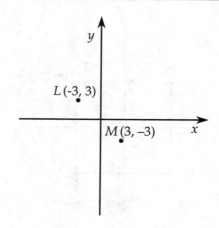

---

**8** If the slope of a line containing the points (3, $a$) and ($b$, 3) is 2, what is $a$ in terms of $b$ ?

(A)  $\dfrac{b-3}{2}$

(B)  $2b - 3$

(C)  $\dfrac{2b-3}{2}$

(D)  $9 - 2b$

(E)  $\dfrac{9-b}{2}$          Ⓐ Ⓑ Ⓒ Ⓓ Ⓔ

| 10 | The area of the circle with diameter $LM$ | $9\pi$ |

Ⓐ Ⓑ Ⓒ Ⓓ Ⓔ

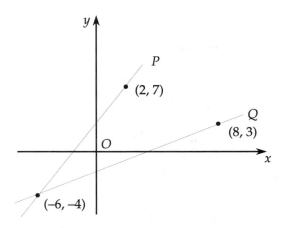

**11** In the figure above, what is the positive difference between the slopes of lines $P$ and $Q$ ?

## HARD

**12** If lines $p$ and $q$ are parallel to each other, which of the following statements must be true?
  I. The slope of $p$ is positive.
  II. The slope of $q$ is the reciprocal of the slope of $p$.
  III. The slopes of $p$ and $q$ are equal.

 (A)  I only
 (B)  II only
 (C)  III only
 (D)  I and II
 (E)  I and III        Ⓐ Ⓑ Ⓒ Ⓓ Ⓔ

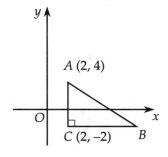

**13** In the rectangular coordinate system above, if the area of right triangle $ABC$ is 24, what are the coordinates of point $B$ ?

 (A)  (10, –2)
 (B)  (10, 2)
 (C)  (2, 6)
 (D)  (8, –2)
 (E)  It cannot be determined from the information given.

Ⓐ Ⓑ Ⓒ Ⓓ Ⓔ

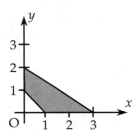

**14** In the figure above, what is the area of the shaded region?

**15** If the slope of a line is $-\dfrac{5}{3}$ and a point on the line is (3, 5), what is the $y$-intercept?

| SCORECARD | |
|---|---|
| Number of Questions Right: | |
| Number of Questions Wrong: | |
| Number of Questions Omitted: | |
| Number of Correct Guesses: | |
| Number of Wrong Guesses: | |
| Time Used: | |

### Answers and Explanations

#### BASIC

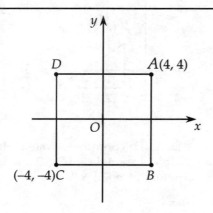

**1** **C**—We are told that the origin is the center of square *ABCD*. Since the center of the square bisects the diagonals, point *C* must be the same distance from the origin as point *A*, and directly opposite point *A*. Since *A* is 4 units above the *x*-axis, *C* will be 4 units *below* it, so the *y*-coordinate is negative. Likewise, since *A* is 4 units to the right of the *y*-axis, *C* will be 4 units to the left of it, so the *x*-coordinate is also negative. This makes the coordinates of point *C* (–4, –4).

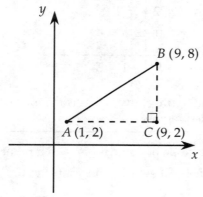

**2** **A**—Draw a diagram. Plotting the points shows that *AB* isn't parallel to one of the axes, so, to find its length, treat it as the hypotenuse of a right triangle. Draw a line from point *A* parallel to the *x*-axis and draw a line from point *B* parallel to the *y*-axis. The point where they meet, *C*, has coordinates (9, 2). Since $\triangle ABC$ is a right triangle, $AB^2 = AC^2 + BC^2$. Since *AC* is parallel to the *x*-axis, its length is determined by the difference between the *x*-coordinates of its endpoints: $9 - 1 = 8$. Since *BC* is

parallel to the *y*-axis, its length is determined by the difference between the *y*-coordinates of its endpoints: $8 - 2 = 6$. You should recognize this as a 6-8-10 right triangle, making the hypotenuse $AB = 10$. If not, you can use the Pythagorean theorem to solve for *AB*: $AB^2 = AC^2 + BC^2$, $AB^2 = 8^2 + 6^2$, $AB^2 = 64 + 36$, $AB^2 = 100$, $AB = 10$.

**3** **C**—Since the slope of a line = (difference of the *y*-coordinates) ÷ (difference of the *x*-coordinates), you can plug the given coordinates and slope into the formula and solve for *a* :

$$\text{Slope} = \frac{\text{change in } y}{\text{change in } x} \quad \frac{4}{9} = \frac{3 - a}{5 - (-4)}$$

$$\frac{4}{9} = \frac{3 - a}{9}$$

$$4 = 3 - a$$

$$a = -1$$

**4** **B**—Since the slope remains the same between any two points on a given line, the slope between the correct answer and *P* or *Q* will be the same as the slope between *P* and *Q*. First find the slope of the line:

$$\text{Slope} = \frac{\text{change in } y}{\text{change in } x}$$

$$= \frac{8 - 3}{5 - 1}$$

$$= \frac{5}{4}$$

Now see which answer choice also gives a slope of $\frac{5}{4}$:

Choice (A): $\frac{8 - (-5)}{5 - (-4)} = \frac{13}{9}$. Eliminate.

Choice (B): $\frac{8 - (-2)}{5 - (-3)} = \frac{10}{8} = \frac{5}{4}$. So choice (B) is

correct because the line between it and point *Q* has

a slope of $\frac{5}{4}$. At this point on the actual test you

would move on to the next question. However, we'll

go through the remaining choices to prove that

they're false.

Choice (C): $\dfrac{8-(-3)}{5-(-2)}=\dfrac{11}{7}$ . Eliminate.

Choice (D): $\dfrac{8-(-4)}{5-(-1)}=\dfrac{12}{6}$ . Eliminate.

Choice (E): $\dfrac{8-(-1)}{5-(-0)}=\dfrac{9}{5}$ . Eliminate.

**5** **B**—Point $(a, b)$ falls to the left of and below the origin, so both coordinates $a$ and $b$ are negative. Point $(c, d)$ falls to the right of the origin so its $x$-coordinate, $c$, is positive, but since it lies below the origin, its $y$-coordinate, $d$, is negative. In Column A, $a$, which is negative, times $c$, which is positive, results in a negative product. As for Column B: $b$, which is negative, times $d$, which is also negative, results in a positive product.

**6** **1/3 or .333**—The slope of a line equals the rise over the run, which you can determine by finding the difference between the $y$-coordinates of the two points and dividing that by the difference between the $x$-coordinates of the two points. So the slope of the line containing points (3, 8) and (9, 10) equals $\dfrac{10-8}{9-3}=\dfrac{2}{6}=\dfrac{1}{3}$ .

**MEDIUM**

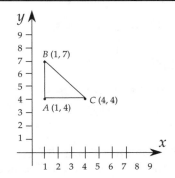

**7** **D**—Start by plotting the points and labeling them. Let $A$ be (1, 4), $B$ be (1, 7), and $C$ be (4, 4). Notice that we have a triangle with side $AB$ parallel to the $y$-axis, $AC$ parallel to the $x$-axis, and

$BC$ as the third side. Since the $x$- and $y$-axes are perpendicular, $AB$ and $AC$ must be perpendicular, so we have a right triangle with $BC$ as the hypotenuse. We need to find the length of the sides. The length of $AB$ is the distance from (1, 4) to (1, 7). Since the $x$-coordinates are the same, the horizontal distance between the points is 0, so all we need is the vertical distance. This is the difference of the $y$-coordinates: $7 - 4 = 3$. Similarly, the distance from $A$ to $C$ is just the horizontal distance: $4 - 1 = 3$. So far we have a right triangle with two legs of length 3. Since the legs are equal, it must be an isosceles right triangle, and the hypotenuse must be $\sqrt{2} \times$ one of the legs, or $3\sqrt{2}$. Now we can find the perimeter.

Perimeter = $AB + AC + BC$
$= 3 + 3 + 3\sqrt{2}$
$= 6 + 3\sqrt{2}$

**8** **D**—Since slope = $\dfrac{\text{change in } y}{\text{change in } x}$ , plug the given coordinates and slope into the formula and solve for $a$ in terms of $b$ :

$$2 = \frac{3-a}{b-3}$$
$$2(b-3) = 3-a$$
$$2b-6 = 3-a$$
$$2b-9 = -a$$
$$9-2b = a$$

**9** **C**—The diagram shows that the point with coordinates $(r, s)$ lies on the $x$-axis. Therefore, $s$ must equal 0. Similarly, the point with coordinates $(t, u)$ lies on the $y$-axis. Therefore, $t$ must equal 0. So the two columns are equal, and choice (C) is correct.

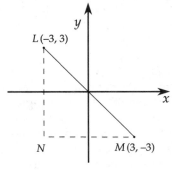

**10** **A**—To find the area of a circle with diameter $LM$, we need to find the length of $LM$, so start by drawing in line segment $LM$. We can find the length of $LM$ by treating it as the hypotenuse of a right triangle. Draw a line down from point $L$ parallel to the $y$-axis and draw a line from point $M$ parallel to the $x$-axis. The point where they meet—let's call it $N$—has coordinates $(-3, -3)$. The length of $LN = 3 - (-3) = 6$; the length of $MN = 3 - (-3) = 6$. So $LMN$ is an isosceles right triangle, and the hypotenuse $LM$ must equal $6\sqrt{2}$. If $LM$ is the diameter of a circle, its radius is $3\sqrt{2}$, and its area is $\pi r^2 = \pi (3\sqrt{2})^2 = 18\pi$, which is greater than $9\pi$ in Column B.

**11** **7/8 or .875**—First, you need to find the slopes of lines P and Q, respectively:

$$\text{Slope} = \frac{\text{change in } y}{\text{change in } x}$$

$$\text{Slope of line } P = \frac{7 - (-4)}{2 - (-6)} = \frac{11}{8}$$

$$\text{Slope of line } Q = \frac{3 - (-4)}{8 - (-6)} = \frac{7}{14} = \frac{1}{2}$$

So the positive difference between the slopes is

$$\frac{11}{8} - \frac{1}{2} = \frac{11}{8} - \frac{4}{8} = \frac{7}{8}, \text{ or .875 expressed as a decimal.}$$

## HARD

**12** **C**—Go through each of the statements to see which one(s) must be true:

Statement I is not necessarily true. All you're given is that lines $p$ and $q$ are parallel. You're not given the coordinates of any points on line $p$. So you can't determine the actual slope of line $p$. Parallel lines have equal slopes. So statement II is only true if the line $p$ has a slope of 1 or $-1$, i.e., it is not always true. Since the lines are parallel, statement III is true. Therefore, choice (C) is correct.

**13** **A**—Notice that point $B$ is on the base of the right triangle. So we need the length of the base to determine the coordinates of point $B$. We can quickly get the height of the triangle, since we're given the coordinates of points $A$ and $C$. The height is the difference in their $y$-coordinates: $4 - (-2) = 4 + 2 = 6$. We're given that the area of right triangle $ABC$ is 24, so we can use the area formula to find the length of the base:

$$\text{Area} = \frac{1}{2} b \times h$$

$$24 = \frac{1}{2} b(6)$$

$$\frac{24 \times 2}{6} = b$$

$$8 = b$$

Since $BC$ has a length of 8, point $B$ must be 8 units directly to the right of point $C$, so add 8 to the $x$-coordinate of C to get the $x$-coordinate of B: $2 + 8 = 10$. Points B and C are at the same height, so their $y$-coordinates are the same. So point $B$ has coordinates $(10, -2)$. You could have eliminated choices (B) and (C) immediately, since point $B$ lies below the $x$-axis and must therefore have a negative $y$-coordinate.

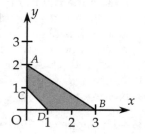

**14** **5/2 or 2.5**—To get the area of the shaded region, we can subtract the area of right triangle $COD$ from the area of right triangle $AOB$. (We've labeled these points in the diagram for clarity.) $OB$ lies along the $x$-axis, so its length is just the difference in $x$-coordinates between $O$ and $B$ : $3 - 0 = 3$. Similarly, the length of $OD$ is $1 - 0$, or 1. $OA$ lies along the $y$-axis, so its length is just the difference in $y$-coordinates between $O$ and $A$: $2 - 0 = 2$. Similarly, the length of $OC$ is $1 - 0$, or 1. Now we can get the respective areas of the triangles:

$$\text{Area of } \triangle AOB = \frac{1}{2}(3)(2) = 3$$

$$\text{Area of } \triangle COD = \frac{1}{2}(1)(1) = \frac{1}{2}$$

Now we take the difference in areas:

$$3 - \frac{1}{2} = 2\frac{1}{2} = \frac{5}{2}$$

**15** **10**—The $y$-intercept of a line is the $y$-coordinate of the point where the line intersects the $y$-axis. Therefore, the $x$-coordinate of the $y$-intercept must be 0. Since you're given the slope of the line and the coordinates of another point on the line, you can plug the given information into the slope formula and solve for the $y$-intercept:

$$\text{Slope} = \frac{\text{change in } y}{\text{change in } x}$$

$$-\left(\frac{5}{3}\right) = \frac{5-y}{3-0}$$

$$-\left(\frac{5}{3}\right) = \frac{5-y}{3}$$

$$-5 = 5 - y$$

$$-10 = -y$$

$$10 = y$$

You could also have found the $y$-intercept if you used the slope-intercept equation of a line: $y = mx + b$ (where $m$ is the slope and $b$ is the $y$ intercept).

Plug in the coordinates of the given point for $x$ and $y$, and plug in $-\left(\frac{5}{3}\right)$ for the slope:

$$5 = -\left(\frac{5}{3}\right)(3) + b$$

$$5 = -5 + b$$

$$10 = b$$

Solids are relatively rare on the SAT. None of the skills listed below is essential to SAT success—but this is a great review of possible problems on the test (you'll find these skills in the SAT Math in a Nutshell section):

98. Surface Area of a Rectangular Solid
99. Volume of a Rectangular Solid
100. Volume of a Cylinder

Note: It's not necessary to memorize any formulas because they're printed in the test booklet.

## PRACTICE SET

### BASIC

| Column A | Column B |
| --- | --- |
| 1 The volume of a cylinder with diameter 6 and height 6 | The volume of a cube with edges of length 6 |

(A) (B) (C) (D) (E)

2  A cube and a rectangular solid are equal in volume. If the lengths of the edges of the rectangular solid are 4, 8, and 16, what is the length of an edge of the cube?

3  What is the maximum number of rectangular blocks, each measuring 3 inches by 8 inches by 12 inches, that can fit inside a rectangular box with dimensions 27 inches by 60 inches by 64 inches?

(A)  72
(B)  144
(C)  288
(D)  360
(E)  540

(A) (B) (C) (D) (E)

A rectangular wood block measuring 120 inches by 200 inches by 150 inches is completely divided into $x$ smaller rectangular blocks, each 24 inches by 40 inches by 50 inches.

4  $x$                              80

(A) (B) (C) (D) (E)

5  What is the volume of a cube with a surface area of 96?

(A)   8
(B)  16
(C)  27
(D)  48
(E)  64

(A) (B) (C) (D) (E)

### MEDIUM

6  A cylinder has a volume of $72\pi$ cubic inches and a height of 8 inches. If the height is increased by 4 inches, what will be the new volume of the cylinder, in cubic inches?

(A)   $84\pi$
(B)   $96\pi$
(C)  $108\pi$
(D)  $120\pi$
(E)  $144\pi$

(A) (B) (C) (D) (E)

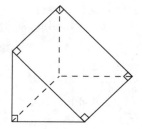

**7** If the solid above is half of a cube, then the volume of the solid is

(A) 16
(B) 32
(C) 42
(D) 64
(E) $64\sqrt{2}$    Ⓐ Ⓑ Ⓒ Ⓓ Ⓔ

**8** Milk is poured from a full rectangular container with dimensions 4 inches by 9 inches by 10 inches into a cylindrical container with a diameter of 6 inches. Assuming the milk does not overflow the container, how many inches high will the milk reach?

(A) $\dfrac{60}{\pi}$

(B) 24

(C) $\dfrac{40}{\pi}$

(D) 10

(E) $3\pi$    Ⓐ Ⓑ Ⓒ Ⓓ Ⓔ

**HARD**

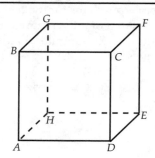

**9** If the length of an edge in the cube above is 3, what is the length of $AF$ ?

(A) $2\sqrt{3}$

(B) $3\sqrt{2}$

(C) $3\sqrt{3}$

(D) 6

(E) 9    Ⓐ Ⓑ Ⓒ Ⓓ Ⓔ

**10** A rectangular block with a volume of 250 cubic inches was sliced into 2 cubes of equal volume. How much greater, in square inches, is the combined surface area of the 2 cubes than the original surface area of the rectangular block?

| SCORECARD | |
|---|---|
| Number of Questions Right: | |
| Number of Questions Wrong: | |
| Number of Questions Omitted: | |
| Number of Correct Guesses: | |
| Number of Wrong Guesses: | |
| Time Used: | |

**KAPLAN**

## Answers and Explanations

### BASIC

**1** **B**—The volume of a cylinder is $\pi r^2 h$, with $r$ as the radius and $h$ as the height. So Column A is $\pi \times 3^2 \times 6 = \pi \times 9 \times 6$, which is about 169.64. The volume of a cube is $e^3$, where $e$ is an edge of the cube. So Column B is $6^3 = 6 \times 6 \times 6 = 216$, which is greater than Column A.

**2** **8**—We can determine the volume of the rectangular solid since we're given all its dimensions: 4, 8, and 16. The volume of a rectangular solid is equal to $l \times w \times h$. So the volume of this solid is $16 \times 8 \times 4$, and this must equal the volume of the cube as well. The volume of a cube is the length of an edge cubed, so we can set up an equation to solve for $e$:
$$e^3 = 16 \times 8 \times 4.$$
To avoid the multiplication, let's break the 16 down into $2 \times 8$:
$$e^3 = 2 \times 8 \times 8 \times 4$$
We can now combine $2 \times 4$ to get another 8:
$$e^3 = 8 \times 8 \times 8$$
$$e = 8$$
The length of an edge of the cube is 8.

**3** **D**—To find the maximum number of rectangular blocks that can fit inside the given box, try to place the blocks in the box so that there is no space left over. Line up the blocks along each dimension of the box to see how many will fit. The blocks are 3 inches wide, so 9 of them can be lined up across the 27-inch width of the box. Similarly, the blocks are 12 inches wide, so 5 of them can be lined up across the 60-inch dimension of the box. Finally, the blocks are 8 inches high, so 8 of them can be placed along the 64-inch dimension of the box. The total number of blocks then $= 9 \times 5 \times 8 = 360$. Choice (D) is correct.

**4** **B**—The value of $x$ in Column A is equal to the volume of the original larger block divided by the volume of a smaller block:
Volume of larger block: $120 \times 200 \times 150 = 3{,}600{,}000$.
Volume of smaller block: $24 \times 40 \times 50 = 48{,}000$.

So the value of $x$ in Column A is $\dfrac{3{,}600{,}000}{48{,}000} = 75$, which is less than 80 in Column B. Therefore, choice (B) is correct.

### MEDIUM

**5** **E**—To find the volume of the cube, you need to know the length of an edge. The surface area of a cube equals six times the area of one face of the cube, or $6e^2$, where $e$ is the length of an edge. Since you're given the surface area of the cube, plug it into the formula and solve for $e$:
$$6e^2 = 96$$
$$e^2 = 16$$
$$e = 4$$
So the length of an edge is 4. Since the volume of a cube equals the length of an edge cubed, the volume of this cube is $4^3$, or 64, so choice (E) is correct.

**6** **C**—To find the volume of the new cylinder, you have to find the area of its circular base. The volume of a cylinder is the area of the base × height, or $\pi r^2 \times h$. You're given the original height of the cylinder and its volume. So you can plug these values into the formula and solve for the area of the base:
$$\text{volume} = \pi r^2 h$$
$$72\pi = \pi r^2 \times 8$$
$$9\pi = \pi r^2$$
The area of the base equals $9\pi$. Since the height of the new cylinder is 4 inches more, its height is $8 + 4$, or 12. The volume of the new cylinder equals $9\pi r^2 \times 12$, or $108\pi$, and choice (C) is correct.

You could also use logic to solve this problem. If the height were increased by 8 inches, you'd double the volume of the cylinder—an increase of $72\pi$ cubic inches. Increasing the height by 4 inches will increase the volume by 50% of the original $72\pi$, or $36\pi$. So $36\pi + 72\pi = 108\pi$, and again, choice (C) is correct.

**7** **B**—This figure is an unfamiliar solid, so we shouldn't try to calculate the volume directly. We are told that the solid in question is half of a cube. We can imagine the other half lying on top of the solid, forming a complete cube.

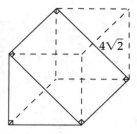

Notice that the diagonal with length $4\sqrt{2}$ and two of the cube's edges form an isosceles right triangle. In an isosceles right triangle, the hypotenuse is $\sqrt{2}$ times the length of a leg. Here the hypotenuse has length $4\sqrt{2}$, so the legs have length 4. So the volume of the whole cube is $4 \times 4 \times 4$, or 64. The volume of the solid in question is $\frac{1}{2}$ of this, or 32.

**8** C—After it's poured, the volume of the milk in the cylinder will still be the same volume as the rectangular container. The volume of the rectangular container is $4 \times 9 \times 10$, or 360 cubic inches. The volume of a cylinder equals the area of its base times its height, or $\pi r^2 h$. Since the diameter is 6 inches, the radius, $r$, is 3 inches. Now we're ready to set up an equation to solve for $h$ (which is the height of the milk):

Volume of milk = Volume of rectangular container

$$\pi(3)^2 h = 360$$

$$h = \frac{360}{9\pi} = \frac{40}{\pi}$$

**HARD**

**9** C—Draw in $AE$ and $AF$ to get right triangle $AEF$.

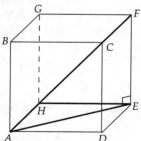

To find the diagonal $AF$, we can first find the lengths of $AE$ and $EF$ and then use the Pythagorean theorem. Since the cube has edge length 3, $EF$ is 3. $AE$ is the hypotenuse of right triangle $ADE$. $\triangle ADE$ is an isosceles right triangle, since legs $AD$ and $DE$ are edges of the cube and, therefore, both have length 3. Since the ratio of the length of a leg to the hypotenuse in an isosceles right triangle is 1 to $\sqrt{2}$, $AE$ has length $3\sqrt{2}$.

Now, looking at triangle $AEF$, we can use the Pythagorean theorem to find $AF$. The theorem states that the hypotenuse squared equals the sum of the squares of the legs. So $AF^2 = AE^2 + EF^2$, or $AF^2 = (3\sqrt{2})^2 + 3^2 = (9 \times 2) + 9 = 18 + 9 = 27$. Therefore, $AF = \sqrt{27} = \sqrt{9 \times 3} = 3\sqrt{3}$.

**10** 50—When the rectangular solid was cut into 2 identical cubes, 2 new faces were formed: 1 on each cube along the line of the cut. So the difference between the original surface area and the combined surface area of the resulting cubes is equal to the surface area of the 2 new faces. To find the area of each of these faces, you need to find the length of an edge of the cube. Since the rectangular block was divided into 2 equal cubes, the volume of each of these cubes is equal to $\frac{1}{2}$ the volume of the original solid, or 250 cubic inches ÷ 2 = 125 cubic inches. So an edge of one of these cubes has a length equal to the cube root of 125, which is 5. Therefore, the area of 1 face of the cube equals $5 \times 5$, or 25. So 2 of these faces have a total area of $2 \times 25$, or 50 square inches.

# THE TOP 100
# SAT MATH FACTS

Listed on the following pages are **100 Things You Need to Know** for the SAT.

## NUMBER PROPERTIES

1.  **Integer/Noninteger**
    Integers are **whole numbers;** they include negative whole numbers and zero.

2.  **Rational/Irrational Numbers**
    A rational number is a number that can be expressed as a **ratio of two integers. Irrational numbers** are real numbers—they have locations on the number line—but they **can't be expressed precisely as a fraction or decimal.** For the purposes of the SAT, the most important **irrational numbers** are $\sqrt{2}$, $\sqrt{3}$, and $\pi$.

3.  **Adding/Subtracting Signed Numbers**
    To **add a positive and a negative,** first ignore the signs and find the positive difference between the number parts. Then attach the sign of the original number with the larger number part. For example, to add 23 and –34, first ignore the minus sign and find the positive difference between 23 and 34—that's 11. Then attach the sign of the number with the larger number part—in this case it's the minus sign from the –34. So, 23 + (–34) = –11.

    Make **subtraction** situations simpler by turning them into addition. For example, think of –17 – (–21) as –17 + (+21).

    To **add or subtract a string of positives and negatives,** first turn everything into addition. Then combine the positives and negatives so that the string is reduced to the sum of a single positive number and a single negative number.

4.  **Multiplying/Dividing Signed Numbers**
    To multiply and/or divide positives and negatives, treat the number parts as usual and **attach a minus sign if there were originally an odd number of negatives.** For example, to multiply –2, –3, and –5, first multiply the number parts: $2 \times 3 \times 5 = 30$. Then go back and note that there were *three*—an *odd* number—negatives, so the product is negative: $(–2) \times (–3) \times (–5) = –30$.

5.  **PEMDAS**
    When performing multiple operations, remember **PEMDAS,** which means **Parentheses** first,

then **Exponents,** then **Multiplication and Division** (left to right), and lastly **Addition and Subtraction** (left to right). In the expression $9 – 2 \times (5 – 3)^2 + 6 \div 3$, begin with the parentheses: $(5 – 3) = 2$. Then do the exponent: $2^2 = 4$. Now the expression is: $9 – 2 \times 4 + 6 \div 3$. Next do the multiplication and division to get: $9 – 8 + 2$, which equals 3. If you have difficulty remembering PEMDAS, use this sentence to recall it: **P**lease **E**xcuse **M**y **D**ear **A**unt **S**ally.

6.  **Counting Consecutive Integers**
    To count consecutive integers, **subtract the smallest from the largest and add 1.** To count the integers from 13 through 31, subtract: $31 – 13 = 18$. Then add 1: $18 + 1 = 19$.

## DIVISIBILITY

7.  **Factor/Multiple**
    The **factors** of integer $n$ are the positive integers that divide into $n$ with no remainder. The **multiples** of $n$ are the integers that $n$ divides into with no remainder. For example, 6 is a factor of 12, and 24 is a multiple of 12. 12 is both a factor and a multiple of itself, since $12 \times 1 = 12$ and $12 \div 1 = 12$.

8.  **Prime Factorization**
    To find the prime factorization of an integer, just keep breaking it up into factors until **all the factors are prime.** To find the prime factorization of 36, for example, you could begin by breaking it into $4 \times 9$: $36 = 4 \times 9 = 2 \times 2 \times 3 \times 3$.

9.  **Relative Primes**
    Relative primes are integers that have no common factor other than 1. To determine whether two integers are relative primes, break them both down to their prime factorizations. For example: $35 = 5 \times 7$, and $54 = 2 \times 3 \times 3 \times 3$. They have **no prime factors in common,** so 35 and 54 are relative primes.

10. **Common Multiple**
    A common multiple is a number that is a multiple of two or more integers. You can always get a common multiple of two integers by **multiplying** them, but, unless the two numbers are

relative primes, the product will not be the *least* common multiple. For example, to find a common multiple for 12 and 15, you could just multiply: $12 \times 15 = 180$.

**11. Least Common Multiple (LCM)**
To find the least common multiple, check out the **multiples of the larger integer** until you find one that's also **a multiple of the smaller.** To find the LCM of 12 and 15, begin by taking the multiples of 15: 15 is not divisible by 12; 30's not; nor is 45. But the next multiple of 15, 60, *is* divisible by 12, so it's the LCM.

**12. Greatest Common Factor (GCF)**
To find the greatest common factor, break down both integers into their prime factorizations and multiply **all the prime factors they have in common.** $36 = 2 \times 2 \times 3 \times 3$, and $48 = 2 \times 2 \times 2 \times 2 \times 3$. What they have in common is two 2s and one 3, so the GCF is $2 \times 2 \times 3 = 12$.

**13. Even/Odd**
To predict whether a sum, difference, or product will be even or odd, just **take simple numbers like 1 and 2 and see what happens.** There are rules—"odd times even is even," for example—but there's no need to memorize them. What happens with one set of numbers generally happens with all similar sets.

**14. Multiples of 2 and 4**
An integer is divisible by 2 (even) if the **last digit is even.** An integer is divisible by 4 if the **last two digits form a multiple of 4.** The last digit of 562 is 2, which is even, so 562 is a multiple of 2. The last two digits form 62, which is *not* divisible by 4, so 562 is not a multiple of 4. The integer 512, however is divisible by four because the last two digits form 12, which is a multiple of 4.

**15. Multiples of 3 and 9**
An integer is divisible by 3 if the **sum of its digits is divisible by 3.** An integer is divisible by 9 if the **sum of its digits is divisible by 9.** The sum of the digits in 957 is 21, which is divisible by 3 but not by 9, so 957 is divisible by 3 but not by 9.

**16. Multiples of 5 and 10**
An integer is divisible by 5 if the **last digit is 5 or 0.** An integer is divisible by 10 if the **last**
digit is 0. The last digit of 665 is 5, so 665 is a multiple of 5 but *not* a multiple of 10.

**17. Remainders**
The remainder is the **whole number left over after division.** 487 is 2 more than 485, which is a multiple of 5, so when 487 is divided by 5, the remainder will be 2.

## FRACTIONS AND DECIMALS

**18. Reducing Fractions**
To reduce a fraction to lowest terms, **factor out and cancel** all factors the numerator and denominator have in common.

$$\frac{28}{36} = \frac{4 \times 7}{4 \times 9} = \frac{7}{9}$$

**19. Adding/Subtracting Fractions**
To add or subtract fractions, first find a **common denominator,** then add or subtract the numerators.

$$\frac{2}{15} + \frac{3}{10} = \frac{4}{30} + \frac{9}{30} = \frac{4+9}{30} = \frac{13}{30}$$

**20. Multiplying Fractions**
To multiply fractions, **multiply** the numerators and **multiply** the denominators.

$$\frac{5}{7} \times \frac{3}{4} = \frac{5 \times 3}{7 \times 4} = \frac{15}{28}$$

**21. Dividing Fractions**
To divide fractions, **invert** the second one and **multiply.**

$$\frac{1}{2} \div \frac{3}{5} = \frac{1}{2} \times \frac{5}{3} = \frac{1 \times 5}{2 \times 3} = \frac{5}{6}$$

**22. Converting a Mixed Number to an Improper Fraction**

To convert a mixed number to an improper fraction, **multiply** the whole number part by the denominator, then **add** the numerator. The result is the new numerator (over the same denominator). To convert $7\frac{1}{3}$, first multiply 7 by 3, then add 1, to get the new numerator of

22. Put that over the same denominator, 3, to get $\frac{22}{3}$.

23. **Converting an Improper Fraction to a Mixed Number**

To convert an improper fraction to a mixed number, divide the denominator into the numerator to get a **whole number quotient with a remainder.** The quotient becomes the whole number part of the mixed number, and the remainder becomes the new numerator— with the same denominator. For example, to convert $\frac{108}{5}$, first divide 5 into 108, which yields 21 with a remainder of 3. Therefore, $\frac{108}{5} = 21\frac{3}{5}$.

24. **Reciprocal**

To find the reciprocal of a fraction, switch the numerator and the denominator. The reciprocal of $\frac{3}{7}$ is $\frac{7}{3}$. The reciprocal of 5 is $\frac{1}{5}$. The product of reciprocals is 1.

25. **Comparing Fractions**

One way to compare fractions is to re-express them with a common denominator. $\frac{3}{4} = \frac{21}{28}$ and $\frac{5}{7} = \frac{20}{28}$. $\frac{21}{28}$ is greater than $\frac{20}{28}$, so $\frac{3}{4}$ is greater than $\frac{5}{7}$. Another method is to convert them both to decimals. $\frac{3}{4}$ converts to .75 , and $\frac{5}{7}$ converts to approximately .714.

26. **Converting Fractions to Decimals**

To convert a fraction to a decimal, **divide the bottom into the top.** To convert $\frac{5}{8}$, divide 8 into 5, yielding .625.

27. **Converting Decimals to Fractions**

To convert a decimal to a fraction, set the decimal over 1 and **multiply the numerator and denominator by ten raised to the number of digits to the right of the decimal point.**

To convert .625 to a fraction, you would multiply $\frac{.625}{1}$ by $\frac{10^3}{10^3}$, or $\frac{1000}{1000}$. Then simplify: $\frac{625}{1000} = \frac{5 \times 125}{8 \times 125} = \frac{5}{8}$.

28. **Repeating Decimal**

To find a particular digit in a repeating decimal, note the **number of digits in the cluster that repeats.** If there are 2 digits in that cluster, then every second digit is the same. If there are 3 digits in that cluster, then every third digit is the same. And so on. For example, the decimal equivalent of $\frac{1}{27}$ is .037037037..., which is best written $.\overline{037}$. There are 3 digits in the repeating cluster, so every third digit is the same: 7. To find the fiftieth digit, look for the multiple of 3 just less than 50—that's 48. The forty-eigth digit is 7, and with the forty-ninth digit the pattern repeats with 0. The 50th digit is 3.

### 29. Identifying the Parts and the Whole

The key to solving most fractions and percents story problems is to identify the part and the whole. Usually you'll find the **part** associated with the verb *is/are* and the **whole** associated with the word *of*. In the sentence, "Half of the boys are blonds," the whole is the boys ("*of* the boys"), and the part is the blonds ("*are* blonds").

## PERCENTS

### 30. Percent Formula

Whether you need to find the part, the whole, or the percent, use the same formula:

**Part = Percent × Whole**

**Example:** What is 12% of 25?
**Setup:** Part = .12 × 25

**Example:** 15 is 3% of what number?
**Setup:** 15 = .03 × Whole

**Example:** 45 is what percent of 9?
**Setup:** 45 = Percent × 9

### 31. Percent Increase and Decrease

To increase a number by a percent, **add the percent to 100%,** convert to a decimal, and multiply. To increase 40 by 25%, add 25% to 100%, convert 125% to 1.25, and multiply by 40. 1.25 × 40 = 50.

### 32. Finding the Original Whole

To find the **original whole before a percent increase or decrease,** set up an equation. Think of the result of a 15% increase over $x$ as $1.15x$.

**Example:** After a 5% increase, the population was 59,346. What was the population before the increase?
**Setup:** $1.05x = 59{,}346$

### 33. Combined Percent Increase and Decrease

To determine the combined effect of multiple percent increases and/or decreases, **start with 100 and see what happens.**

**Example:** A price went up 10% one year, and the new price went up 20% the next year. What was the combined percent increase?

**Setup:** First year: 100 + (10% of 100) = 110. Second year: 110 + (20% of 110) = 132. That's a combined 32% increase.

## RATIOS, PROPORTIONS, AND RATES

### 34. Setting Up a Ratio

To find a ratio, put the number associated with the word *of* **on top** and the quantity associated with the word *to* **on the bottom** and reduce. The ratio of 20 oranges to 12 apples is $\frac{20}{12}$, which reduces to $\frac{5}{3}$.

### 35. Part-to-Part Ratios and Part-to-Whole Ratios

If the parts add up to the whole, a part-to-part ratio can be turned into 2 part-to-whole ratios by putting **each number in the original ratio over the sum of the numbers.** If the ratio of males to females is 1 to 2, then the males-to-people ratio is $\frac{1}{1+2} = \frac{1}{3}$ and the females-to-people ratio is $\frac{2}{1+2} = \frac{2}{3}$. In other words, $\frac{2}{3}$ of all the people are female.

### 36. Solving a Proportion

To solve a proportion, **cross multiply:**

$$\frac{x}{5} = \frac{3}{4}$$
$$4x = 3 \times 5$$
$$x = \frac{15}{4} = 3.75$$

### 37. Rate

To solve a rates problem, **use the units** to keep things straight.

**Example:** If snow is falling at the rate of 1 foot every 4 hours, how many inches of snow will fall in 7 hours?

**Setup:**
$$\frac{1 \text{ foot}}{4 \text{ hours}} = \frac{x \text{ inches}}{7 \text{ hours}}$$

$$\frac{12 \text{ inches}}{4 \text{ hours}} = \frac{x \text{ inches}}{7 \text{ hours}}$$

$$4x = 12 \times 7$$

$$x = 21$$

### 38. Average Rate

Average rate is *not* simply the average of the rates.

$$\text{Average } A \text{ per } B = \frac{\text{Total } A}{\text{Total } B}$$

$$\text{Average Speed} = \frac{\text{Total distance}}{\text{Total time}}$$

To find the average speed for 120 miles at 40 mph and 120 miles at 60 mph, **don't just average the two speeds.** First figure out the total distance and the total time. The total distance is 120 + 120 = 240 miles. The times are 2 hours for the first leg and 3 hours for the second leg, or 5 hours total. The average speed, then, is $\frac{240}{5} = 48$ miles per hour.

## AVERAGES

### 39. Average Formula

To find the average of a set of numbers, **add them up and divide by the number of numbers.**

$$\text{Average} = \frac{\text{Sum of the terms}}{\text{Number of terms}}$$

To find the average of the 5 numbers 12, 15, 23, 40, and 40, first add them: 12 + 15 + 23 + 40 + 40 = 130. Then divide the sum by 5: 130 ÷ 5 = 26.

### 40. Average of Evenly Spaced Numbers

To find the average of evenly spaced numbers, just **average the smallest and the largest.** The average of all the integers from 13 through 77 is the same as the average of 13 and 77:

$$\frac{13 + 77}{2} = \frac{90}{2} = 45$$

### 41. Using the Average to Find the Sum Sum = (Average) × (Number of terms)

If the average of 10 numbers is 50, then they add up to 10 × 50, or 500.

### 42. Finding the Missing Number

To find a missing number when you're given the average, **use the sum.** If the average of 4 numbers is 7, then the sum of those 4 numbers is 4 × 7, or 28. Suppose that 3 of the numbers are 3, 5, and 8. These 3 numbers add up to 16 of that 28, which leaves 12 for the fourth number.

### 43. Median

The median of a set of numbers is the value that falls in the middle of the set. If you have five test scores, and they are 88, 86, 57, 94, and 73, you must first list the scores in increasing or decreasing order: 57, 73, 86, 88, 94.

The median is the middle number, or 86. If there is an even number of values in a set (six test scores, for instance), simply take the average of the two middle numbers.

### 44. Mode

The mode of a set of numbers is the value that appears most often. If your test scores were 88, 57, 68, 85, 99, 93, 93, 84, and 81, the mode of the scores would be 93 because it appears more often than any other score. If there is a tie for the most common value in a set, the set has more than one mode.

## POSSIBILITIES AND PROBABILITY

### 45. Counting the Possibilities

The fundamental counting principle: If there are **m ways** one event can happen and **n ways** a second event can happen, then there are **m × n ways** for the two events to happen. For example, with 5 shirts and 7 pairs of pants to choose from, you can have 5 × 7 = 35 different outfits.

### 46. Probability

$$\text{Probability} = \frac{\text{Favorable Outcomes}}{\text{Total Possible Outcomes}}$$

For example, if you have 12 shirts in a drawer and 9 of them are white, the probability of picking a white shirt at random is $\frac{9}{12} = \frac{3}{4}$. This probability can also be expressed as .75 or 75%.

## POWERS AND ROOTS

### 47. Multiplying and Dividing Powers

To multiply powers with the same base, **add the exponents and keep the same base:**

$$x^3 \times x^4 = x^{3+4} = x^7$$

To divide powers with the same base, **subtract the exponents and keep the same base:**

$$y^{13} \div y^8 = y^{13-8} = y^5$$

### 48. Raising Powers to Powers

To raise a power to a power, **multiply the exponents:**

$$(x^3)^4 = x^{3\times4} = x^{12}$$

### 49. Simplifying Square Roots

To simplify a square root, **factor out the perfect squares** under the radical, un-square them and put the result in front.

$$\sqrt{12} = \sqrt{4\times3} = \sqrt{4} \times \sqrt{3} = 2\sqrt{3}$$

### 50. Adding and Subtracting Roots

You can add or subtract radical expressions **when the part under the radicals is the same:**

$$2\sqrt{3} + 3\sqrt{3} = 5\sqrt{3}$$

Don't try to add or subtract when the radical parts are different. There's not much you can do with an expression like:

$$3\sqrt{5} + 3\sqrt{7}$$

### 51. Multiplying and Dividing Roots

The product of square roots is equal to the **square root of the product:**

$$\sqrt{3} \times \sqrt{5} = \sqrt{3\times5} = \sqrt{15}$$

The quotient of square roots is equal to the **square root of the quotient:**

$$\frac{\sqrt{6}}{\sqrt{3}} = \sqrt{\frac{6}{3}} = \sqrt{2}$$

## ALGEBRAIC EXPRESSIONS

### 52. Evaluating an Expression

To evaluate an algebraic expression, **plug in** the given values for the unknowns and calculate according to PEMDAS. To find the value of $x^2 + 5x - 6$ when $x = -2$, plug in $-2$ for $x$: $(-2)^2 + 5(-2) - 6 = -12$.

### 53. Adding and Subtracting Monomials

To combine like terms, **keep the variable part unchanged while adding or subtracting the coefficients:**

$$2a + 3a = (2+3)a = 5a$$

### 54. Adding and Subtracting Polynomials

To add or subtract polynomials, **combine like terms.**

$$(3x^2+5x-7)-(x^2+12)=$$
$$(3x^2-x^2)+5x+(-7-12)=$$
$$2x^2+5x-19=$$

### 55. Multiplying Monomials

To multiply monomials, **multiply the coefficients and the variables separately:**

$$2a \times 3a = (2\times3)(a\times a) = 6a^2$$

### 56. Multiplying Binomials—FOIL

To multiply binomials, use FOIL. To multiply $(x + 3)$ by $(x + 4)$, first multiply the First terms: $x \times x = x^2$. Next the Outer terms: $x \times 4 = 4x$. Then the Inner terms: $3 \times x = 3x$. And finally the Last terms: $3 \times 4 = 12$. Then add and combine like terms:

$$x^2 + 4x + 3x + 12 = x^2 + 7x + 12$$

### 57. Multiplying Other Polynomials

FOIL works only when you want to multiply two binomials. If you want to multiply polynomials with more than two terms, make sure you **multiply each term in the first polynomial by each term in the second.**

$$(x^2 + 3x + 4)(x + 5) =$$
$$x^2(x + 5) + 3x(x + 5) + 4(x + 5) =$$
$$x^3 + 5x^2 + 3x^2 + 15x + 4x + 20 =$$
$$x^3 + 8x^2 + 19x + 20$$

After multiplying two polynomials together, the number of terms in your expression before simplifying should equal the number of terms in one polynomial multiplied by the number of terms in the second. In the example above, you should have $3 \times 2 = 6$ terms in the product before you simplify like terms.

## FACTORING ALGEBRAIC EXPRESSIONS

**58. Factoring Out a Common Divisor**
A factor common to all terms of a polynomial can be **factored out.** All three terms in the polynomial $3x^3 + 12x^2 - 6x$ contain a factor of $3x$. Pulling out the common factor yields $3x(x^2 + 4x - 2)$.

**59. Factoring the Difference of Squares**
One of the test maker's favorite factorables is the **difference of squares.**

$$a^2 - b^2 = (a - b)\ (a + b)$$

$x^2 - 9$, for example, factors to $(x - 3)(x + 3)$.

**60. Factoring the Square of a Binomial**
Recognize polynomials that are squares of binomials:

$$a^2 + 2ab + b^2 = (a + b)^2$$
$$a^2 - 2ab + b^2 = (a - b)^2$$

For example, $4x^2 + 12x + 9$ factors to $(2x + 3)^2$, and $n^2 - 10n + 25$ factors to $(n - 5)^2$.

**61. Factoring Other Polynomials—FOIL in Reverse**
To factor a quadratic expression, **think about what binomials you could use FOIL on to get that quadratic expression.** To factor $x^2 - 5x + 6$, think about what First terms will produce $x^2$, what Last terms will produce $+6$, and what Outer and Inner terms will produce $-5x$. Some common sense—and some trial and error—lead you to $(x - 2)(x - 3)$.

**62. Simplifying an Algebraic Fraction**
Simplifying an algebraic fraction is a lot like simplifying a numerical fraction. The general idea is to **find factors common to the numerator and denominator and cancel them.** Thus, simplifying an algebraic fraction begins with factoring.

For example, to simplify $\dfrac{x^2 - x - 12}{x^2 - 9}$, first factor the numerator and denominator:

$$\frac{x^2 - x - 12}{x^2 - 9} = \frac{(x - 4)(x + 3)}{(x - 3)(x + 3)}$$

Canceling $x + 3$ from the numerator and denominator leaves you with $\dfrac{x - 4}{x - 3}$.

## SOLVING EQUATIONS

**63. Solving a Linear Equation**
To solve an equation, do whatever is necessary to both sides to **isolate the variable.** To solve the equation $5x - 12 = -2x + 9$, first get all the $x$s on one side by adding $2x$ to both sides: $7x - 12 = 9$. Then add 12 to both sides: $7x = 21$. Then divide both sides by 7: $x = 3$.

**64. Solving "In Terms Of"**
To solve an equation for one variable **in terms of** another means to **isolate the one variable on one side of the equation,** leaving an expression containing the other variable on the other side of the equation. To solve the equation $3x - 10y = -5x + 6y$ for $x$ in terms of $y$, isolate $x$:

$$3x - 10y = -5x + 6y$$
$$3x + 5x = 6y + 10y$$
$$8x = 16y$$
$$x = 2y$$

**65. Translating from English into Algebra**
To translate from English into algebra, look for the key words and systematically turn phrases into algebraic expressions and sentences into equations. Be careful about order, especially when subtraction is called for.

**Example:** The charge for a phone call is $r$ cents for the first 3 minutes and $s$ cents for each minute thereafter.

What is the cost, in cents, of a phone call lasting exactly $t$ minutes? ($t > 3$)

**Setup:** The charge begins with $r$, and then something more is added, depending on the length of the call. The amount added is $s$ times the number of minutes past 3 minutes. If the total number of minutes is $t$, then the number of minutes past 3 is $t - 3$. So the charge is $r + s(t - 3)$.

**66. Solving a Quadratic Equation**
To solve a quadratic equation, put it in the "$ax^2 + bx + c = 0$" form, **factor** the left side (if you can), and set each factor equal to 0 separately to get the two solutions. To solve $x^2 + 12 = 7x$, first rewrite it as $x^2 - 7x + 12 = 0$. Then factor the left side:

$$(x-3)(x-4)=0$$
$$x-3=0 \ \text{or} \ x-4=0$$
$$x=3 \ \text{or} \ 4$$

**67. Solving a System of Equations**
You can solve for two variables only if you have two distinct equations. Two forms of the same equation will not be adequate. **Combine the equations** in such a way that **one of the variables cancels out.** To solve the two equations $4x + 3y = 8$ and $x + y = 3$, multiply both sides of the second equation by $-3$ to get: $-3x - 3y = -9$. Now add the two equations; the $3y$ and the $-3y$ cancel out, leaving: $x = -1$. Plug that back into either one of the original equations and you'll find that $y = 4$.

**68. Solving an Inequality**
To solve an inequality, do whatever is necessary to both sides to **isolate the variable.** Just remember that when you **multiply or divide both sides by a negative number,** you must **reverse the sign.** To solve $-5x + 7 < -3$, subtract 7 from both sides to get: $-5x < -10$. Now divide both sides by $-5$, remembering to reverse the sign: $x > 2$.

**COORDINATE GEOMETRY**

**69. Finding the Distance Between Two Points**
To find the distance between points, **use the Pythagorean theorem or special right triangles.** The difference between the $x$s is one leg and the difference between the $y$s is the other.

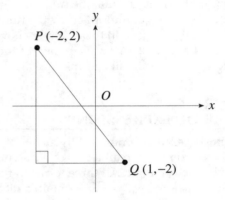

In the figure above, $PQ$ is the hypotenuse of a 3-4-5 triangle, so $PQ = 5$.

You can also use the **distance formula:**

$$d = \sqrt{(x_1 - x_2)^2 + (y_1 - y_2)^2}$$

To find the distance between $R(3, 6)$ and $S(5, -2)$:

$$\begin{aligned} d &= \sqrt{(3 - 5)^2 + [6 - (-2)]^2} \\ &= \sqrt{(-2)^2 + (8)^2} \\ &= \sqrt{68} = 2\sqrt{17} \end{aligned}$$

**70. Using Two Points to Find the Slope**

$$\text{Slope} = \frac{\text{Change in } y}{\text{Change in } x} = \frac{\text{Rise}}{\text{Run}}$$

The slope of the line that contains the points $A(2, 3)$ and $B(0, -1)$ is:

$$\frac{y_A - y_B}{x_A - x_B} = \frac{3 - (-1)}{2 - 0} = \frac{4}{2} = 2$$

**71. Using an Equation to Find the Slope**
To find the slope of a line from an equation, put the equation into the **slope-intercept** form:

$$y = mx + b$$

The **slope is** $m$. To find the slope of the equation $3x + 2y = 4$, rearrange it:

$$3x + 2y = 4$$
$$2y = -3x + 4$$
$$y = -\frac{3}{2}x + 2$$

The slope is $-\frac{3}{2}$.

## 72. Using an Equation to Find an Intercept

To find the $y$-intercept, you can either put the equation into $y = mx + b$ (**slope-intercept**) form—in which case $b$ **is the** $y$-**intercept**—or you can just **plug** $x = 0$ into the equation and **solve for** $y$. To find the $x$-intercept, **plug** $y = 0$ into the equation and **solve for** $x$.

## LINES AND ANGLES

### 73. Intersecting Lines

When two lines intersect, **adjacent angles are supplementary and vertical angles are equal.**

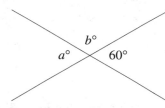

In the figure above, the angles marked $a°$ and $b°$ are adjacent and supplementary, so $a + b = 180$. Furthermore, the angles marked $a°$ and $60°$ are vertical and equal, so $a = 60$.

### 74. Parallel Lines and Transversals

A transversal across parallel lines forms **four equal acute angles and four equal obtuse angles.**

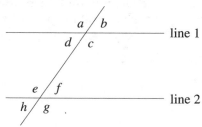

In the figure above, line 1 is parallel to line 2. Angles $a$, $c$, $e$, and $g$ are obtuse, so they are all

equal. Angles $b$, $d$, $f$, and $h$ are acute, so they are all equal.

Furthermore, **any of the acute angles is supplementary to any of the obtuse angles.** Angles $a$ and $h$ are supplementary, as are $b$ and $e$, $c$ and $f$, and so on.

## TRIANGLES—GENERAL

### 75. Interior Angles of a Triangle

The three angles of any triangle **add up to 180°.**

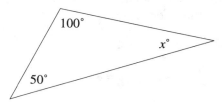

In the figure above, $x + 50 + 100 = 180$, so $x = 30$.

### 76. Exterior Angles of a Triangle

An exterior angle of a triangle is equal to the **sum of the remote interior angles.**

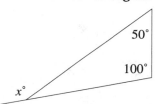

In the figure above, the exterior angle labeled $x°$ is equal to the sum of the remote angles: $x = 50 + 100 = 150$.

The three exterior angles of a triangle add up to 360°.

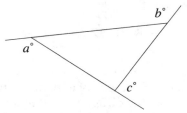

In the figure above, $a + b + c = 360$.

### 77. Similar Triangles

Similar triangles have the same shape: **corresponding angles are equal and corresponding sides are proportional.**

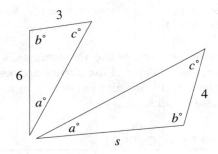

The triangles above are similar because they have the same angles. The 3 corresponds to the 4 and the 6 corresponds to the *s*.

$$\frac{3}{4}=\frac{6}{s}$$
$$3s = 24$$
$$s = 8$$

### 78. Area of a Triangle

$$\textbf{Area of Triangle} = \frac{1}{2}\textbf{(base)(height)}$$

The height is the perpendicular distance between the side that's chosen as the base and the opposite vertex.

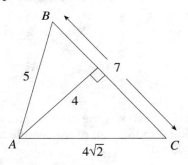

In the triangle above, 4 is the height when the 7 is chosen as the base.

$$\text{Area } = \frac{1}{2}bh = \frac{1}{2}(7)(4) = 14$$

### 79. Triangle Inequality Theorem

The length of one side of a triangle must be **greater than the difference and less than the sum** of the lengths of the other two sides. For example, if it is given that the length of one side is 3 and the length of another side is 7, then you know that the length of the third side must be greater than $7 - 3 = 4$ and less than $7 + 3 = 10$.

### 80. Isosceles Triangles

An isosceles triangle is a triangle that has **two equal sides.** Not only are two sides equal, but the angles opposite the equal sides, called base angles, are also equal.

### 81. Equilateral Triangles

Equilateral triangles are triangles in which **all three sides are equal.** Since all the sides are equal, all the angles are also equal. All three angles in an equilateral triangle measure 60 degrees, regardless of the lengths of sides.

## RIGHT TRIANGLES

### 82. Pythagorean Theorem

For all right triangles:

$$\textbf{(leg}_1\textbf{)}^2 + \textbf{(leg}_2\textbf{)}^2 = \textbf{(hypotenuse)}^2$$

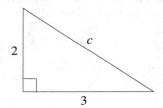

If one leg is 2 and the other leg is 3, then:

$$2^2 + 3^2 = c^2$$
$$c^2 = 4 + 9$$
$$c = \sqrt{13}$$

### 83. The 3-4-5 Triangle

If a right triangle's leg-to-leg ratio is 3:4, or if the leg-to-hypotenuse ratio is 3:5 or 4:5, it's a 3-4-5 triangle and you don't need to use the Pythagorean theorem to find the third side. Just figure out what multiple of 3-4-5 it is.

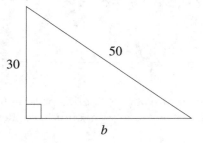

**KAPLAN**

In the right triangle shown, one leg is 30 and the hypotenuse is 50. This is 10 times 3–4–5. The other leg is 40.

## 84. The 5-12-13 Triangle

If a right triangle's leg-to-leg ratio is 5:12, or if the leg-to-hypotenuse ratio is 5:13 or 12:13, then it's a 5-12-13 triangle and you don't need to use the Pythagorean theorem to find the third side. Just figure out what multiple of 5-12-13 it is.

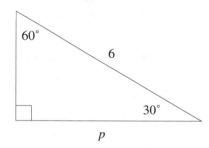

Here one leg is 36 and the hypotenuse is 39. This is 3 times 5-12-13. The other leg is 15.

## 85. The 30-60-90 Triangle

The sides of a 30-60-90 triangle are in a ratio of $x : x\sqrt{3} : 2x$. You don't need the Pythagorean theorem.

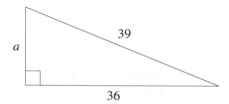

If the hypotenuse is 6, then the shorter leg is half that, or 3; and then the longer leg is equal to the short leg times $\sqrt{3}$, or $3\sqrt{3}$.

## 86. The 45-45-90 Triangle

The sides of a 45-45-90 triangle are in a ratio of $x : x : x\sqrt{2}$.

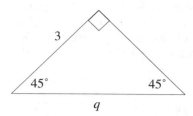

If one leg is 3, then the other leg is also 3, and the hypotenuse is equal to a leg times $\sqrt{2}$, or $3\sqrt{2}$.

## OTHER POLYGONS

## 87. Characteristics of a Rectangle

A rectangle is a **4-sided figure with 4 right angles.** Opposite sides are equal. Diagonals are equal.

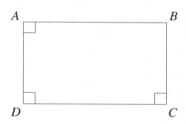

Quadrilateral *ABCD* above is shown to have three right angles. The fourth angle therefore also measures 90°, and *ABCD* is a rectangle. The perimeter of a rectangle is equal to the sum of the lengths of the four sides, which is equivalent to 2(Length + Width).

## 88. Area of a Rectangle

**Area of Rectangle = Length × Width**

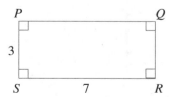

The area of a 7-by-3 rectangle is $7 \times 3 = 21$.

**89. Characteristics of a Parallelogram**
A parallelogram has **two pairs of parallel sides.** Opposite sides are equal. Opposite angles are equal. Consecutive angles add up to 180°.

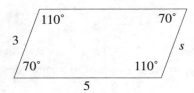

In the figure above, $s$ is the length of the side opposite the 3, so $s = 3$.

**90. Area of a Parallelogram**
**Area of Parallelogram = base × height**

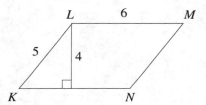

In parallelogram $KLMN$ above, 4 is the height when $LM$ or $KN$ is used as the base. Base × height = $6 \times 4 = 24$.

**91. Characteristics of a Square**
A square is a **rectangle with 4 equal sides.**

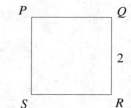

If $PQRS$ is a square, all sides are the same length as $QR$. The perimeter of a square is equal to 4 times the length of one side.

**92. Area of a Square**
**Area of Square = (side)²**

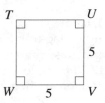

The square above, with sides of length 5, has an area of $5^2 = 25$.

**93. Interior Angles of a Polygon**
The **sum of the measures of the interior angles of a polygon = $(n - 2) \times 180$,** where $n$ is the number of sides.

**Sum of the Angles = $(n - 2) \times 180$**

The eight angles of an octagon, for example, add up to $(8 - 2) \times 180 = 1,080$.

**CIRCLES**

**94. Circumference of a Circle**
**Circumference = $2\pi r$**

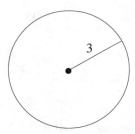

In the circle above, the radius is 3, and so the circumference is $2\pi(3) = 6\pi$.

**95. Length of an Arc**
An **arc** is a piece of the circumference. If $n$ is the degree measure of the arc's central angle, then the formula is:

**Length of an Arc = $\left(\dfrac{n}{360}\right)(2\pi r)$**

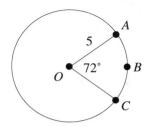

In the figure above, the radius is 5 and the measure of the central angle is 72°. The arc length is $\frac{72}{360}$ or $\frac{1}{5}$ of the circumference:

$$\left(\frac{72}{360}\right)(2\pi)(5)=\left(\frac{1}{5}\right)(10\pi)=2\pi$$

**96. Area of a Circle**

$$\text{Area of a Circle} = \pi r^2$$

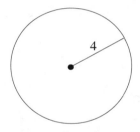

The area of the circle is $\pi(4)^2 = 16\pi$.

**97. Area of a Sector**

A **sector** is a piece of the area of a circle. If $n$ is the degree measure of the sector's central angle, then the formula is:

$$\text{Area of a Sector} = \left(\frac{n}{360}\right)\left(\pi r^2\right)$$

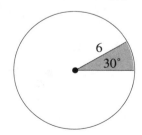

In the figure above, the radius is 6 and the measure of the sector's central angle is 30°. The

sector has $\frac{30}{360}$ or $\frac{1}{12}$ of the area of the circle:

$$\left(\frac{30}{360}\right)\left(\pi\right)\left(6^2\right)=\left(\frac{1}{12}\right)\left(36\pi\right)=3\pi$$

## SOLIDS

**98. Surface Area of a Rectangular Solid**

The surface of a rectangular solid consists of 3 pairs of identical faces. To find the surface area, find the area of each face and add them up. If the length is $l$, the width is $w$, and the height is $h$, the formula is:

$$\text{Surface Area} = 2lw + 2wh + 2lh$$

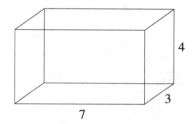

The surface area of the box above is: $2 \times 7 \times 3 + 2 \times 3 \times 4 + 2 \times 7 \times 4 = 42 + 24 + 56 = 122$

**99. Volume of a Rectangular Solid**

$$\text{Volume of a Rectangular Solid} = lwh$$

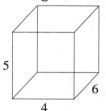

The volume of a 4-by-5-by-6 box is

$$4 \times 5 \times 6 = 120$$

A cube is a rectangular solid with length, width, and height all equal. If $e$ is the length of an edge of a cube, the volume formula is:

$$\text{Volume of a Cube} = e^3$$

The volume of this cube is $2^3 = 8$.

**100. Volume of a Cylinder**

**Volume of a Cylinder = $\pi r^2 h$**

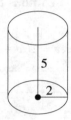

In the cylinder above, $r = 2$, $h = 5$, so:

Volume $= \pi(2^2)(5) = 20\pi$

# PRACTICE TESTS

# PRACTICE TEST A

Before taking this practice test, find a quiet room where you can work uninterrupted for 75 minutes. Make sure you have a comfortable desk, your calculator, and several No. 2 pencils.

Use the scoresheet on the reverse side of this page to record your answers.

Once you start this practice test, don't stop until you've finished. Remember—you can review any questions within a section, but you may not go back or forward a section.

Use the answer key following the test to count up the number of questions you got right and the number you got wrong. (Remember not to count omitted questions as wrong.) The "Compute Your Score" section at the back of the book will show you how to find your score.

Good luck.

# ANSWER SHEET

Start with number 1 for each new section. If a section has fewer questions than answer spaces, leave the extra spaces blank.

**SECTION 1**

| 1 Ⓐ Ⓑ Ⓒ Ⓓ Ⓔ | 11 Ⓐ Ⓑ Ⓒ Ⓓ Ⓔ | 21 Ⓐ Ⓑ Ⓒ Ⓓ Ⓔ | 31 Ⓐ Ⓑ Ⓒ Ⓓ Ⓔ |
| 2 Ⓐ Ⓑ Ⓒ Ⓓ Ⓔ | 12 Ⓐ Ⓑ Ⓒ Ⓓ Ⓔ | 22 Ⓐ Ⓑ Ⓒ Ⓓ Ⓔ | 32 Ⓐ Ⓑ Ⓒ Ⓓ Ⓔ |
| 3 Ⓐ Ⓑ Ⓒ Ⓓ Ⓔ | 13 Ⓐ Ⓑ Ⓒ Ⓓ Ⓔ | 23 Ⓐ Ⓑ Ⓒ Ⓓ Ⓔ | 33 Ⓐ Ⓑ Ⓒ Ⓓ Ⓔ |
| 4 Ⓐ Ⓑ Ⓒ Ⓓ Ⓔ | 14 Ⓐ Ⓑ Ⓒ Ⓓ Ⓔ | 24 Ⓐ Ⓑ Ⓒ Ⓓ Ⓔ | 34 Ⓐ Ⓑ Ⓒ Ⓓ Ⓔ |
| 5 Ⓐ Ⓑ Ⓒ Ⓓ Ⓔ | 15 Ⓐ Ⓑ Ⓒ Ⓓ Ⓔ | 25 Ⓐ Ⓑ Ⓒ Ⓓ Ⓔ | 35 Ⓐ Ⓑ Ⓒ Ⓓ Ⓔ |
| 6 Ⓐ Ⓑ Ⓒ Ⓓ Ⓔ | 16 Ⓐ Ⓑ Ⓒ Ⓓ Ⓔ | 26 Ⓐ Ⓑ Ⓒ Ⓓ Ⓔ | 36 Ⓐ Ⓑ Ⓒ Ⓓ Ⓔ |
| 7 Ⓐ Ⓑ Ⓒ Ⓓ Ⓔ | 17 Ⓐ Ⓑ Ⓒ Ⓓ Ⓔ | 27 Ⓐ Ⓑ Ⓒ Ⓓ Ⓔ | 37 Ⓐ Ⓑ Ⓒ Ⓓ Ⓔ |
| 8 Ⓐ Ⓑ Ⓒ Ⓓ Ⓔ | 18 Ⓐ Ⓑ Ⓒ Ⓓ Ⓔ | 28 Ⓐ Ⓑ Ⓒ Ⓓ Ⓔ | 38 Ⓐ Ⓑ Ⓒ Ⓓ Ⓔ |
| 9 Ⓐ Ⓑ Ⓒ Ⓓ Ⓔ | 19 Ⓐ Ⓑ Ⓒ Ⓓ Ⓔ | 29 Ⓐ Ⓑ Ⓒ Ⓓ Ⓔ | 39 Ⓐ Ⓑ Ⓒ Ⓓ Ⓔ |
| 10 Ⓐ Ⓑ Ⓒ Ⓓ Ⓔ | 20 Ⓐ Ⓑ Ⓒ Ⓓ Ⓔ | 30 Ⓐ Ⓑ Ⓒ Ⓓ Ⓔ | 40 Ⓐ Ⓑ Ⓒ Ⓓ Ⓔ |

# right in section 1

# wrong in section 1

**SECTION 2**

| 1 Ⓐ Ⓑ Ⓒ Ⓓ Ⓔ | 11 Ⓐ Ⓑ Ⓒ Ⓓ Ⓔ | 21 Ⓐ Ⓑ Ⓒ Ⓓ Ⓔ | 31 Ⓐ Ⓑ Ⓒ Ⓓ Ⓔ |
| 2 Ⓐ Ⓑ Ⓒ Ⓓ Ⓔ | 12 Ⓐ Ⓑ Ⓒ Ⓓ Ⓔ | 22 Ⓐ Ⓑ Ⓒ Ⓓ Ⓔ | 32 Ⓐ Ⓑ Ⓒ Ⓓ Ⓔ |
| 3 Ⓐ Ⓑ Ⓒ Ⓓ Ⓔ | 13 Ⓐ Ⓑ Ⓒ Ⓓ Ⓔ | 23 Ⓐ Ⓑ Ⓒ Ⓓ Ⓔ | 33 Ⓐ Ⓑ Ⓒ Ⓓ Ⓔ |
| 4 Ⓐ Ⓑ Ⓒ Ⓓ Ⓔ | 14 Ⓐ Ⓑ Ⓒ Ⓓ Ⓔ | 24 Ⓐ Ⓑ Ⓒ Ⓓ Ⓔ | 34 Ⓐ Ⓑ Ⓒ Ⓓ Ⓔ |
| 5 Ⓐ Ⓑ Ⓒ Ⓓ Ⓔ | 15 Ⓐ Ⓑ Ⓒ Ⓓ Ⓔ | 25 Ⓐ Ⓑ Ⓒ Ⓓ Ⓔ | 35 Ⓐ Ⓑ Ⓒ Ⓓ Ⓔ |
| 6 Ⓐ Ⓑ Ⓒ Ⓓ Ⓔ | →16 Ⓐ Ⓑ Ⓒ Ⓓ Ⓔ | 26 Ⓐ Ⓑ Ⓒ Ⓓ Ⓔ | 36 Ⓐ Ⓑ Ⓒ Ⓓ Ⓔ |
| 7 Ⓐ Ⓑ Ⓒ Ⓓ Ⓔ | 17 Ⓐ Ⓑ Ⓒ Ⓓ Ⓔ | 27 Ⓐ Ⓑ Ⓒ Ⓓ Ⓔ | 37 Ⓐ Ⓑ Ⓒ Ⓓ Ⓔ |
| 8 Ⓐ Ⓑ Ⓒ Ⓓ Ⓔ | 18 Ⓐ Ⓑ Ⓒ Ⓓ Ⓔ | 28 Ⓐ Ⓑ Ⓒ Ⓓ Ⓔ | 38 Ⓐ Ⓑ Ⓒ Ⓓ Ⓔ |
| 9 Ⓐ Ⓑ Ⓒ Ⓓ Ⓔ | 19 Ⓐ Ⓑ Ⓒ Ⓓ Ⓔ | 29 Ⓐ Ⓑ Ⓒ Ⓓ Ⓔ | 39 Ⓐ Ⓑ Ⓒ Ⓓ Ⓔ |
| 10 Ⓐ Ⓑ Ⓒ Ⓓ Ⓔ | 20 Ⓐ Ⓑ Ⓒ Ⓓ Ⓔ | 30 Ⓐ Ⓑ Ⓒ Ⓓ Ⓔ | 40 Ⓐ Ⓑ Ⓒ Ⓓ Ⓔ |

# right in section 2

# wrong in section 2

Continue to item 16 →

Grid-in items 16, 17, 18, 19, 20, 21, 22, 23, 24, 25 (each with numeric bubble grids 0–9)

**SECTION 3**

| 1 Ⓐ Ⓑ Ⓒ Ⓓ Ⓔ | 11 Ⓐ Ⓑ Ⓒ Ⓓ Ⓔ | 21 Ⓐ Ⓑ Ⓒ Ⓓ Ⓔ | 31 Ⓐ Ⓑ Ⓒ Ⓓ Ⓔ |
| 2 Ⓐ Ⓑ Ⓒ Ⓓ Ⓔ | 12 Ⓐ Ⓑ Ⓒ Ⓓ Ⓔ | 22 Ⓐ Ⓑ Ⓒ Ⓓ Ⓔ | 32 Ⓐ Ⓑ Ⓒ Ⓓ Ⓔ |
| 3 Ⓐ Ⓑ Ⓒ Ⓓ Ⓔ | 13 Ⓐ Ⓑ Ⓒ Ⓓ Ⓔ | 23 Ⓐ Ⓑ Ⓒ Ⓓ Ⓔ | 33 Ⓐ Ⓑ Ⓒ Ⓓ Ⓔ |
| 4 Ⓐ Ⓑ Ⓒ Ⓓ Ⓔ | 14 Ⓐ Ⓑ Ⓒ Ⓓ Ⓔ | 24 Ⓐ Ⓑ Ⓒ Ⓓ Ⓔ | 34 Ⓐ Ⓑ Ⓒ Ⓓ Ⓔ |
| 5 Ⓐ Ⓑ Ⓒ Ⓓ Ⓔ | 15 Ⓐ Ⓑ Ⓒ Ⓓ Ⓔ | 25 Ⓐ Ⓑ Ⓒ Ⓓ Ⓔ | 35 Ⓐ Ⓑ Ⓒ Ⓓ Ⓔ |
| 6 Ⓐ Ⓑ Ⓒ Ⓓ Ⓔ | 16 Ⓐ Ⓑ Ⓒ Ⓓ Ⓔ | 26 Ⓐ Ⓑ Ⓒ Ⓓ Ⓔ | 36 Ⓐ Ⓑ Ⓒ Ⓓ Ⓔ |
| 7 Ⓐ Ⓑ Ⓒ Ⓓ Ⓔ | 17 Ⓐ Ⓑ Ⓒ Ⓓ Ⓔ | 27 Ⓐ Ⓑ Ⓒ Ⓓ Ⓔ | 37 Ⓐ Ⓑ Ⓒ Ⓓ Ⓔ |
| 8 Ⓐ Ⓑ Ⓒ Ⓓ Ⓔ | 18 Ⓐ Ⓑ Ⓒ Ⓓ Ⓔ | 28 Ⓐ Ⓑ Ⓒ Ⓓ Ⓔ | 38 Ⓐ Ⓑ Ⓒ Ⓓ Ⓔ |
| 9 Ⓐ Ⓑ Ⓒ Ⓓ Ⓔ | 19 Ⓐ Ⓑ Ⓒ Ⓓ Ⓔ | 29 Ⓐ Ⓑ Ⓒ Ⓓ Ⓔ | 39 Ⓐ Ⓑ Ⓒ Ⓓ Ⓔ |
| 10 Ⓐ Ⓑ Ⓒ Ⓓ Ⓔ | 20 Ⓐ Ⓑ Ⓒ Ⓓ Ⓔ | 30 Ⓐ Ⓑ Ⓒ Ⓓ Ⓔ | 40 Ⓐ Ⓑ Ⓒ Ⓓ Ⓔ |

# right in section 3

# wrong in section 3

*Solve each of the following problems, decide which is the best answer choice, and darken the corresponding oval on the answer sheet. Use available space in the test booklet for scratchwork.\**

**Notes:**

(1)  Calculator use is permitted.
(2)  All numbers used are real numbers.
(3)  Figures are provided for some problems. All figures are drawn to scale and lie in a plane UNLESS otherwise indicated.

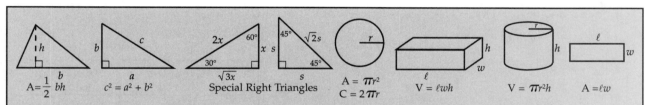

$A = \dfrac{1}{2}bh$          $c^2 = a^2 + b^2$          Special Right Triangles          $A = \pi r^2$
$C = 2\pi r$          $V = \ell wh$          $V = \pi r^2 h$          $A = \ell w$

The sum of the degree measures of the angles of a triangle is 180.
The number of degrees of arc in a circle is 360.
A straight angle has a degree measure of 180.

Reference Information

---

**1**  What is the smallest positive integer that is evenly divisible by both 21 and 9?

(A)  189
(B)  126
(C)  63
(D)  42
(E)  21

**2**  If $5 - 2x = 15$, then $x =$

(A)  −10
(B)  −5
(C)  1
(D)  5
(E)  10

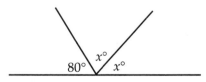

**3**  In the figure above, what is the value of $x$ ?

(A)  40
(B)  50
(C)  60
(D)  80
(E)  100

**4**  At a certain photography store it costs Pete $1.65 for the first print of a photograph and $0.85 for each additional print. How many prints of a particular photograph can Pete get for $20?

(A)  19
(B)  20
(C)  21
(D)  22
(E)  23

**5**  What is the value of $a$ if $ab + ac = 21$ and $b + c = 7$?

(A)  −3
(B)  −1
(C)  0
(D)  1
(E)  3

**6**  A laboratory has 55 rabbits, some white and the rest brown. Which of the following could be the ratio of white rabbits to brown rabbits in the lab?

(A)  3:8
(B)  5:11
(C)  3:4
(D)  3:1
(E)  5:1

*\*The directions on the actual SAT will vary slightly.*

**7** If $x = 9a^2$ and $a > 0$, then $\sqrt{x} =$

(A) $-3a$
(B) $3a$
(C) $9a$
(D) $3a^2$
(E) $81a^4$

**8** For all $x$ and $y$, $(x + 1)(y + 1) - x - y =$

(A) $xy - x - y + 1$
(B) $xy + 1$
(C) $-x - y + 1$
(D) $x^2 + y^2 - 1$
(E) $1$

**9** What percent of 4 is $\frac{2}{3}$ of 8?

(A) $25\%$
(B) $66\frac{2}{3}\%$
(C) $120\%$
(D) $133\frac{1}{3}\%$
(E) $150\%$

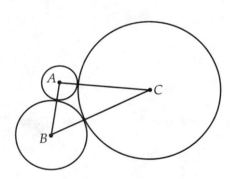

**10** If points $A$, $B$, and $C$ are the centers of the above circles, and the circles have radii of 2, 3, and 4, respectively, what is the perimeter of triangle $ABC$ ?

(A) 18
(B) 12
(C) $3\pi$
(D) 9
(E) 6

**11** If $n$ is an odd number, which of the following must be even?

(A) $\dfrac{n + 1}{2}$
(B) $\dfrac{n - 1}{2}$
(C) $n^2 + 2n$
(D) $2n + 2$
(E) $3n^2 - 2n$

| Contribution to Charity | Number of People |
|---|---|
| $10 | 4 |
| $15 | 3 |
| $20 | 2 |
| $25 | 4 |
| $30 | 2 |

**12** The contributions of 15 people to a certain charity are shown above. What is the difference between the median contribution and the average (arithmetic mean) contribution?

(A) $5
(B) $4
(C) $3
(D) $2
(E) $1

**13** If $m \blacktriangle n$ is defined by the equation

$m \blacktriangle n = \dfrac{m^2 - n + 1}{mn}$, for all nonzero $m$ and $n$,

then $3 \blacktriangle 1 =$

(A) $\dfrac{9}{4}$
(B) $3$
(C) $\dfrac{11}{3}$
(D) $6$
(E) $9$

GO ON TO THE NEXT PAGE

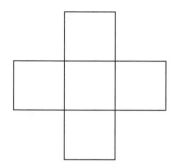

**14** The figure above is made of 5 squares of equal area. If the area of the figure is 20, what is the perimeter of the figure?

(A)  24
(B)  30
(C)  36
(D)  48
(E)  100

**15** A lighthouse blinks regularly 5 times a minute. A neighboring lighthouse blinks 4 times a minute. If they blink simultaneously, after how many seconds will they blink together again?

(A)  20
(B)  24
(C)  30
(D)  60
(E)  300

**16** What is the radius of the largest sphere that can be placed inside a cube of volume 64?

(A)  $6\sqrt{2}$
(B)  8
(C)  4
(D)  $2\sqrt{2}$
(E)  2

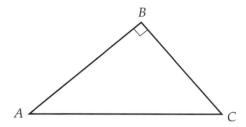

Note: Figure not drawn to scale.

**17** In the figure above, the area of $\triangle ABC$ is 6. If the length of $BC$ is $\frac{1}{3}$ the length of $AB$, then $AC =$

(A)  $\sqrt{2}$
(B)  2
(C)  4
(D)  6
(E)  $2\sqrt{10}$

**18** If $d = \dfrac{c - b}{a - b}$, then $b =$

(A)  $\dfrac{c - d}{a - d}$

(B)  $\dfrac{c + d}{a + d}$

(C)  $\dfrac{ca - d}{ca + d}$

(D)  $\dfrac{c - ad}{1 - d}$

(E)  $\dfrac{c + ad}{d - 1}$

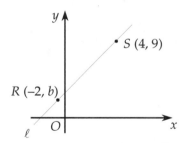

Note: Figure not drawn to scale.

**19** In the figure above, the slope of line $\ell$ is $\frac{4}{3}$. What is the value of $b$ ?

(A)  $-2$
(B)  $-1$
(C)  1
(D)  2
(E)  3

**20** If snow falls at the rate of $x$ centimeters per minute, how many hours would it take $y$ centimeters to fall?

(A)  $\dfrac{x}{60y}$

(B)  $\dfrac{y}{60x}$

(C)  $\dfrac{60x}{y}$

(D)  $\dfrac{60y}{x}$

(E)  $60xy$

**21** What is the set of all values of $x$ for which $x^2 - 3x - 18 = 0$?

(A)  $\{-6\}$
(B)  $\{-3\}$
(C)  $\{-3, 6\}$
(D)  $\{3, 6\}$
(E)  $\{2, 6\}$

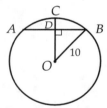

Note: Figure not drawn to scale.

**22** In the figure above, if $AB$ has a length of 16 and $OB$ has a length of 10, what is the length of $CD$ ?

(A)  4
(B)  $2\sqrt{3}$
(C)  $8 - \sqrt{35}$
(D)  2
(E)  $8 - \sqrt{39}$

**23** If $N$ is the square of a positive integer, which of the following must be equal to the square of the next greater integer?

(A)  $\sqrt{N} + 1$
(B)  $N + 1$
(C)  $N^2 + 1$
(D)  $N^2 + 2N + 1$
(E)  $N + 2\sqrt{N} + 1$

**24** A motorist travels 90 miles at a rate of 20 miles per hour. If he returns the same distance at a rate of 40 miles per hour, what is his average speed for the entire trip, in miles per hour?

(A)  20

(B)  $\dfrac{65}{3}$

(C)  $\dfrac{80}{3}$

(D)  30

(E)  $\dfrac{130}{3}$

**25** A factory cut its labor force by 16 percent, but then increased it by 25 percent of the new amount. What was the overall change in the size of the workforce?

(A)  A 5% decrease
(B)  No net change
(C)  A 5% increase
(D)  A 9% increase
(E)  A 10% increase

**STOP**  IF YOU FINISH BEFORE TIME IS CALLED, YOU MAY CHECK YOUR WORK ON THIS SECTION ONLY. **DO NOT** TURN TO ANY OTHER SECTION IN THE TEST.

*Solve each of the following problems, decide which is the best answer choice, and darken the corresponding oval on the answer sheet. Use available space in the test booklet for scratchwork.\**

**Notes:**

(1)     Calculator use is permitted.
(2)     All numbers used are real numbers.
(3)     Figures are provided for some problems. All figures are drawn to scale and lie in a plane UNLESS otherwise indicated.

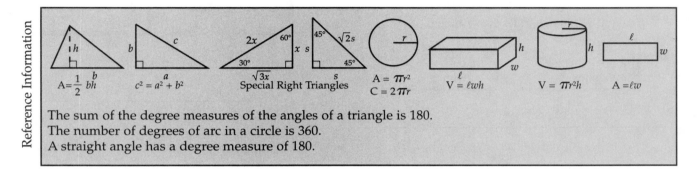

The sum of the degree measures of the angles of a triangle is 180.
The number of degrees of arc in a circle is 360.
A straight angle has a degree measure of 180.

## DIRECTIONS FOR QUANTITATIVE COMPARISON QUESTIONS

Compare the boxed quantity in Column A with the boxed quantity in Column B. Select answer choice

A    if Column A is greater;
B    if Column B is greater;
C    if the columns are equal; or
D    if more information is needed to determine the relationship.

An E response will be treated as an omission.

Notes:

1.    Some questions include information about one or both quantities. That information is centered and unboxed.
2.    A symbol that appears in both Column A and Column B stands for the same thing in both columns.
3.    All numbers used are real numbers.

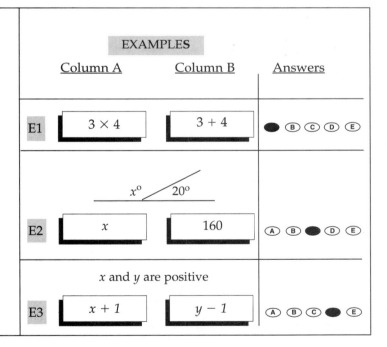

| **Column A** | **Column B** |
|---|---|
| | |

**1** | 0.04504 | 0.045134 |

---

John is older than Karen.

**2** | John's weight, in pounds | Karen's weight, in pounds |

---

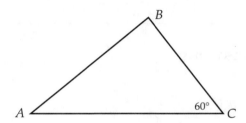

Note: Figure not drawn to scale.

$\angle CAB = \angle CBA$

**3** | AB | AC |

---

$$a + 7 = 10$$
$$b - 2 = 5$$

**4** | $\dfrac{a + 7}{b - 2}$ | $\dfrac{(a + 7)(b - 2)}{20}$ |

| **Column A** | **Column B** |
|---|---|
| | |

The lost-sock bin at a laundromat contains 5 black socks, 3 brown socks, and 3 white socks. One sock is pulled out at random.

**5** | The probability that the sock is black | The probability that the sock is not black |

---

$AB = BC = CD = DA$

**6** | $x$ | 45 |

---

$$a > b > 0$$

**7** | $\dfrac{1}{a}$ | $b$ |

KAPLAN

GO ON TO THE NEXT PAGE

| Column A | Column B |
|---|---|

The finance plan for the purchase of a certain television requires 25 percent of the cost as an initial down payment and 12 monthly payments of $30 each.

**8** | Total cost of the television | $480

$$13 < a < 15$$
$$15 < b < 17$$

**9** | $a + b$ | 30

**10** | The perimeter of a triangle with area 4 | The circumference of a circle with area $4\pi$

The "play" of a number $x$ is defined as the result when $\frac{1}{x}$ is subtracted from 1.

**11** | The "play" of $-\frac{1}{2}$ | The "play" of $-2$

On a 50-question test, 1 point is given for each question answered correctly and $\frac{1}{2}$ point is deducted for each question answered incorrectly. A student who answered 48 questions received a total of 36 points.

**12** | Number of questions the student answered incorrectly | 9

| Column A | Column B |
|---|---|

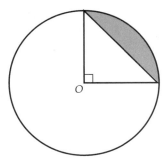

$O$ is the center of the circle with radius 6.

**13** | Area of the shaded region | 18

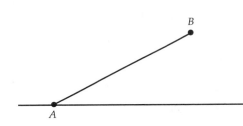

**14** | The number of possible right triangles that have $AB$ as a hypotenuse | 2

$$a - b = c$$
$$c - a = 5$$
$$b + c = -2$$

**15** | $a$ | $b$

## DIRECTIONS FOR STUDENT-PRODUCED RESPONSE QUESTIONS

For each of the questions below (16–25), solve the problem and indicate your answer by darkening the ovals in the special grid. For example:

Answer: 1.25 or $\frac{5}{4}$ or 5/4

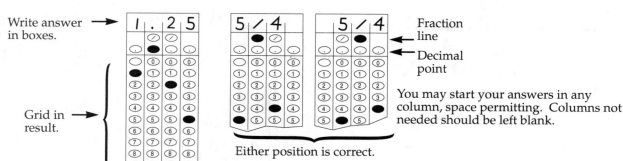

Write answer in boxes.

Grid in result.

Either position is correct.

Fraction line

Decimal point

You may start your answers in any column, space permitting. Columns not needed should be left blank.

- It is recommended, though not required, that you write your answer in the boxes at the top of the columns. However, you will receive credit only for darkening the ovals correctly.

- Grid only one answer to a question, even though some problems have more than one correct answer.

- Darken no more than one oval in a column.

- No answers are negative.

- Mixed numbers cannot be gridded. For example: the number $1\frac{1}{4}$ must be gridded as 1.25 or 5/4.

   (If $\boxed{1\,1\,/\,4}$ is gridded, it will be interpreted as $\frac{11}{4}$, not $1\frac{1}{4}$.)

- Decimal Accuracy: Decimal answers must be entered as accurately as possible. For example, if you obtain an answer such as 0.1666. . ., you should record the result as .166 or .167. **Less accurate values such as .16 or .17 are not acceptable.**

Acceptable ways to grid $\frac{1}{6}$ = .1666. . .

16  A certain book costs $12 more in hardcover than softcover. If the softcover price is $\frac{2}{3}$ of the hardcover price, how much does the book cost, in dollars, in hardcover? (Ignore the dollar sign when gridding your answer.)

17  If $4a - 1 = 64$, what is the value of $6a$ ?

18  The average (arithmetic mean) of six numbers is $7\frac{1}{2}$. If the average of 4 of these numbers is 2, what is the average of the other two numbers?

KAPLAN

GO ON TO THE NEXT PAGE

19  In a certain dairy store, $\frac{1}{3}$ of all the yogurts are fruit flavored. If $\frac{1}{8}$ of all yogurts are peach flavored, what fraction of the fruit flavored yogurts are peach flavored?

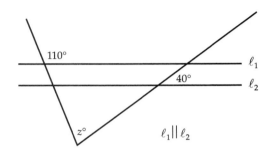

20  In the figure above, what is the value of $z$ ?

21  If $m$ and $n$ are prime numbers such that the sum of $m$ and $n$ is greater than 20 and the product of $m$ and $n$ is less than 50, what is a possible value of $mn$ ?

22  What is the area of a triangle with vertices $(2, 3)$, $(8, 3)$, and $(13, 6)$ in the $xy$-plane?

23  If $y > 0$ and $x$ is $2\frac{1}{2}$ percent of $y$, then $y$ is what percent of $x$ ? (Ignore the percent sign when gridding your answer.)

24  For how many positive integers $x$ is $\frac{130}{x}$ an integer?

25  The area of a circle is $16\pi$ square inches. What is the area, in square inches, of the largest square that can be drawn within this circle?

*Solve each of the following problems, decide which is the best answer choice, and darken the corresponding oval on the answer sheet. Use available space in the test booklet for scratchwork.\**

**Notes:**

(1)   Calculator use is permitted.
(2)   All numbers used are real numbers.
(3)   Figures are provided for some problems. All figures are drawn to scale and lie in a plane UNLESS otherwise indicated.

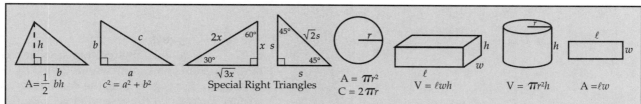

The sum of the degree measures of the angles of a triangle is 180.
The number of degrees of arc in a circle is 360.
A straight angle has a degree measure of 180.

---

**1**   If the three-digit number 5W2 is evenly divisible by 8, which of the following could be the value for the digit $W$ ?

(A)   2
(B)   3
(C)   4
(D)   5
(E)   6

**2**   If $\frac{3}{11} + \frac{3}{11} + \frac{3}{11} = \frac{x}{33}$, what is the value of $\frac{x}{3}$?

(A)   27
(B)    9
(C)    6
(D)    3
(E)    1

**3**   If $gh > 0$, which of the following must be true?

(A)   $\frac{g}{h} > 0$

(B)   $\frac{h}{g} < 0$

(C)   $g + h > 0$

(D)   $g - h > 0$

(E)   $g + h < 0$

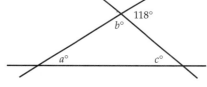

Note: Figure not drawn to scale.

**4**   In the figure above, what is the value of $a + c - b$ ?

(A)   45
(B)   56
(C)   59
(D)   62
(E)   64

**5**   The first term of a certain sequence is 5. If every term after the first term is 3 less than 2 times the term immediately preceding it, what is the difference between the third and fourth terms?

(A)    8
(B)   11
(C)   16
(D)   19
(E)   32

---

*\*The directions on the actual SAT will vary slightly.*

6  The sum of two positive numbers $x$ and $z$ is 50. If $x$ is greater than 10 more than four times $z$, which of the following includes the entire range of values for $z$ ?

(A)  $0 < z < 4$
(B)  $0 < z < 8$
(C)  $0 < z < 10$
(D)  $8 < z < 10$
(E)  $8 < z < 50$

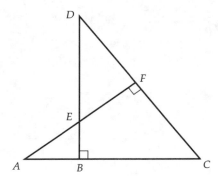

Note: Figure not drawn to scale.

7  In the figure above, if $AC = 12$, $DC = 18$, and $DB = 15$, what is the length of $AF$ ?

(A)  8
(B)  9
(C)  10
(D)  11
(E)  12

8  A radioactive chemical decays 20 percent each day. If 48 pounds of this chemical remain today, how many pounds of this chemical were present two days ago?

(A)  75
(B)  72
(C)  70
(D)  66
(E)  60

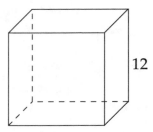

12

9  The figure above is a cube with an edge of 12. If this cube is divided into smaller rectangular solids with dimensions 2 by 2 by 4, how many times greater is the combined surface areas of all these smaller rectangular solids than the surface area of the larger cube?

(A)  16
(B)  12
(C)  10
(D)  8
(E)  5

10  If $k$ is a positive integer less than 17, what is the total number of possible integral solutions for the equation $x^2 + 8x + k = 0$?

(A)  4
(B)  5
(C)  6
(D)  7
(E)  8

**STOP**  IF YOU FINISH BEFORE TIME IS CALLED, YOU MAY CHECK YOUR WORK ON THIS SECTION ONLY. **DO NOT** TURN TO ANY OTHER SECTION IN THE TEST.

**KAPLAN**

# PRACTICE TEST A—ANSWERS AND EXPLANATIONS

## Section 1

**1** C—The fastest method is to start with the smallest answer choice and test each one for divisibility. Choice (E) is divisible by 21, but not by 9. Similarly, choice (D) is 2 × 21, but it is not divisible by 9. Choice (C), 63, is divisible by both 21 (21 × 3 = 63) and 9 (9 × 7 = 63). Since the remaining answer choices are larger, this must be the correct answer.

A more mathematical approach is to find the prime factors of 9 and 21, and, by eliminating shared factors, find the least common multiple. Breaking each into prime factors:

$$21 = 3 \times 7$$
$$9 = 3 \times 3$$

We can drop one factor of 3 from the 9, since it is already present in the factors of 21. The least common multiple is $3 \times 3 \times 7$, or 63.

**2** B—Solve for $x$:
$$5 - 2x = 15$$
$$-2x = 10$$
$$x = -5$$

**3** B—Since the three marked angles form a straight angle, the sum of their measures is 180°. So we can set up an equation to solve for $x$:
$$x + x + 80 = 180$$
$$2x + 80 = 180$$
$$2x = 100$$
$$x = 50$$

**4** D—The first print uses up $1.65 of the $20 Pete has available. This leaves him $20 – $1.65 or $18.35 for the rest of the prints, at a rate of $0.85 per print. Divide 0.85 into 18.35 to find out how many additional prints can be purchased. It comes out to 21 prints (with change left over), and that, plus the first print, means he can buy 22 prints all together.

**5** E—To use the first equation we need to factor out $a$:
$$ab + ac = 21$$
$$a(b + c) = 21$$
Since $b + c = 7$, substitute 7 for $b + c$:
$$a(7) = 21$$
Solve for $a$:
$$a = \frac{21}{7} = 3$$

**6** A—There are 55 rabbits in the laboratory. So the sum of the terms in the ratio must be a factor of 55. There are only four factors of 55: 1, 5, 11, and 55. The only answer choice with terms that add up to one of these numbers is choice (A): the sum of the terms in a 3:8 ratio is 11.

**7** B—We can find the value of $\sqrt{x}$ by substituting $9a^2$ for $x$.
$$\sqrt{x} = \sqrt{9a^2}$$
$$= \sqrt{9} \times \sqrt{a^2}$$
$$= 3a$$

Note: We could only arrive at this answer because we know that $a > 0$. The radical sign refers to the *positive* square root of a number.

**8** B—To simplify the expression, first use the FOIL method (**F**irst terms, **O**uter terms, **I**nner terms, and **L**ast terms) to multiply the binomials $x + 1$ and $y + 1$. Then combine terms:
$$(x + 1)(y + 1) = xy + 1$$
$$(x + 1)(y + 1) - x - y = xy + x + y + 1 - x - y$$
$$= xy + 1$$

**9** D—First, translate the words into algebra: *of* means "times," *is* means "equals." Call the percent you're looking for $p$:
$$\frac{2}{3} \times 8 = p \times 4$$
$$\frac{\frac{2}{3} \times 8}{4} = p$$
$$\frac{4}{3} = p$$

To convert $\frac{4}{3}$ to a percent, multiply by 100%:
$$\frac{4}{3} = \frac{4}{3} \times 100\% = \frac{400}{3}\% = 133\frac{1}{3}\%$$

**10** A—Each side of triangle $ABC$ connects the centers of two tangent circles, and each side passes through the point where the circumferences of the circles touch. Therefore, each side is composed of the radii of two of the circles: $AB$ is made up of a radius of $A$ and a radius of $B$, $BC$ is made up of a radius of $B$ and a radius of $C$, and $AC$ is made up of a radius of $A$ and a radius of $C$. The sum of the lengths of these sides is the perimeter of the triangle. Since we have two radii of each circle, the perimeter is twice the sum of the radii: 2(2 + 3 + 4) = 18.

**11** **D**—The simplest approach here is to pick an odd value for $n$, such as 3. When working with addition, subtraction, or multiplication, *any* odd or even number will behave the same way (in terms of whether the *result* is odd or even). In this particular problem we have to be careful, though, because two answer choices involve division, and the problem asks for a choice that *must* be even. If choices (A) or (B) produce an even result, we'll have to make sure there's not another possibility.

Choice (A): $\frac{n+1}{2} = \frac{3+1}{2} = \frac{4}{2} = 2$. Even. But this choice involves division, so we need to try another value, such as 1: $\frac{1+1}{2} = \frac{2}{2} = 1$. So this doesn't have to be even, and that means it's not the correct answer.

Choice (B): $\frac{n-1}{2} = \frac{3-1}{2} = \frac{2}{2} = 1$. Not even, so this choice can't be correct.

Choice (C): $n^2 + 2n = 3^2 + 2(3) = 9 + 6 = 15$. No.
Choice (D): $2n + 2 = 2(3) + 2 = 6 + 2 = 8$. Even. Since no division is involved, we can safely assume any odd value for $n$ will cause the result here to be even. So this is the correct choice.
Just for practice:
Choice (E): $3n^2 - 2n = 3(3)^2 - 2(3) = 21$. As expected, it doesn't produce an even result.

**12** **E**—The median is the middle term in a group of terms arranged in numerical order. Since there were 15 contributions made, the median contribution will be the eighth term. The eighth term coincides with a $20 contribution, so the median contribution is $20. Remember that average = $\frac{\text{sum of the terms}}{\text{number of terms}}$. You know there were 15 contributions, so all you need to find is the total amount of contributions: $(4 \times \$10) + (3 \times \$15) + (2 \times \$20) + (4 \times \$25) + (2 \times \$30) = \$285$. So the average = $\frac{\$285}{15}$, or $19. So the difference between the median contribution and the average contribution is $20 – $19, or $1, and choice (E) is correct.

**13** **B**—Here we have a symbolism problem, involving a symbol—▲—that doesn't exist in mathematics. All you need to do is follow the directions given in the definition of this symbol. To find the value of $3 \triangle 1$, plug 3 and 1 into the formula given for $m \triangle n$, substituting 3 for $m$ and 1 for $n$. Then the equation becomes:

$$3 \triangle 1 = \frac{(3)^2 - (1) + 1}{(3)(1)}$$
$$= \frac{9 - 1 + 1}{3}$$
$$= \frac{9}{3}$$
$$= 3$$

**14** **A**—Each of these squares must have an area equal to one-fifth of the area of the whole figure: $\frac{1}{5} \times 20 = 4$. For squares, area = side², or $\sqrt{\text{area}}$ = side. Since $\sqrt{4} = 2$, the length of each side of each square must be 2.

The perimeter consists of 3 sides from each of four squares, for a total of $3 \times 4$, or 12 sides. Each side has a length of 2, for a total perimeter of $12 \times 2$, or 24.

**15** **D**—There are 60 seconds in a minute, so if the first lighthouse blinks 5 times a minute, it must blink once every $\frac{60}{5}$, or 12 seconds. The neighboring lighthouse, at 4 times a minute, works out to once every $\frac{60}{4}$ or 15 seconds.

If they start out together, the next time they blink simultaneously will be when the number of seconds gone by is a multiple of both 12 and 15. So we need to find the least common multiple of 12 and 15. You could work this out by finding the prime factors, but it's probably easier to go through the multiples of the

**KAPLAN**

larger number, 15, until you find one that is also a multiple of 12.

$1 \times 15 = 15$
$2 \times 15 = 30$
$3 \times 15 = 45$
$4 \times 15 = 60$—This is a multiple of 12, since $5 \times 12 = 60$.
So the two lighthouses will blink together after 60 seconds.

**16** **E**—It may be helpful to draw a quick diagram, like this one:

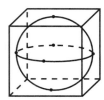

The sphere will touch the cube at six points. Each point will be an endpoint of a diameter and will be at the center of one of the cubic faces. (Imagine putting a beach ball inside a tight-fitting, cube-shaped box.) Therefore the diameter extends directly from one face of the cube to the other, and is perpendicular to both faces that it touches. This means that the diameter must have the same length as an edge of the cube. The cube's volume is 64, so the length of each edge is the cube root of 64, or 4. So the diameter of the sphere is 4, which means that the radius is 2.

**17** **E**—The area of any right triangle equals one-half the product of the legs. Since $AB$ is three times as long as $BC$, we can call the length of $BC$ $x$, and the length of $AB$ $3x$. The area of the triangle is one-half their product, or $\frac{1}{2}(x)(3x)$. Since we know the area is 6, we can say:

$$\frac{1}{2}(x)(3x) = 6$$
$$3x^2 = 12$$
$$x^2 = 4$$
$$x = 2$$

So $BC$ has a length of 2. $AB$, which is $3x$, is 6. Now use the Pythagorean theorem to find $AC$.

$$AC^2 = AB^2 + BC^2$$
$$AC^2 = (6)^2 + (2)^2$$
$$AC^2 = 36 + 4$$
$$AC = \sqrt{40} = \sqrt{4} \times \sqrt{10} = 2\sqrt{10}.$$

**18** **D**—Solve for $b$ in terms of $a$, $c$, and $d$. First, multiply both sides by $(a - b)$:

$$d = \frac{c-b}{a-b}$$
$$d(a - b) = c - b$$

Distribute the $d$:

$$da - db = c - b$$

Gather the $b$ factors on one side and factor out:

$$b - db = c - da$$
$$b(1 - d) = c - da$$

Divide both sides by $1 - d$ to isolate $b$:

$$b = \frac{c-ad}{1-d}$$

**19** **C**—The slope of a line is defined as *rise over run*, which means the difference between the $y$-coordinates of any two points on the line, divided by the difference between the $x$-coordinates of the same two points. We're given the value of the slope and three of the four coordinates, so we can write an equation to solve for the missing coordinate. Since both coordinates of point $S$ will be greater than those of point $R$, we'll put those numbers first when we compute the difference:

$$\frac{9-b}{4-(-2)} = \frac{4}{3}$$
$$\frac{9-b}{6} = \frac{4}{3}$$
$$6\left(\frac{9-b}{6}\right) = 6\left(\frac{4}{3}\right)$$
$$9-b = 8$$
$$-b = -1$$
$$b = 1$$

**20** **B**—The easiest method to solve this problem is to pick numbers. Choose numbers that will be easy to work with. Let $x = 2$, that is, say that the snow falls at a rate of 2 centimeters per minute. Let $y = 60$, since there are a lot of 60s to divide by in the answer choices. Now we figure out how many hours it would take for 60 centimeters to fall at this rate. At 2 centimeters per minute, 60 centimeters would fall in half an hour.

Next, let's plug 2 and 60 into each answer choice and see which one equals half an hour. (When using this method, remember that more than one answer choice *could* have the right value depending on the numbers we happen to pick, so we need to try them all. If more than one works, we try different values until only one choice works.)

Choice (A): $\dfrac{2}{(60)(60)} = \dfrac{1}{1,800}$. Discard.

Choice (B): $\dfrac{60}{(60)(2)} = \dfrac{60}{120} = \dfrac{1}{2}$. Choice (B) is probably correct, but we have to make sure by checking the other choices.

Choice (C): $\dfrac{(60)(2)}{60} = 2$. Discard.

Choice (D): $\dfrac{(60)(60)}{2} = 1,800$. Discard.

Choice (E): $(60)(2)(60) = 7,200$. Since none of the other choices yields $\dfrac{1}{2}$, choice (B) is indeed the correct answer.

**21** C—Factor the quadratic:
$x^2 - 3x - 18 = (x + a)(x + b)$
The product of $a$ and $b$ is $ab = -18$
The sum of $a$ and $b$ is $a + b = -3$.
What pair of numbers has a product of $-18$ and a sum of $-3$? By trial and error we find that the two numbers must be positive 3 and $-6$. So:
$x^2 - 3x - 18 = (x + 3)(x - 6) = 0$
If this equals zero, either $x + 3 = 0$ (i.e., $x = -3$) or $x - 6 = 0$ (i.e., $x = 6$).
The set of values is therefore $\{-3, 6\}$.

This can also be solved by trying the values given in each answer choice in the original equation. But since you're looking for all values of $x$, it would be wrong to choose choice (B) as correct, even though it works.

**22** A—We're looking for the length of $CD$. Note that $OC$ is a radius of the circle, so if we knew the lengths of $OC$ and $OD$, we could find $CD$, since $CD = OC - OD$. We're given that $OB$ has a length of 10, which means the circle has a radius of 10, and therefore $OC$ is 10. All that remains is to find $OD$ and subtract.

The only other piece of information we have to work with is that $AB$ has length 16. If we connect $O$ and $A$, we create two right triangles, $ADO$ and $BDO$:

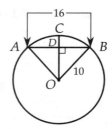

Since both these right triangles have a radius as the hypotenuse and both have leg $OD$ in common, they must be equal in size. Therefore, the other legs, $AD$ and $DB$, must also be equal. That means that $D$ is the midpoint of $AB$, so $DB$ is $\dfrac{1}{2}$ (16), or 8. So right triangle $BDO$ has a hypotenuse of 10 and a leg of 8; thus its other leg has length 6. If you didn't recognize this as a 6-8-10 Pythagorean Triplet—a multiple of the 3-4-5 triangle—you could have used the Pythagorean theorem to find the length of $OD$. So $OD$ has length 6, and $CD = 10 - 6 = 4$.

**23** E—$N$ is the square of a positive integer $t$, or $N = t^2$. Then, the integer $t = \sqrt{N}$. The next greater integer is one more, or $t + 1$, which equals $\sqrt{N} + 1$. To find the square, we use the distributive law (FOIL):

$$(\sqrt{N} + 1)^2 = (\sqrt{N} + 1)(\sqrt{N} + 1)$$

$$= (\sqrt{N})^2 + \sqrt{N} \times 1 + 1 \times \sqrt{N} + 1^2$$

$$= N + 2\sqrt{N} + 1$$

Or you can easily solve this problem by picking numbers. We know $N$ is the square of a positive integer. So let's say $N$ is 4, the square of 2. The next greater integer after 2 is 3, and the square of 3 is 9. Therefore, we can eliminate any answer choice that does not result in a value of 9 when $N$ is 4.

Choice (A): $\sqrt{4+1} + 1 = \sqrt{5}$. Discard.

Choice (B): $4 + 1 = 5$. Discard.

Choice (C): $4^2 + 1 = 16 + 1 = 17$. Discard.

Choice (D): $4^2 + (2 \times 4) + 1 = 16 + 8 + 1 = 25$. Discard.

Choice (E): $4 + 2\sqrt{4} + 1 = 4 + 4 + 1 = 9$. This is what we're looking for, so choice (E) is correct.

**24** **C**—Since he traveled the same distance both ways, it's tempting to think we can simply average the speeds to find the answer. But rates can't be averaged in that way. It's necessary to compute the total distance and the total time and use these numbers in the average formula.

Total miles: He travels 90 miles there and 90 miles back, for a total of 180 miles. To find the total time, we must calculate the time for each part of the trip, and then add them together. Going there, he travels 90 miles at 20 miles per hour.

Since rate × time = distance, time = $\frac{\text{distance}}{\text{rate}}$. So it takes him $\frac{90 \text{ miles}}{20 \text{ miles per hour}} = \frac{9}{2}$ hours to travel there. Coming back, he travels 90 miles at 40 miles per hour, so it takes him $\frac{90}{40} = \frac{9}{4}$ hours to return home.

The total time spent was therefore $\frac{9}{2} + \frac{9}{4} = \frac{18}{4} + \frac{9}{4} = \frac{27}{4}$, or $6\frac{3}{4}$ hours.

So his average speed for the whole trip was $\frac{\text{Total miles}}{\text{Total hours}} = \frac{180 \text{ miles}}{\frac{27}{4}\text{ hours}} = \left(180 \times \frac{4}{27}\right) = \frac{80}{3}$ miles per hour.

**25** **C**—Many students will assume that a loss of 16 percent followed by an increase of 25 percent adds up to an overall increase of 25 − 16, or 9 percent. This works if both percents are percents of the same amount. But the 25 percent is a percent of a *different* amount. To find the actual result, assume a starting value of 100 (since we're working with percents) and see what happens.

If the factory cuts its labor force by 16 percent, it eliminates 16 percent of 100 jobs or 16 jobs, leaving a work force of 100 − 16, or 84 people. It then increases this work force by 25 percent. Twenty-five percent of 84 is the same as $\frac{1}{4}$ of 84, or 21. So the facto-

ry adds 21 jobs to the 84 it had, for a total of 105 jobs. Since the factory started with 100 jobs and finished with 105, it gained 5 jobs overall. This represents $\frac{5}{100}$, or 5 percent, of the total we started with. So there was a 5 percent overall increase after both changes were made.

## Section 2

**1** **B**—Compare the digits after the decimal in each column. The first three digits after the decimal (0, 4, and 5) are the same in both columns. However, the fourth digits are different: 0 in Column A and 1 in Column B. Since 1 is greater than 0, the quantity in Column B is larger.

**2** **D**—You're told that John is older than Karen. Does that mean John is heavier than Karen? Of course not. There is no way to determine someone's weight given only his or her relative age, so the correct answer is (D).

**3** **C**—The sum of the measures of the three angles in any triangle equals 180 degrees. If ∠ACB measures 60 degrees, then the sum of the other two angles, ∠CAB and ∠CBA, is 120 degrees. Since ∠CAB and ∠CBA are equal in measure, ∠CAB and ∠CBA each measures $\frac{1}{2}$ of 120, or 60 degrees.

Now we have a triangle with three 60 degree angles; therefore, it is an equilateral triangle, and all the sides are equal. Line segment *AB* is equal to line segment *AC*, and the columns are equal.

**4** **B**—Plug the values of *a* + 7 and *b* − 2 directly into the expressions. Column A becomes $\frac{10}{5}$ or 2. Column B becomes $\frac{(10)(5)}{20} = \frac{50}{20} = 2\frac{1}{2}$. Since $2\frac{1}{2}$ is greater than 2, Column B is larger.

**5** **B**—Probability is simply the number of desired outcomes divided by the total number of *possible* outcomes. So the probability that the sock will be black is the number of *desired* outcomes that could occur (there are 5 black socks, so 5 possible outcomes are desirable) divided by the total number of possible outcomes, which is 11 (because there are 11 socks in the bin). So the probability that the sock will be black is $\frac{5}{11}$.

You might have been tempted to think the probability in Column B was $\frac{3}{11}$, because there are only 3 brown socks and 3 white socks. But the condition is simply that the sock *is not black*. That means 6 of the socks would fit the description, and 6 of the 11 possible outcomes would be acceptable. So the probability that the sock will not be black is $\frac{6}{11}$, which is greater than $\frac{5}{11}$ in Column A.

**6** **A**—The angle at $D$ is marked 89 degrees, so this isn't a square; it's a parallelogram with equal sides. If it were a square, $x$ would equal 45°.

The best way to find the answer is to *redraw the diagram,* exaggerating the difference between the angles.

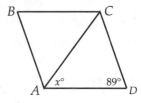

Now it's clear that angle $x$ has increased as a result of angle $D$ shrinking, so whatever the actual value of $x$ in the given diagram, it must be slightly greater than 45.

**7** **D**—If you assumed that $a$ and $b$ must be different positive integers, then Column B would have to be greater than Column A. But in a problem like this, it's crucial to remember that the variables can represent something besides positive integers—in this case, fractions smaller than 1.

Suppose, for instance, $a = \frac{2}{3}$, while $b = \frac{1}{3}$. Then $\frac{1}{a} = \frac{1}{\frac{2}{3}}$, which equals $\frac{3}{2}$. This is greater than $\frac{1}{3}$, so in this situation, Column A is greater than Column B.

Since more than one relationship is possible between the columns, the correct answer has to be (D).

**8** **C**—Since the payment for the TV starts with a 25 percent down payment, the 12 monthly payments of $30 each must represent the other 75 percent of the cost.

Twelve times $30 = $360, so this is 75 percent, or $\frac{3}{4}$, of the total cost of the TV. So $x\left(\frac{3}{4}\right) = \$360$, where $x$ represents the total cost of the TV. Multiplying both sides by $\frac{4}{3}$ gives us $x = \$480$. This is the total cost of the TV, and the columns are equal.

**9** **D**—Don't forget: Not all numbers are integers. If $a$ were 14 and $b$ were 16, then the columns would be equal. But $a$ could equal 13.5 and $b$ equal 15.5, in which case their sum would be 29, and Column B would be larger. Or $a$ could equal 14.5 and $b$ could equal 16.5, and their sum would be 31, making Column A larger. Since there is more than one possibility, the answer is (D).

**10** **D**—Draw some diagrams. When drawing the triangle we have to remember that the area = $\frac{1}{2}$ base times height = 4. Keeping this in mind, you can easily draw the following:

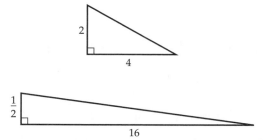

Triangles with equal areas can have very different perimeters. We also know, from the area formula of a circle, $A = \pi r^2$, that the radius of the circle is 2. So its circumference is $2\pi r = 4\pi$ which is approximately 12.56.

The circumference of the circle is obviously greater than the perimeter of the first triangle, but less than the perimeter of the second. However, the area of both triangles is 4. So Column A can be less than or greater than Column B. Therefore, choice (D) is correct.

**11** **A**—This is a symbolism question, but instead of a symbol, it gives us a definition. All that's required is to carefully follow the given instructions, plugging in the values given in each column. To find the "play" of $-\frac{1}{2}$, we find the value of $\frac{1}{\frac{1}{2}}$ and then

subtract that from 1: $\frac{1}{-\frac{1}{2}} = -2.$ $1 - (-2) = 1 + 2,$ or 3.

In Column B, the "play" of $-2$ is $1 - \left(\frac{1}{-2}\right)$, which

equals $1 - \left(-\frac{1}{2}\right)$, or $1 + \frac{1}{2}$. This is clearly less than

3, so Column A is greater.

**12** **B**—To solve this one, you need to set up an equation. We know that 48 questions were answered. Some number of them, which we can call

$x$, were answered correctly. The rest of the 48 were answered incorrectly, so those questions can be represented by $48 - x$. Each correct answer added 1 point, and each incorrect answer deducted $\frac{1}{2}$ point. Since the result was 36 points, we can now set up our equation: $x - \dfrac{48 - x}{2} = 36.$ Multiplying both sides by 2 gives us $2x - (48 - x) = 72$, or $2x - 48 + x = 72$, when we remove the parentheses and distribute the minus sign. Simplifying, we get $3x - 48 = 72$, or $3x = 120$, and $x = 40$. So 40 questions were answered correctly, and 8 incorrectly. (And 8 times $\frac{1}{2}x$ is 4, so this would indeed lower the student's score to 36.) Therefore, Column B is greater than Column A.

**13** **B**—The area of the shaded region can be found by subtracting the area of the right triangle from the area of the quarter circle. Since the radius of the circle is 6, the area of the whole circle is $\pi 6^2$, or $36\pi$. The central angle of 90 degrees is one-quarter of 360 degrees, so this is a quarter circle, with one-quarter the area of the whole circle, or an area of $9\pi$. The area of the right triangle inside the circle is equal to $\frac{1}{2}$(base × height). Since the legs of the triangle are both radii of the circle, and since the circle has radius 6, the area of the triangle must be $\left(\frac{1}{2}\right)(6)(6)$, or 18. So the area of the shaded region is $9\pi - 18$. Since $p$ is slightly greater than 3, $9\pi - 18$ is slightly greater than $9(3) - 18 = 9$, so the value of Column A is slightly greater than 9. Thus, Column B is clearly greater.

You might have saved time by realizing that 18—the area of the right triangle—is also the quantity in Column B, so you can simply compare the area of the triangle with the area of the shaded region. From the diagram you can probably tell that the area of the triangle is larger than the area of the shaded region. Either way, Column B is greater.

**14** A—The illustration is designed to make you think along certain lines and overlook other possibilities. At first glance you might notice only 2 possible right triangles with *AB* as hypotenuse, illustrated in Diagram 1. In fact, there are an infinite number of different right triangles that could have *AB* as their hypotenuse, for example, those shown in Diagram 2.

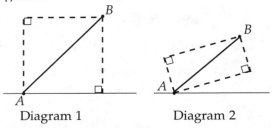

Diagram 1            Diagram 2

Again, when a problem close to the end of a question set has a seemingly obvious answer, it must be wrong. Be suspicious near the end.

**15** A—Since we have three variables and three equations, solve for the value of one variable in terms of the others and then plug that value into another equation.

Since $a - b = c$, we can plug this value for c into the second equation. It becomes $(a - b) - a = 5$, or $-b = 5$, so $b = -5$. Plugging this value into the third equation gives us the value of $c$: $(-5) + c = -2$, so $c = 3$. Now we can use the first equation to solve for *a*: $a - (-5) = 3$, or $a + 5 = 3$, so $a = -2$. That means the value of Column A is $-2$, and the value of Column B is $-5$, so Column A is greater.

**16** 36—The price of the softcover is $\frac{2}{3}$ the price of the hardcover. So the difference between the prices—the extra money you pay to get the hardcover edition—must be the remaining third of the hardcover price. That amount is $12. If $12 is one-third the cost of the hardcover, the full cost must be 3 times that, or $36.

**17** 97.5—Solve the given equation for a :
$$4a - 1 = 64$$
$$4a = 65$$
$$a = 16.25$$
So $6a = 97.5$

**18** 18.5 or 37/2 – To solve a problem like this we have to use the formula for average (average = $\frac{\text{Sum of terms}}{\text{Number of terms}}$ or, restated in the way most useful for this problem, average × the number of terms = the sum of the terms) to find the sum of each set of terms. If the average of 6 numbers is $7\frac{1}{2}$, then the sum of the six terms must be 6 times $7\frac{1}{2}$, or 45. If the average of four of those numbers is 2, then the sum of those four numbers must be 4 times 2, or 8. If those four numbers add up to only 8, then the other two numbers in the group of six must account for the rest of the overall total of 45. Taking away 8 from 45 leaves 37, so that must be the sum of the two remaining numbers. To find their average, we simply divide by two, for a result of $\frac{37}{2}$, or 18.5.

**19** 3/8 or .375—Since $\frac{1}{3}$ of all the yogurts are fruit flavored and $\frac{1}{8}$ are peach, we just need to know what fraction of $\frac{1}{3}$ $\frac{1}{8}$ is. To find that, we simply divide $\frac{1}{8}$ by $\frac{1}{3}$. Dividing by a fraction is the same as multiplying by the reciprocal of the fraction, so $\frac{1}{8} \div \frac{1}{3}$ is the same as $\frac{1}{8} \times \frac{3}{1}$, or $\frac{3}{8}$.

**20** 70—Neither one of the two marked angles can tell us the value of z by itself, but angle z is an interior angle of a triangle, and the marked angles can help us find the value of the other two interior angles. The angle marked 40 degrees is a vertical angle to one of the interior angles of the triangle, so that interior angle must also have a measure of 40 degrees. Since $\ell_1$ and $\ell_2$ are parallel and the two lines that form angle $z$ are transversals, all the obtuse angles formed by the line on the left are equal. That means the obtuse angle right above $\angle z$ on the left is 110 degrees. And that angle, in turn, is supplementary to the remaining interior angle. So the remaining interior angle has a measure of 180 − 110, or 70 degrees.

Now we have the measure of two of the three interior angles. Since they must add up to 180 degrees, we can write an equation: $40 + 70 + z = 180$, and then $110 + z = 180$. Subtracting 110 from both sides gives us $z = 70$.

**21** **38 or 46**—If you list the first several prime numbers—2, 3, 5, 7, 11, 13, 17, 19, 23, 29—you can see that there aren't many pairs that will work. Lots of pairs add up to more than 20, but most have products much greater than 50. In fact, the only way to keep the product under 50 is to combine a prime number close to 20 with 2. But two pairs of prime numbers *will* work. Two and 19 sum to 21 and their product is 38, less than 50. Likewise, 2 and 23 sum to 25, but have a product of only 46. But the next prime after 23, 29, breaks the 50 limit when multiplied by 2. So the only pairs that work are 2 and 19, and 2 and 23, with products of 38 and 46, respectively.

**22** **9**—You'll probably find it helpful to draw a diagram for this one. If you do, you'll see that the triangle in question has a base that runs from (2, 3) to (8, 3), parallel to the $x$-axis. Since it is parallel to the $x$-axis, we can find the length of the base by subtracting the $x$-coordinates: $8 − 2 = 6$, and that's the length of the base.

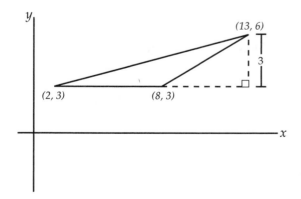

To find the area, we need both the base and height. The vertex of this triangle is off to one side, but all we need to know is the vertical distance from the base to the vertex, and the $y$-coordinates of the points make this easy to find. The base line is parallel to the $x$-axis, so the whole line is at a height of 3, measured along the $y$-axis. The vertex of the triangle has a $y$-coordinate of 6, or 3 units above the base, measured vertically. So the base is 6 and the height is 3.

Area = $\frac{1}{2}$ base times height, or $\frac{1}{2} \times 6 \times 3 = 9$.

**23** **4,000**—This question is easily solved by picking numbers. If we let $y = 100$, then $x$ is $2\frac{1}{2}$ percent of 100, or 2.5. Now what percent of 2.5 is 100? Percent = $\frac{\text{part}}{\text{whole}} \times 100\% = \frac{100}{2.5} \times 100\% = 40 \times 100\% = 4,000\%$.

**24** **8**—$\frac{130}{x}$ will be an integer whenever $x$ is a factor of 130. So we need to find *every number* that's a factor of 130. Perhaps the best approach is to break down 130 into its prime factorization. Obviously $130 = 13 \times 10$. Thirteen is prime, but we can break down 10 into $5 \times 2$. So the prime factorization of 130 is $13 \times 5 \times 2$. That doesn't mean the correct answer is 3, though; these are just the *prime* factors. We can find other factors by multiplying the prime factors together in different combinations: $5 \times 2 = 10$, and 10 is a factor; $5 \times 13 = 65$, and 65 is a factor; $13 \times 2 = 26$, another factor. Also, 130 and 1 are factors of 130. So any of these 8 numbers, divided into 130, will produce an integer value.

**25** **32**—The largest square that can be drawn within a circle is a square that's inscribed in the circle. Draw a diagram:

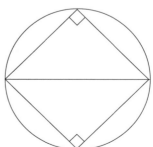

Note that the diagonal of the square is a diameter of the circle. We can find this length from the area of the circle. Since area = $\pi r^2 = 16\pi$, in this case $r^2 = 16$, so the radius of the circle is 4. The diameter is double that, or 8.

So a diagonal of the square has a length of 8. The diagonal divides the square into 2 isosceles right triangles, so the ratio of the diagonal to a side of the square is $\sqrt{2}$:1. Since the diagonal is the length of a side times $\sqrt{2}$, the side is the length of the diagonal *divided by* $\sqrt{2}$. In this case, that means $\frac{8}{\sqrt{2}}$.

Now that we know the length of a side, it's easy to find the area of the square by squaring that side:

$$\left(\frac{8}{\sqrt{2}}\right) = \frac{8^2}{(\sqrt{2})^2} = \frac{64}{2} = 32.$$

## Section 3

**1** **D**—Any number that is divisible by 8 must also be divisible by 4. A number is divisible by 4 if its last two digits form a number that is divisible by 4; the only answer choices for $W$ that will make $5W2$ divisible by 4 are 3 and 5 (since 32 and 52 are both divisible by 4). Dividing 532 and 552 by 8, you see that only 552 leaves no remainder, so $W$ must be 5, answer choice (D).

**2** **B**—Add the terms on the left side of the equation: $\frac{9}{11} = \frac{x}{33}$

Multiply both sides by 33:

$\frac{9}{11} \times 33 = x$

Simplify: $27 = x$.

So $\frac{x}{3} = \frac{27}{3} = 9$.

**3** **A**—For the product $gh$ to be positive, $g$ and $h$ are either both positive or both negative (since a negative times a negative is a positive). Looking at the answer choices, (A) says $\frac{g}{h}$ is positive. If $g$ and $h$ are both positive, this will be true; if $g$ and $h$ are both negative this will also be true. So choice (A) must be correct.

**4** **B**—The angle marked 118 degrees is an exterior angle of the triangle, so its measure is equal to the sum of the two nonadjacent interior angles. This means $a + c = 118$. Angle $b$ is supplementary to the 118 degree angle, so $b = 62$. So $a + c - b = 118 - 62 = 56$, answer choice (B).

**5** **A**—Every term after the first term in this sequence is 3 less than 2 times the term before it, or $2n - 3$, where $n$ represents the term before it. Since the first term is 5, the second term is $2(5) - 3 = 7$. The third term is $2(7) - 3 = 11$. So the fourth term is $2(11) - 3 = 19$. Therefore, the difference between the third term and the fourth terms is $19 - 11 = 8$.

**6** **B**—According to the given information, $x + z = 50$ and $x > 4z + 10$. To find the range of values of $z$, solve for $x$ in terms of $z$ in the first equation:

$x + z = 50$
$x = 50 - z$

Now plug this expression for $x$ into the inequality and solve for $z$ :

$x > 4z + 10$
$50 - z > 4z + 10$
$40 > 5z$
$8 > z$

Since you're given that $z$ is positive, it must be greater than 0. Therefore, $0 < z < 8$.

**7** C—Draw $AD$ as shown below to create $\triangle ADC$:

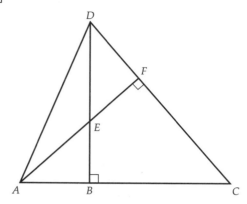

The area of a triangle $= \frac{1}{2}$ (base × height), so the area of $\triangle ADC$ is equal to $\frac{1}{2}(DB \times AC)$ and also equal to $\frac{1}{2}(AF \times DC)$. Therefore, $DB \times AC = AF \times DC$. Now plug in the given measurements to find the length of $AF$:

$$(15)(12) = (AF)(18)$$
$$180 = 18AF$$
$$10 = AF$$

You could have also solved this problem using similar triangles. Since $\triangle AFC$ and $\triangle DBC$ are both right triangles and share $\angle C$, they are similar, and therefore, the lengths of their sides are in proportion. So $\frac{AF}{AC} = \frac{DB}{DC}$, or $\frac{AF}{12} = \frac{15}{18}$. Multiply both sides of the equation by 12 to solve for $AF$: $AF = 10$.

**8** A—Let $x$ = the amount of the chemical two days ago. Since it decays at a rate of 20% each day, the amount of the chemical remaining yesterday is equal to 80% of $x$, or $.8x$. So the amount of the chemical remaining today equals 80% of $.8x$, or $.64x$. Therefore, $.64x$ is equal to 48 pounds of the chemical. So, $.64x = 48$, and $x = 75$.

**9** E—First figure out the number of small 2 by 2 by 4 rectangular solids there are by dividing each dimension of the cube by one of the dimensions of the small solids.

The cube has dimensions 12 by 12 by 12. So along the length, we have $\frac{12}{2}$ or 6 solids. Along the width, we have $\frac{12}{2}$ or 6 solids. Along the height, we have $\frac{12}{4}$ or 3 solids. That gives us a total of $6 \times 6 \times 3$, or 108 small solids.

The surface area of each small solid is the sum of the areas of the six faces. There are four faces that are 2 by 4. They each have an area of 8. The two faces that are 2 by 2 each have an area of 4. So the surface area of each small solid is $4(8) + 2(4) = 32 + 8 = 40$. The combined surface areas of all the smaller rectangular solids is equal to the number of solids times the surface area of each, or $108 \times 40 = 4,320$.

The surface area of the cube is 6 times the area of one face, or 6 times $12^2$, which equals 864.

Since $\frac{4320}{864} = 5$, the combined surface area of all the smaller solids is 5 times greater than the surface area of the original cube.

**10** D—The $8x$ in the quadratic equation represents the sum of the products of the outer and inner terms of the equation in factored form, $(x + \_)(x + \_)$. The $k$ represents the product of the last terms. So to factor the equation, think of pairs of numbers that sum to 8 and whose product is a positive integer less than 17. List the pairs:
$$(x + 1)(x + 7) = 0$$
2 solutions.
$$(x + 2)(x + 6) = 0$$
2 solutions.
$$(x + 3)(x + 5) = 0$$
2 solutions.
$$(x + 4)(x + 4) = 0$$
1 solution.
Since there are 7 different solutions to this equation, answer choice (D) is correct.

## PRACTICE TEST B

Before taking this practice test, find a quiet room where you can work uninterrupted for 75 minutes. Make sure you have a comfortable desk, your calculator, and several No. 2 pencils.

Use the scoresheet on the reverse side of this page to record your answers.

Once you start this practice test, don't stop until you've finished. Remember—you can review any questions within a section, but you may not go back or forward a section.

Good luck.

# ANSWER SHEET

Start with number 1 for each new section. If a section has fewer questions than answer spaces, leave the extra spaces blank.

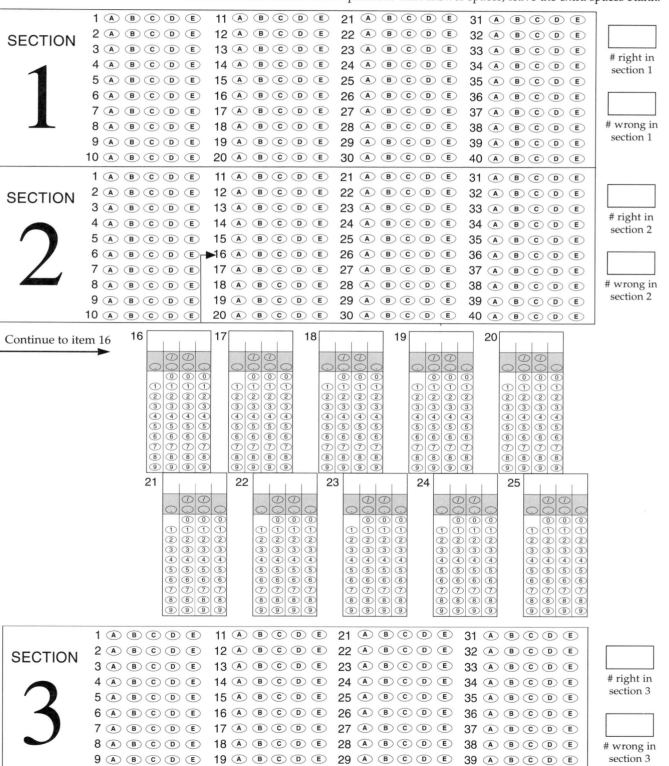

Continue to item 16 →

*Solve each of the following problems, decide which is the best answer choice, and darken the corresponding oval on the answer sheet. Use available space in the test booklet for scratchwork.**

**Notes:**

(1)    Calculator use is permitted.
(2)    All numbers used are real numbers.
(3)    Figures are provided for some problems. All figures are drawn to scale and lie in a plane UNLESS otherwise indicated.

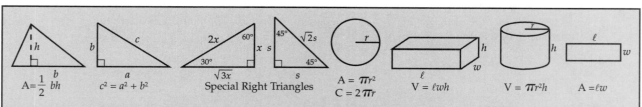

Reference Information

$A = \frac{1}{2} bh$     $c^2 = a^2 + b^2$     Special Right Triangles     $A = \pi r^2$     $V = \ell wh$     $V = \pi r^2 h$     $A = \ell w$
                                                                                   $C = 2\pi r$

The sum of the degree measures of the angles of a triangle is 180.
The number of degrees of arc in a circle is 360.
A straight angle has a degree measure of 180.

---

**1**  Which of the following must be equal to 30 percent of $x$ ?

(A)    $30x$

(B)    $3x$

(C)    $\dfrac{3x}{10}$

(D)    $\dfrac{3x}{100}$

(E)    $\dfrac{3x}{1000}$

**2**  $(2 \times 10^4) + (5 \times 10^3) + (6 \times 10^2) + (4 \times 10^1) =$

(A)    2,564
(B)    20,564
(C)    25,064
(D)    25,604
(E)    25,640

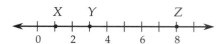

**3**  On the number line shown above, the length of $YZ$ is how much greater than the length of $XY$ ?

(A)    3
(B)    4
(C)    5
(D)    6
(E)    7

**4**  If $2^{x+1} = 16$, what is the value of $x$ ?

(A)    2
(B)    3
(C)    4
(D)    5
(E)    6

---

*The directions on the actual SAT will vary slightly.*

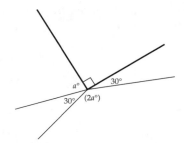

Note: Figure not drawn to scale.

**5** In the figure above, what is the value of $a$ ?

(A)  50
(B)  55
(C)  60
(D)  65
(E)  70

**6** A machine labels 150 bottles in 20 minutes. At this rate, how many minutes does it take to label 60 bottles?

(A)  2
(B)  4
(C)  6
(D)  8
(E)  10

**7** If $x - 1$ is a multiple of 3, which of the following must be the next greater multiple of 3?

(A)  $x$
(B)  $x + 2$
(C)  $x + 3$
(D)  $3x$
(E)  $3x - 3$

**8** When $x$ is divided by 5, the remainder is 4. When $x$ is divided by 9, the remainder is 0. Which of the following is a possible value for $x$ ?

(A)  24
(B)  45
(C)  59
(D)  109
(E)  144

**9** In triangle $ABC$, $AB = 6$, $BC = 12$, and $AC = x$. Which of the following cannot be a value of $x$ ?

(A)  6
(B)  7
(C)  8
(D)  9
(E)  10

**10** The average of 20, 70, and $x$ is 40. If the average of 20, 70, $x$, and $y$ is 50, then $y =$

(A)  100
(B)  80
(C)  70
(D)  60
(E)  30

NUMBER OF BOOKS BORROWED
FROM MIDVILLE PUBLIC LIBRARY

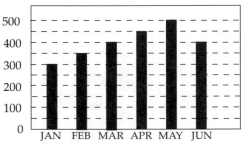

**11** According to the graph above, the number of books borrowed during the month of January was what fraction of the total number of books borrowed during the first six months of the year?

(A)  $\dfrac{1}{8}$

(B)  $\dfrac{1}{7}$

(C)  $\dfrac{1}{6}$

(D)  $\dfrac{3}{16}$

(E)  $\dfrac{5}{12}$

**KAPLAN**

GO ON TO THE NEXT PAGE

**12** If 40 percent of $r$ is equal to $s$, then which of the following is equal to 10 percent of $r$ ?

(A)  $4s$

(B)  $2s$

(C)  $\dfrac{s}{2}$

(D)  $\dfrac{s}{4}$

(E)  $\dfrac{s}{8}$

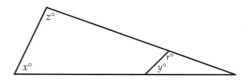

**13** In the figure above, which of the following must be true?

(A)  $x + r = z + y$
(B)  $x + r = z - y$
(C)  $x - y = z + r$
(D)  $x - r = y - z$
(E)  $x + y = z + r$

**14** If a "prifact number" is a nonprime integer such that each factor of the integer other than 1 and the integer itself is a prime number, which of the following is a "prifact number"?

(A)  12
(B)  18
(C)  21
(D)  24
(E)  28

**15** If $3x + y = 14$, and $x$ and $y$ are positive integers, each of the following could be the value of $x + y$ EXCEPT

(A)  12
(B)  10
(C)  8
(D)  6
(E)  4

**16** A certain deck of cards contains $r$ cards. After the cards are distributed evenly among $s$ people, 8 cards are left over. In terms of $r$ and $s$, how many cards did each person receive?

(A)  $\dfrac{s}{8-r}$

(B)  $\dfrac{r-s}{8}$

(C)  $\dfrac{r-8}{s}$

(D)  $s - 8r$

(E)  $rs - 8$

**17** If $d$ is an integer, which of the following CANNOT be an integer?

(A)  $\dfrac{d}{2}$

(B)  $\dfrac{\sqrt{d}}{2}$

(C)  $2d$

(D)  $d\sqrt{2}$

(E)  $d + 2$

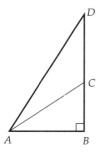

**18** In the figure above, the area of triangle $ABC$ is 6. If $BC = CD$, what is the area of triangle $ACD$ ?

(A)  6
(B)  8
(C)  9
(D)  10
(E)  12

**19** The ratio of $x$ to $y$ to $z$ is 3 to 6 to 8. If $y = 24$, what is the value of $x + z$ ?

(A)  11
(B)  33
(C)  44
(D)  66
(E)  88

**20** What is the minimum number of rectangular tiles, each 12 centimeters by 18 centimeters, needed to completely cover 5 flat rectangular surfaces, each 60 centimeters by 180 centimeters?

(A)   50
(B)  100
(C)  150
(D)  200
(E)  250

**21** If $x + y = 11$, $y + z = 14$, and $x + z = 13$, what is the value of $x + y + z$ ?

(A)  16
(B)  17
(C)  18
(D)  19
(E)  20

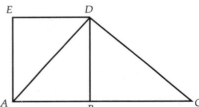

**22** In the figure above, side $AB$ of square $ABDE$ is extended to point $C$. If $BC = 8$ and $CD = 10$, what is the perimeter of triangle $ACD$ ?

(A)  $18 + 6\sqrt{2}$
(B)  $24 + 6\sqrt{2}$
(C)  $26 + 6\sqrt{2}$
(D)  30
(E)  36

**23** If $r < 0$ and $(4r - 4)^2 = 36$, what is the value of $r$ ?

(A)  $-2$
(B)  $-1$
(C)  $-\dfrac{1}{2}$
(D)  $-\dfrac{1}{4}$
(E)  $-\dfrac{1}{8}$

**24** Five liters of water were poured from tank $A$ into tank $B$, and ten liters of water were then poured from tank $A$ into tank $C$. If tank $A$ originally had 10 more liters of water than tank $C$, how many more liters of water does tank $C$ now have than tank $A$ ?

(A)   0
(B)   5
(C)  10
(D)  15
(E)  20

**25** If a cube has a surface area of $36n^2$ square feet, what is its volume in cubic feet, in terms of $n$ ?

(A)  $n^3\sqrt{6}$
(B)  $6n^3\sqrt{6}$
(C)  $36n^3$
(D)  $36n^3\sqrt{6}$
(E)  $216n^3$

**STOP**  IF YOU FINISH BEFORE TIME IS CALLED, YOU MAY CHECK YOUR WORK ON THIS SECTION ONLY. **DO NOT** TURN TO ANY OTHER SECTION IN THE TEST.

*Solve each of the following problems, decide which is the best answer choice, and darken the corresponding oval on the answer sheet. Use available space in the test booklet for scratchwork.\**

**Notes:**

(1)   Calculator use is permitted.
(2)   All numbers used are real numbers.
(3)   Figures are provided for some problems. All figures are drawn to scale and lie in a plane UNLESS otherwise indicated.

Reference Information

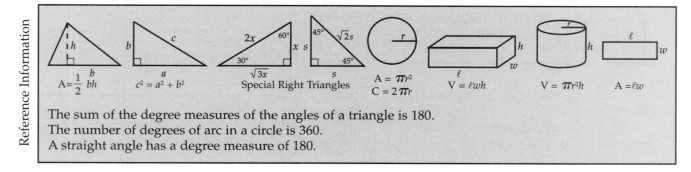

$$A = \frac{1}{2} bh \qquad c^2 = a^2 + b^2 \qquad \text{Special Right Triangles} \qquad \begin{array}{l} A = \pi r^2 \\ C = 2\pi r \end{array} \qquad V = \ell wh \qquad V = \pi r^2 h \qquad A = \ell w$$

The sum of the degree measures of the angles of a triangle is 180.
The number of degrees of arc in a circle is 360.
A straight angle has a degree measure of 180.

## DIRECTIONS FOR QUANTITATIVE COMPARISON QUESTIONS

Compare the boxed quantity in Column A with the boxed quantity in Column B. Select answer choice

   A   if Column A is greater;
   B   if Column B is greater;
   C   if the columns are equal; or
   D   if more information is needed to determine the relationship.

An E response will be treated as an omission.

Notes:

1.   Some questions include information about one or both quantities. That information is centered and unboxed.
2.   A symbol that appears in both Column A and Column B stands for the same thing in both columns.
3.   All numbers used are real numbers.

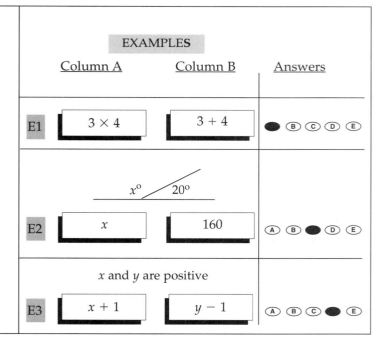

| **Column A** | **Column B** |
|---|---|

**1**    $\dfrac{3}{8} + \dfrac{2}{5}$      1

**2**    The cost of 6 pens at 2 for 22 cents      The cost of 5 pens at 22 cents each

$$2a + b = 17$$
$$b - 3 = 2$$

**3**    $a$      $b$

**4**    $x - 2(y + z)$      $x - 2y - 2z$

$a$, $b$, and $c$ are positive integers such that $a + b + c = 150$.

**5**    The mean of $a$, $b$, and $c$      The median of $a$, $b$, and $c$

For all numbers $x$ and $y$, let $x * y = (x + y)^3$.

**6**    $4 * 5$      $0 * 9$

| **Column A** | **Column B** |
|---|---|

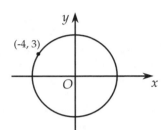

(-4, 3)

**7**    The circumference of circle $O$      30

Jimmy owns a plant he waters every other day.

**8**    The number of times Jimmy waters the plant during a certain week      The number of times Jimmy waters the plant during the following week

A certain line in the rectangular coordinate plane contains the points $(1, 1)$, $(3, r)$, $(s, 9)$, and $(6, 11)$.

**9**    $r$      $s$

$$r^2 + 4 = 21$$

**10**    $r$      4

**KAPLAN**

GO ON TO THE NEXT PAGE

| Column A | Column B | | Column A | Column B |
|----------|----------|--|----------|----------|

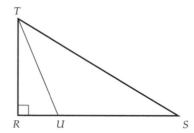

In right triangle *RST,*
*RT = US* = 6 and *RU* < 2.

**11**

| The perimeter of RST | 24 |
|----------------------|----|

At a science fair, 5 students are semifinalists for 1st and 2nd place prizes.

**12**

| The total number of ways to select the two science fair prize winners | 10 |
|---|---|

$x > 0$
$0 < x^2 < 1$

**13**

| $1 - x^2$ | $1 - x$ |
|-----------|---------|

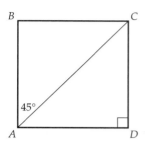

Note: Figure not drawn to scale.

**14**

| The length of *AB* | 4 |
|--------------------|---|

*t* is a positive integer.

**15**

| The number of distinct prime factors of 2t | The number of distinct prime factors of 8t |
|---|---|

GO ON TO THE NEXT PAGE

### DIRECTIONS FOR STUDENT-PRODUCED RESPONSE QUESTIONS

For each of the questions below (16–25), solve the problem and indicate your answer by darkening the ovals in the special grid. For example:

Answer: 1.25 or $\frac{5}{4}$ or 5/4

Write answer in boxes. →

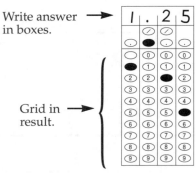

Grid in result. →

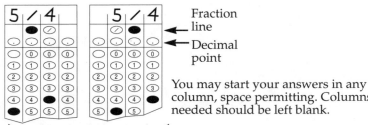

← Fraction line

← Decimal point

You may start your answers in any column, space permitting. Columns not needed should be left blank.

Either position is correct.

- It is recommended, though not required, that you write your answer in the boxes at the top of the columns. However, you will receive credit only for darkening the ovals correctly.

- Grid only one answer to a question, even though some problems have more than one correct answer.

- Darken no more than one oval in a column.

- No answers are negative.

- Mixed numbers cannot be gridded. For example: the number $1\frac{1}{4}$ must be gridded as 1.25 or 5/4.

  (If $\boxed{1\,1\,/\,4}$ is gridded, it will be interpreted as $\frac{11}{4}$, not $1\frac{1}{4}$.)

- Decimal Accuracy: Decimal answers must be entered as accurately as possible. For example, if you obtain an answer such as 0.1666. . ., you should record the result as .166 or .167. **Less accurate values such as .16 or .17 are not acceptable.**

Acceptable ways to grid $\frac{1}{6}$ = .1666. . .

**16** If $A = 2.54$ and $20B = A$, what is the value of $B$ ?

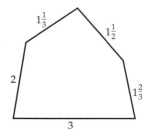

**17** What is the perimeter of the figure above?

**GO ON TO THE NEXT PAGE**

**18** If $\frac{h}{3}$ and $\frac{h}{4}$ are integers, and if $75 < h < 100$, what is one possible value of $h$ ?

**19** A retailer buys 16 shirts at $4.50 each and she sells all 16 shirts for $6.75 each. If the retailer purchases more of these shirts at $4.50 each, what is the greatest number of these shirts that she can buy with the profit she made on the 16 shirts?

**20** Lines $\ell$ and $m$ intersect at a point to form four angles. If one of the angles formed is 15 times as large as an adjacent angle, what is the measure, in degrees, of the smaller angle?

**21** If $x = -4$ when $x^2 + 2xr + r^2 = 0$, what is the value of $r$ ?

**22** Let $n\ast = n^2 - n$ for all positive numbers $n$. What is the value of $\frac{1}{4}\ast - \frac{1}{2}\ast$ ?

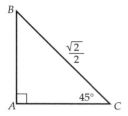

**23** What is the area of $\triangle ABC$ shown above?

**24** If $x$ is a factor of 8,100 and if $x$ is an odd integer, what is the greatest possible value of $x$ ?

**25** In a certain class, $\frac{1}{2}$ of the male students and $\frac{2}{3}$ of the female students speak French. If there are $\frac{3}{4}$ as many girls as boys in the class, what fraction of the entire class speaks French?

**STOP** IF YOU FINISH BEFORE TIME IS CALLED, YOU MAY CHECK YOUR WORK ON THIS SECTION ONLY. **DO NOT** TURN TO ANY OTHER SECTION IN THE TEST.

*Solve each of the following problems, decide which is the best answer choice, and darken the corresponding oval on the answer sheet. Use available space in the test booklet for scratchwork.\**

**Notes:**

(1)   Calculator use is permitted.
(2)   All numbers used are real numbers.
(3)   Figures are provided for some problems. All figures are drawn to scale and lie in a plane UNLESS otherwise indicated.

Reference Information

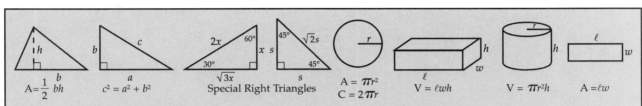

$A = \dfrac{1}{2} bh$    $c^2 = a^2 + b^2$    Special Right Triangles    $A = \pi r^2$ $C = 2\pi r$    $V = \ell wh$    $V = \pi r^2 h$    $A = \ell w$

The sum of the degree measures of the angles of a triangle is 180.
The number of degrees of arc in a circle is 360.
A straight angle has a degree measure of 180.

**1**   If $p = -2$ and $q = 3$, then $p^3 q^2 + p^2 q =$

(A)   −84
(B)   −60
(C)   36
(D)   60
(E)   84

| N | P |
|---|---|
| 2 | 7 |
| 4 | 13 |
| 6 | 19 |
| 8 | 25 |

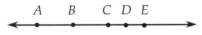

A    B    C D E

Note: Figure not drawn to scale.

**2**   In the figure above, $B$ is the midpoint of $AC$ and $D$ is the midpoint of $CE$. If $AB = 5$ and $BD = 8$, what is the length of $DE$ ?

(A)   8
(B)   6
(C)   5
(D)   4
(E)   3

**3**   Which of the following equations describes the relationship of each pair of numbers $(N, P)$ in the table above?

(A)   $P = N + 5$
(B)   $P = 2N + 3$
(C)   $P = 2N + 5$
(D)   $P = 3N + 1$
(E)   $P = 3N - 1$

*\*The directions on the actual SAT will vary slightly.*

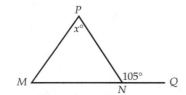

Note: Figure not drawn to scale.

4  In the figure above, *MQ* is a straight line. If *PM* = *PN*, what is the value of *x* ?

(A)  30
(B)  45
(C)  60
(D)  75
(E)  90

5  Marty has exactly 5 blue pens, 6 black pens, and 4 red pens in his knapsack. If he pulls out one pen at random from his knapsack, what is the probability that the pen is either red or black?

(A)  $\frac{11}{15}$

(B)  $\frac{2}{3}$

(C)  $\frac{1}{2}$

(D)  $\frac{1}{3}$

(E)  $\frac{1}{5}$

6  Two hot dogs and a soda cost $3.25. If three hot dogs and a soda cost $4.50, what is the cost of two sodas?

(A)  $0.75
(B)  $1.25
(C)  $1.50
(D)  $2.50
(E)  $3.00

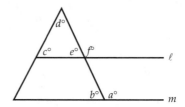

7  In the figure above, if $\ell \parallel m$, which of the following must be equal to *a* ?

(A)  *b* + *c*
(B)  *b* + *e*
(C)  *c* + *d*
(D)  *d* + *e*
(E)  *d* + *f*

8  A certain phone call cost 75 cents for the first 3 minutes plus 15 cents for each additional minute. If the call lasted *x* minutes and *x* is an integer greater than 3, which of the following expresses the cost of the call, in dollars?

(A)  0.75(3) + 0.15*x*
(B)  0.75(3) + 0.15(*x* + 3)
(C)  0.75 + 0.15(3 − *x*)
(D)  0.75 + 0.15(*x* − 3)
(E)  0.75 + 0.15*x*

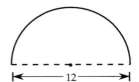

9   The figure above shows a piece of wire in the shape of a semicircle. If the piece of wire is bent to form a circle without any of the wire overlapping, what is the area of the circle?

(A)   $6\pi$
(B)   $9\pi$
(C)   $12\pi$
(D)   $18\pi$
(E)   $36\pi$

10   If $a^2 - a = 72$, and $b$ and $n$ are integers such that $b^n = a$, which of the following cannot be a value for $b$ ?

(A)   $-8$
(B)   $-2$
(C)   $2$
(D)   $3$
(E)   $9$

**STOP**   IF YOU FINISH BEFORE TIME IS CALLED, YOU MAY CHECK YOUR WORK ON THIS SECTION ONLY. **DO NOT** TURN TO ANY OTHER SECTION IN THE TEST.

# PRACTICE TEST B—ANSWERS AND EXPLANATIONS

## SECTION 1

**1** **C**—Use the formula Percent × Whole = Part. Thirty percent is $\frac{30}{100}$, or $\frac{3}{10}$. So $\frac{3}{10} \times x$ = part, and choice (C) is correct.

**2** **E**—$2 \times 10^4 = 20,000$. $5 \times 10^3 = 5,000$. $6 \times 10^2 = 600$. $4 \times 10^1 = 40$. So the sum is 25,640.

**3** **A**—Find the length of each segment, and then subtract the length of $XY$ from the length of $YZ$. $Y$ is at 3 on the number line and $Z$ is at 8, so the length of $YZ$ is $8 - 3 = 5$. $X$ is at 1 on the number line and $Y$ is at 3, so the length of $XY$ is $3 - 1 = 2$. So the length of $YZ$ is $5 - 2 = 3$ greater than the length of $XY$.

**4** **B**—To find the value of $x$, you need to change 16 into a power of 2: $16 = 2^4$. Therefore, $2^{x+1} = 2^4$. So $x + 1 = 4$, or $x = 3$.

**5** **E**—The number of degrees around a point is 360. Therefore:
$$90 + 30 + 2a + 30 + a = 360$$
$$150 + 3a = 360$$
$$3a = 210$$
$$a = 70$$

**6** **D**—If a machine labels 150 bottles in 20 minutes, it labels 15 bottles every 2 minutes. To label 60, or $4 \times 15$, bottles would take $4 \times 2$, or 8 minutes.

**7** **B**—To find the next multiple of 3, simply add 3 to the expression: $x - 1 + 3 = x + 2$, choice (B).

If this is unclear, pick a number for $x$. If $x = 4$, $4 - 1 = 3$; the next greatest multiple of 3 is 6. Plugging 4 for $x$ into each answer choice, we find that only choice (B) gives us 6.

**8** **E**—Since $x$ leaves a remainder of 4 when divided by 5, it must end in either a 4 or a 9, so choice (B) can be eliminated. Since $x$ leaves no remainder when divided by 9, it is evenly divisible by 9. Of the remaining choices only 144 is divisible by 9.

**9** **A**—The sum of the lengths of any two sides of a triangle must be greater than the length of the third side. So $AB + AC$ must be greater than $BC$; $6 + x > 12$. If $x = 6$, $6 + 6 = 12$ is not greater than 12, so $x$ cannot equal 6.

**10** **B**—Number of terms × average = sum of the terms. For the first group, $3 \times 40 = 120$, so the sum of 20, 70, and $x$ is 120. For the second group, $4 \times 50 = 200$, so $20 + 70 + x + y = 200$. Since the sum of the first three terms is 120, $120 + y = 200$, $y = 80$.

**11** **A**—Looking at the graph, you can see that the number of books borrowed in January was 300. To find the total number of books borrowed during the first six months of the year, add the values of each bar: $300 + 350 + 400 + 450 + 500 + 400 = 2,400$ books. So the number of books borrowed in January is $\frac{300}{2400}$ or $\frac{1}{8}$ of the total number of books borrowed during the first six months of the year.

**12** **D**—We're told that 40% of $r = s$. The value of 40% of $r$ is 4 times the value of 10% of $r$, so 10% of $r = \frac{1}{4} \times s = \frac{s}{4}$.

An alternative method is to pick numbers. Since you're dealing with percents, let $r = 100$. Forty percent of $r = s$, so 40% of $100 = 40 = s$. You're asked which answer choice is equal to 10% of $r$; 10% of $100 = 10$. Now plug the value for $s$ into the answer choices to see which ones give you 10:

(A)  $4s = 4 \times 40 = 160$. Eliminate.

(B)  $2s = 2 \times 40 = 80$. Eliminate.

(C)  $\frac{s}{2} = \frac{40}{2} = 20$. Eliminate.

(D)  $\frac{s}{4} = \frac{40}{4} = 10$. Works!

(E)  $\frac{s}{8} = \frac{40}{8} = 5$. Eliminate.

Since (D) is the only choice that produces the desired result, it is the correct answer. But remember, when picking numbers you need to check all the answer choices; if more than one works, pick new numbers and plug them in until only one answer choice works.

**13** D—The two overlapping triangles share a common angle, which we can label $p°$. Since the interior angles of any triangle add up to 180°, we have two equations: $x + z + p = 180$ and $y + r + p = 180$. Subtracting $p$ from both sides of each equation, we have $x + z = 180 – p$ and $y + r = 180 – p$. Since $x + z$ and $y + r$ both equal the same quantity, $x + z$ and $y + r$ must be equal to each other. Rearranging $x + z = y + r$, we get $x – r = y – z$, which matches choice (D).

**14** C—Check the answer choices. If a number has even one factor (not including 1 and itself) that is not a prime number, eliminate that choice:
- (A) 12: 4 is not prime. Eliminate.
- (B) 18: 6 is not prime. Eliminate.
- (C) 21: 3 and 7 are its only other factors, and both are prime. Correct!
- (D) 24: 6 is not prime. Eliminate.
- (E) 28: 4 is not prime. Eliminate.

**15** E—Try different possible values for $x$ and $y$, eliminating the incorrect answer choices. Since $x$ is multiplied by 3, let's begin with the smallest positive integer value for $x$: 1. If $3(1) + y = 14$, then $y = 11$, and $x + y = 12$. So choice (A) is out.

If $3(2) + y = 14$, then $y = 8$, and $x + y = 10$. So choice (B) is out. If $3(3) + y = 14$, then $y = 5$, and $x + y = 8$. So choice (C) is also out. If you're really clever, you'll see at this point that answer choice (E) is impossible (which makes it the right choice). After all, the next smallest possible value of $x$ is 4, and since $x$ and $y$ must both be positive integers, neither one can equal 0. (Zero is *not* positive—or negative.) So the sum of $x$ and $y$ must be greater than 4. (Sure enough, if $x = 4$, then $y = 2$, and $x + y = 6$, eliminating choice (D) as well.)

**16** C—When the $r$ cards are distributed, there are 8 left over, so the number of cards distributed is $r – 8$. Divide the number of cards distributed by the number of people. Since there are $s$ people, each person gets $\dfrac{r-8}{s}$ cards.

Another approach is to pick numbers. Let $r = 58$ and $s = 10$; if $58 – 8$ or 50 cards were distributed evenly among 10 people, each would receive 5 cards. Plug the values you picked for $r$ and $s$ into the answer choices to see which ones give you 5:

(A) $\dfrac{s}{8-r} = \dfrac{10}{8-58} = -\dfrac{1}{5}$ Eliminate.

(B) $\dfrac{r-s}{8} = \dfrac{58-10}{8} = 6$. Eliminate.

(C) $\dfrac{r-8}{s} = \dfrac{58-8}{10} = 5$. Works!

(D) $s – 8r = 10 – (8 \times 58) = –454$. Eliminate.

(E) $rs – 8 = (58 \times 10) – 8 = 572$. Eliminate.

Since (C) is the only answer choice that gives you 5, it is the correct answer. But be sure to check all the answer choices when picking numbers.

**17** D—Check each answer choice to see which doesn't work:

(A) $\dfrac{d}{2}$: If $d$ is an even integer, say 2, then $\dfrac{d}{2} = \dfrac{2}{2} = 1$ is an integer. Eliminate.

(B) $\sqrt{d}$: If $d$ is a perfect square with an even square root, say $d = 4$, then $\dfrac{\sqrt{4}}{2} = \dfrac{2}{2} = 1$ is an integer. Eliminate.

(C) $2d$: This will always produce an even integer; if $d = 3$, $2d = 2 \times 3 = 6$ is an integer. Eliminate.

(D) $d\sqrt{2}$ CANNOT produce an integer. An integer would result if $\sqrt{2}$ is multiplied by another multiple of $\sqrt{2}$, which is impossible because $d$ must be an integer. So (D) is correct.

Let's check (E) just to make sure.

(E) $d + 2$: This will always produce an integer; if $d = 5$, $d + 2 = 5 + 2 = 7$ is an integer. Eliminate.

**18** A—The area of a triangle $= \dfrac{1}{2}$(base × height). Since the area of $\triangle ABC$ is 6, $\dfrac{1}{2}(AB \times BC) = 6$. If you consider $CD$ as the base of $\triangle ACD$, you will notice that its height is represented by altitude $AB$. So the area of $\triangle ACD = \dfrac{1}{2}(CD \times AB)$. Since $CD = BC$, the area of $\triangle ACD$ can be expressed as $\dfrac{1}{2}(BC \times AB)$, which you know equals 6.

**19** **C**—Since the ratio of $x$ to $y$ to $z$ is 3:6:8, if $y = 24$ or $4 \times 6$, $x$ and $z$ must also be multiplied by 4 for the ratio to hold. So $x = 4 \times 3 = 12$ and $z = 4 \times 8 = 32$, and $x + z = 44$.

**20** **E**—Each of the five surfaces is 60 by 180 centimeters, so tiles measuring 12 by 18 centimeters can be laid down in 5 rows of 10 to exactly cover one surface. There are 5 surfaces so $5 \times 5 \times 10 = 250$ tiles are needed.

**21** **D**—If you add the 3 equations together, you find that $2x + 2y + 2z = 38$; dividing both sides by 2 shows that $x + y + z = 19$, answer choice (D).

**22** **B**—The perimeter of triangle $ACD = AD + AB + BC + CD$. You are given the lengths of $BC$ and $CD$, so you need to find the lengths of $AD$ and $AB$. Angle $DBC$ is a right angle because it is supplementary to $\angle DBA$, one of the 4 right angles of square $ABDE$. Since right triangle $DBC$ has sides of length 8 and 10, you should recognize it as a 6-8-10 right triangle (a multiple of the 3-4-5 right triangle) and realize that $BD = 6$. (If you didn't recognize this you could have used the Pythagorean theorem to find the length of $BD$.) $BD$ is also a side of the square and since all sides of a square are equal, $AB = 6$.

So triangle $DBA$ is an isosceles right triangle with sides in the ratio of $1:1:\sqrt{2}$. That means hypotenuse $AD$ is equal to the length of a side times $\sqrt{2}$, so $AD = 6\sqrt{2}$. Now you can find the perimeter of triangle $ACD$: $6\sqrt{2} + 6 + 8 + 10 = 24 + 6\sqrt{2}$.

**23** **C**—$(4r - 4)^2 = 36$, so $4r - 4$ could equal 6 or $-6$, since the result is 36 when each of these integers is squared.

But the problem states that $r < 0$, so try $-6$. $4r - 4 = -6$, $4r = -2$, and $r = -\dfrac{2}{4} = -\dfrac{1}{2}$, answer choice (C). (If you try $4r - 4 = 6$ you'll find $r = 2\dfrac{1}{2}$, which cannot be correct for this question since $r < 0$.)

**24** **D**—Tank $A$ originally contained 10 more liters of water than tank $C$, so represent the initial number of liters in each tank in terms of tank $A$:

tank $A = a$
tank $C = a - 10$

5 liters of water are poured from $A$ to $B$, and an additional 10 liters are poured from $A$ to $C$. A total of 15 liters are removed from tank $A$ so it now contains $a - 15$ liters of water. 10 liters are added to tank $C$ so it now contains $a - 10 + 10 = a$ liters. So tank $C$ contains 15 more liters of water than tank $A$.

**25** **B** – The surface area of a cube is $6e^2$, where $e = $ the length of an edge of the cube. Since the surface area is $36n^2$:

$$6e^2 = 36n^2$$
$$e^2 = 6n^2$$
$$e = n\sqrt{6}$$

The volume of a cube is $e^3$. To solve for the volume in terms of $n$, plug in the value for an edge that you just found: Volume $= e^3 = (n6)^3 = 6n^3\sqrt{6}$, answer choice (B).

## SECTION 2

**1** **B**—You could find the answer by calculating the value of Column A, but there's a shortcut. You should see that both fractions in Column A are less than $\dfrac{1}{2}$. Therefore, their sum must be less than 1, and Column B is greater than Column A.

**2** **B**—The cost of 6 pens at 2 for 22 cents is $\dfrac{22}{2}$ cents $\times 6$, or \$0.66, which is the value of Column A. The cost of 5 pens at 22 cents each is \$1.10, and that's the value of Column B. So Column B is greater, and choice (B) is correct.

**3** **A**—You can solve for $b$ using the second equation: $b - 3 = 2$, so $b = 5$. Plug in 5 for $b$ in the first equation and solve for $a$: $2a + 5 = 17$, $2a = 12$, $a = 6$. So Column A is greater than Column B, and choice (A) is correct.

**4** **C**—Make one column look more like the other. Perform the multiplication in Column A: $x - 2(y + z)$ becomes $x - 2y - 2z$, which is the same expression as in Column B. Therefore, choice (C) is correct.

**5** **D**—The mean (or average) of a group of terms is equal to the sum of the terms divided by the number of terms. You don't know the values of $a$, $b$, or $c$, but you do know that they sum to 150. So in Column A their mean is $\frac{150}{3} = 50$.

The median is the middle term in a group of terms in numerical order. All you know about $a$, $b$, and $c$ is that their sum is 150. It is possible that $a = 1$, $b = 2$, and $c = 147$; if so, the median would be 2 and in this case Column A would be greater. But what if $a = b = c = 50$? Then the median would be 50 and the columns would be equal. Since more than one relationship between the columns is possible, the answer must be choice (D).

**6** **C**—Plug the values from each column into the given expression:
Column A = $(4 + 5)^3$ or $(9)^3$. Column B = $(0 + 9)^3$ or $(9)^3$.
Since the values in both columns are equal, choice (C) is correct.

**7** **A**—To find the circumference of circle $O$, you need to find the length of its radius. Draw a right triangle as shown below:

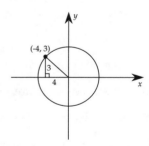

The lengths of the legs of the triangle are 4 and 3. You should recognize that this is a special 3-4-5 right triangle, so the length of the hypotenuse, which is also the radius of the circle, must be 5. Since circumference = $2\pi r$, the circumference of circle $O$ = $10\pi$. Since $\pi$ is approximately 3.14, the circumference of circle $O$ is greater than 30; Column A is greater than Column B.

**8** **D**—If Jimmy waters his plant every other day, the number of times he waters it in one week depends upon whether he waters it the first day of the week or not. If he does, then he will water the plant the first, third, fifth, and seventh days for a total of 4 times that week. So Column A can be 4. Then the following week he will water it on the second, fourth, and sixth days for a total of 3 times. So Column B is 3, which makes Column A greater in this case. However, it's possible that in a given week he doesn't water the plant until the second day of the week. Then he will water it only 3 times that week and 4 times the following week. In this case, Column A is 3 and Column B is 4, making Column B greater. So Column A can be either greater than or less than Column B, and the answer must be choice (D).

**9** **C**—To find the values of $r$ and $s$, you need to find the slope of the line. Plug coordinates (1, 1) and (6, 11) into the slope formula:

$$\text{Slope} = \frac{y_2 - y_1}{x_2 - x_1}$$
$$= \frac{11 - 1}{6 - 1}$$
$$= \frac{10}{5}$$
$$= 2$$

So the slope of the line is 2.
Now find the value of $r$ using coordinates (1, 1) and (3, $r$):

$$2 = \frac{r - 1}{3 - 1}$$
$$2 = \frac{r - 1}{2}$$
$$4 = r - 1$$
$$5 = r$$

Then find the value of $s$ using coordinates ($s$, 9) and (6, 11):

$$2 = \frac{11 - 9}{6 - s}$$
$$2 = \frac{2}{6 - s}$$
$$12 - 2s = 2$$
$$-2s = -10$$
$$s = 5$$

The values in both columns are the same, and choice (C) is correct.

**10** **D**—$r^2 + 4 = 21$, so $r^2 = 17$. You might think this means that $r$ in Column A is greater than 4 in Column B, since $r^2 = 17$ while $4^2$ equals only 16. But $r$ can have a positive or negative value, since a neg-

**KAPLAN**

ative squared also produces a positive. If $r$ has a positive value, Column A is greater; if $r$ has a negative value, Column B is greater. Since more than one relationship is possible, the answer is choice (D).

**11** **B**—The perimeter of a triangle is equal to the sum of the lengths of its sides. You're given that $RT = US = 6$ and $RU < 2$. This means that $RS$ must be less than 8. However, if $RS = 8$, then triangle $RST$ would be a special right triangle with side lengths in a ratio of 3:4:5. So the length of $ST$ would be 10, and the perimeter would be $6 + 8 + 10$, or 24. But $RS$ is less than 8, which means the perimeter must be less than 24. Therefore, Column B is greater than Column A, and choice (B) is correct.

**12** **A**—Think of the 5 students as $A$, $B$, $C$, $D$, and $E$, then systematically consider all of the possible winning combinations. If A wins 1st place, $B$, $C$, $D$, or $E$ could win 2nd; if $B$ wins 1st place, $A$, $C$, $D$, or $E$ could win 2nd; if $C$ wins 1st place, $A$, $B$, $D$, or $E$ could win 2nd; if $D$ wins 1st place, $A$, $B$, $C$, or $E$ could win 2nd; if $E$ wins 1st place, $A$, $B$, $C$, or $D$ could win 2nd. This is a total of 20 different combinations, so column A is greater than 10 in column B.

**13** **A**—Since $x^2$ is a positive fraction less than 1, its positive square root, $x$, must also be a fraction less than 1, which you are told is positive. When a positive fraction less than 1 is squared, the result is a positive fraction smaller than the original. Therefore, $x^2 < x$.

For example, $\left(\frac{1}{2}\right)^2 < \frac{1}{2}$, since $\left(\frac{1}{2}\right)^2 = \frac{1}{4}$. So in Column A you're subtracting a positive value from 1, and in Column B you're subtracting a larger positive value from 1, so Column A must be greater.

**14** **D**—Do not assume that $ABCD$ is a square and that $AB = BC = AD = 4$. You know that triangle $ACD$ is an isosceles right triangle and angle $CAD$ is a 45° angle, which means that angle $BAD$ is a right angle. However, no information is given about the lengths of $AB$ and $BC$, or whether angles $ABC$ and $BCD$ are right angles. If necessary, redraw the diagram to see this. So the relationship cannot be determined and answer choice (D) is correct.

**15** **C**—To determine the number of distinct prime factors of an integer, break the integer down into its prime factors and see how many different prime factors it has. Since you don't know the value of $t$, there is no way to determine how many distinct prime factors it has. This isn't a problem though—since $t$ appears as a factor in both of the columns, we can eliminate it from each without affecting the relationship between the columns. So that leaves 2 in Column A and 8 in Column B. The only prime factor of 2 is 2, and the prime factorization of 8 is $2 \times 2 \times 2$. While 2 appears as a factor three times in Column B, there is still only one distinct prime factor in each, so the columns are equal.

**16** **.127**—If $A = 2.54$ and $20B = A$, then $20B = 2.54$. So $B = \frac{2.54}{20}$ or .127.

**17** **9.5 or 19/2**—The perimeter of the figure is equal to the sum of the lengths of its sides: $2 + 1\frac{1}{3} + 1\frac{1}{2} + 1\frac{2}{3} + 3 = 9\frac{1}{2}$, which is $\frac{19}{2}$ expressed as an improper fraction, or 9.5 expressed as a decimal.

**18** **84 or 96**—If $\frac{h}{3}$ and $\frac{h}{4}$ are both integers, then $h$ must be a multiple of $3 \times 4$, or 12. Since it's given that $h$ is between 75 and 100, $h$ must be 84 or 96.

**19** **8**—The profit made by the retailer on the shirts is equal to the difference between the selling price and the cost for each shirt, multiplied by the number of shirts: ($6.75 – $4.50) × 16 = $2.25 × 16 = $36.00 profit. To find the number of $4.50 shirts that can be bought for $36.00, you need to divide $36.00 by $4.50, and $\frac{36}{4.5} = 8$.

**20** **45/4 or 11.2 or 11.3**—Draw a diagram and label it according to the given information:

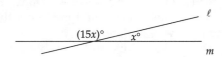

Let the smaller angle measure $x°$. Since the other angle formed is 15 times as large, label it $(15x)°$. Notice that these two angles are supplementary, that is, they add up to 180°. Therefore:

$$x + 15x = 180$$
$$16x = 180$$
$$x = \frac{45}{4}$$

So the smaller angle is $\frac{45}{4}$ degrees, which can also be gridded in decimal form as 11.2 or 11.3.

**21** **4**—Before you plug in –4 for $x$, you should factor the given equation:

$$x^2 + 2xr + r^2 = 0$$
$$(x + r)(x + r) = 0$$
$$(x + r)^2 = 0$$

Now plug in –4 for $x$ to solve for $r$: $(-4 + r)^2 = 0$, $-4 + r = 0$, and $r = 4$.

**22** **1/16 or .062 or .063**—Plug the values into the given definition:

$$\frac{1}{4} * = \left(\frac{1}{4}\right)^2 - \frac{1}{4}$$
$$= \frac{1}{16} - \frac{1}{4}$$
$$= \frac{1}{16} - \frac{4}{16}$$
$$= \frac{-3}{16}$$

$$\frac{1}{2} * = \left(\frac{1}{2}\right)^2 - \frac{1}{2}$$
$$= \frac{1}{4} - \frac{1}{2}$$
$$= \frac{-1}{4}$$

So:

$$\frac{1}{4} * - \frac{1}{2} * = \frac{-3}{16} - \left(\frac{-1}{4}\right)$$
$$= \frac{-3}{16} - \left(-\frac{4}{16}\right)$$
$$= \frac{1}{16}$$

This can also be gridded as .062 or .063.

**23** **1/8 or .125**—You should recognize that right $\triangle ABC$ is a 45-45-90 triangle, with side lengths in a ratio of $1:1:\sqrt{2}$. Therefore, the length of the two equal legs $AB$ and $AC$ is $\frac{1}{2}$.

To find the area of the triangle, plug the values of the base and height (the lengths of the two equal legs) into the area formula:

$$\text{Area of a triangle} = \frac{1}{2}(\text{base} \times \text{height})$$
$$= \frac{1}{2}\left(\frac{1}{2}\right)^2$$
$$= \frac{1}{2}\left(\frac{1}{4}\right)$$
$$= \frac{1}{8}, \text{ or } .125$$

**24** **2,025**—You're given that $x$ is a factor of 8,100 and it's an odd integer. To find the greatest possible value of $x$, begin factoring 8,100 by using its smallest prime factor, 2, as one of the factors. Continue factoring out a 2 from the remaining factors until you find an odd one as shown below:

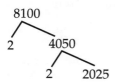

8,100
2 × 4,050
2 × 2,025
Since 2,025 is odd, you can stop factoring; it is the greatest odd factor of 8,100.

**25** **4/7 or .571**—Translate the problem into math: Let $b$ = number of boys; let $g$ = number of girls. So $b + g$ = total number of students in the class.

$\frac{1}{2}$ of the boys speak French, so $\frac{1}{2}b$ = the number of boys who speak French.

$\frac{2}{3}$ of the girls speak French, so $\frac{2}{3}g$ = the number of girls who speak French.

Therefore, $\frac{1}{2}b + \frac{2}{3}g$ = total French speakers.

So the fraction of the class that speaks French

$$= \frac{\frac{1}{2}b + \frac{2}{3}\left(\frac{3}{4}b\right)}{b + g}$$

Since there are $\frac{3}{4}$ as many girls as boys in the class,

$g = \frac{3}{4}b$. Plug in $\frac{3}{4}b$ for $g$ into the fraction above:

Fraction of the class that speaks French:

$$= \frac{\frac{1}{2}b + \frac{2}{3}\left(\frac{3}{4}b\right)}{b + \frac{3}{4}b}$$

$$= \frac{\frac{1}{2}b + \frac{1}{2}b}{\frac{7}{4}b}$$

$$= \frac{b}{\frac{7}{4}b}$$

$$= \frac{4}{7}, \text{ or } .571$$

## SECTION 3

**1** **B**—Plug in –2 for $p$ and 3 for $q$: $p^3q^2 + p^2q = (-2)^3 3^2 + (-2)^2 3 = (-8)(9) + 4(3)$, or $(-72) + 12 = -60$.

(Note that a negative number raised to an *even* power becomes positive, but raised to an *odd* power stays negative.)

**2** **E**—Keep track of the lengths you know on the diagram. $B$ is the midpoint of $AC$ so $AB = BC$. Since $AB = 5$, $BC = 5$. $BD = 8$, so $BC + CD = 8$. $BC = 5$, so $5 + CD = 8$, $CD = 3$. $D$ is the midpoint of $CE$, so $CD = DE = 3$.

**3** **D**—Try each answer choice until you find one that works for all of the pairs of numbers.

Choice (A), $P = N + 5$ works for 2 and 7, but not for 4 and 13.

Choice (B), $P = 2N + 3$ also works for 2 and 7, but not for 4 and 13.

Choice (C), $P = 2N + 5$, doesn't work for 2 and 7.

Choice (D), $P = 3N + 1$, works for all four pairs of numbers, so that's the answer.

**4** **A**—$\angle PNM$ is supplementary to $\angle PNQ$, so $\angle PNM + 105° = 180°$, and $\angle PNM = 75°$. Since $PM = PN$, triangle $MPN$ is an isosceles and $\angle PMN = \angle PNM = 75°$. The interior angles of a triangle sum to 180°, so $75 + 75 + x = 180$, and $x = 30$.

**5** **B**—Probability is defined as the number of desired events divided by the total number of possible events. There are $5 + 6 + 4$, or 15 pens in the knapsack. If he pulls out 1 pen, there are 15 different pens he might pick, or 15 possible outcomes. The desired outcome is that the pen be either red or black.

The group of acceptable pens consists of $4 + 6$, or 10 pens. So the probability that one of these pens will be picked is 10 out of 15, or $\frac{10}{15}$, which we can reduce to $\frac{2}{3}$.

**6** **C**—Pick variables for the two items and translate the given information into algebraic equations. Let $h$ = the price of a hot dog and $s$ = the price of a soda. The first statement is translated as $2h + s = \$3.25$, and the second as $3h + s = \$4.50$. If you subtract the first equation from the second, the $s$ is eliminated so you can solve for $h$:

$$3h + s = \$4.50$$
$$-\ 2h + s = \$3.25$$
$$h \quad = \$1.25$$

Plug this value for $h$ into the first equation to solve for $s$:

$$2(\$1.25) + s = \$3.25$$
$$\$2.50 + s = \$3.25$$
$$s = \$0.75$$

So two sodas would cost $2 \times \$0.75 = \$1.50$.

**7** **C**—$a = f$, since all the obtuse angles formed when two parallel lines are cut by a transversal are equal. $f$ is an exterior angle of the small triangle containing angles $c$, $d$, and e, so it is equal to the sum of the two nonadjacent interior angles, $c$ and $d$. Since $a = f$ and $f = c + d$, $a = c + d$, answer choice (C).

**8** **D**—The first 3 minutes of the phone call cost 75 cents or 0.75 dollars. If the entire call lasted $x$ minutes, the rest of the call lasted $x - 3$ minutes. Each minute after the first 3 cost 15 cents or $0.15, so the rest of the call cost $0.15(x - 3)$. So the cost of the entire call is $0.75 + 0.15(x - 3)$ dollars.

If this isn't clear, pick numbers. Let $x = 5$. The first 3 minutes cost $0.75 and the additional $5 - 3 = 2$ minutes are $0.15 each. So the entire call costs $\$0.75 + 2(\$0.15) = \$1.05$. Plug 5 for $x$ into all the answer choices to see which ones give you 1.05:

(A) $0.75(3) + 0.15x = 2.25 + 0.15(5) = 2.25 + 0.75 = 3.00$. Eliminate.

(B) $0.75(3) + 0.15(x + 3) = 2.25 + 0.15(5 + 3) = 2.25 + 1.20 = 3.45$. Eliminate.

(C) $0.75 + 0.15(3 - x) = 0.75 + 0.15(3 - 5) = 0.75 - 0.30 = 0.45$. Eliminate.

(D) $0.75 + 0.15(x - 3) = 0.75 + 0.15(5 - 3) = 0.75 + 0.30 = 1.05$. Works!

(E) $0.75 + 0.15(5) = 0.75 + 0.75 = 1.50$. Eliminate.

The only choice that yields the desired result is (D), so it must be correct.

**9** **B**—Before you can find the area of the circle, you need to find the length of the wire. The wire is in the shape of a semicircle with diameter 12. Since circumference = $\pi d$, the length of a semicircle is half of that, $\frac{\pi d}{2}$. So the length of the wire is $\frac{\pi(12)}{2}$, or $6\pi$. When this wire is bent to form a circle, the circumference of this circle will equal $6\pi$. So the length of the circle's diameter must equal 6, and the radius must be 3. Now you can find the area of the circle:

$$\text{Area} = \pi r^2$$
$$= \pi(3)^2$$
$$= 9\pi$$

**10** **C**—If $a^2 - a = 72$, then $a^2 - a - 72 = 0$. Factoring this quadratic equation: $(a - 9)(a + 8) = 0$. So $a - 9 = 0$ or $a + 8 = 0$, and $a = 9$ or $a = -8$. $b$ to the $n$th power equals $a$, so $b$ must be a root of either 9 or $-8$. Look through the answer choices to find the choice that is not a root of either 9 or $-8$:

(A) $-8$: $(-8)1 = -8$, so this can be a value for $b$.

(B) $-2$: $(-2)3 = -8$, so this can be a value for $b$.

(C) 2: $23 = 8$, *not* $-8$, so this answer *cannot* be a value for $b$.

(D) 3: $32 = 9$, so this can be a value for $b$.

(E) 9: $91 = 9$, so this can be a value for $b$.

So (C) is the only answer choice that cannot be a value for $b$.

**Step 1: Figure out your Math raw score.** Refer to your answer sheet for the total number right and the total number wrong for all three sections in the practice test you're scoring. (If you haven't scored your results, do that now, using the answer key that follows the test.) You can use the chart below to figure out your Math raw score section by section. Multiply the number wrong in section 1 by .25 and subtract the result from the number right in that section. In section 2, multiply the QCs you got wrong by .33 and subtract the result from the number of QCs you got right. Add the number of Grid-ins you got right without subtracting anything. Section 3 is scored in the same way as section 1. Add the scores together and round the result to the nearest whole number.

## PRACTICE TEST A

|  | NUMBER RIGHT | NUMBER WRONG | RAW SCORE |
|---|---|---|---|
| SECTION 1: | ☐ − | (.25 x ☐) | = ☐ |
| SECTION 2: (QUESTIONS 1–15) | ☐ − | (.33 x ☐) | = ☐ |
| SECTION 2: (QUESTIONS 16–25) | ☐ | (NO GUESSING PENALTY) | = ☐ |
| SECTION 3: | ☐ − | (.25 x ☐) | = ☐ |
| MATH RAW SCORE | | | = ☐ (ROUNDED) |

## PRACTICE TEST B

|  | NUMBER RIGHT | NUMBER WRONG | RAW SCORE |
|---|---|---|---|
| SECTION 1: | ☐ − | (.25 x ☐) | = ☐ |
| SECTION 2: (QUESTIONS 1–15) | ☐ − | (.33 x ☐) | = ☐ |
| SECTION 2: (QUESTIONS 16–25) | ☐ | (NO GUESSING PENALTY) | = ☐ |
| SECTION 3: | ☐ − | (.25 x ☐) | = ☐ |
| MATH RAW SCORE | | | = ☐ (ROUNDED) |

**Step 2: Find your practice test score.** Use the table below to find your practice test score based on your Math raw score.

## Find Your Practice Test Score

| Raw | Scaled | Raw | Scaled | Raw | Scaled |
|-----|--------|-----|--------|-----|--------|
| −1 or | | 19 | 440 | 40 | 600 |
| less | 200 | 20 | 450 | 41 | 610 |
| 0 | 220 | 21 | 460 | 42 | 620 |
| 1 | 240 | 22 | 470 | 43 | 630 |
| 2 | 260 | 23 | 480 | 44 | 640 |
| 3 | 280 | 24 | 480 | 45 | 650 |
| 4 | 300 | 25 | 490 | 46 | 650 |
| 5 | 310 | 26 | 500 | 47 | 660 |
| 6 | 330 | 27 | 510 | 48 | 670 |
| 7 | 340 | 28 | 520 | 49 | 680 |
| 8 | 350 | 29 | 520 | 50 | 690 |
| 9 | 360 | 30 | 530 | 51 | 700 |
| 10 | 370 | 31 | 530 | 52 | 720 |
| 11 | 380 | 32 | 540 | 53 | 730 |
| 12 | 390 | 33 | 550 | 54 | 740 |
| 13 | 400 | 34 | 560 | 55 | 760 |
| 14 | 410 | 35 | 560 | 56 | 770 |
| 15 | 420 | 36 | 570 | 57 | 780 |
| 16 | 430 | 37 | 580 | 58 | 790 |
| 17 | 430 | 38 | 590 | 59 | 800 |
| 18 | 440 | 39 | 600 | 60 | 800 |

Don't take your practice test scores too literally. Practice test conditions cannot precisely mirror real test conditions. Your actual SAT Math score will almost certainly vary from your practice test scores. Your score on a practice test gives you a rough idea of your range on the actual exam.

If you don't like your score, it's not too late to do something about it. Work your way way through this book again, and turn to Kaplan's *SAT & PSAT 1998,* our more comprehensive test prep and college admissions guide, for even more help.

# About

# Educational Centers

Kaplan Educational Centers is one of the nation's premier education companies, providing individuals with a full range of resources to achieve their educational and career goals. Kaplan, celebrating its 60th anniversary, is a wholly-owned subsidiary of The Washington Post Company.

## TEST PREPARATION & ADMISSIONS

Kaplan's nationally-recognized test prep courses cover more than 20 standardized tests, including entrance exams for secondary school, college and graduate school as well as foreign language and professional licensing exams. In addition, Kaplan offers private tutoring and comprehensive, one-to-one admissions and application advice for students applying to graduate school.

## SCORE! EDUCATIONAL CENTERS

SCORE! after-school learning centers help students in grades K-8 build academic skills, confidence and goal-setting skills in a motivating, sports-oriented environment. Kids use a cutting-edge, interactive curriculum that continually assesses and adapts to their academic needs and learning style. Enthusiastic Academic Coaches serve as positive role models, creating a high-energy atmosphere where learning is exciting and fun for kids.With nearly 40 centers today, new centers continue to open nationwide.

## KAPLAN LEARNING SERVICES

Kaplan Learning Services provides customized assessment, education and training programs to K-12 schools, universities and businesses to help students and employees reach their educational and career goals.

## KAPLAN INTERNATIONAL

Kaplan serves international students and professionals in the U.S. through Access America, a series of intensive English language programs, and LCP International Institute, a leading provider of intensive English language programs at on-campus centers in California, Washington and New York. Kaplan and LCP offer specialized services to sponsors including placement at top American universities, fellowship management, academic monitoring and reporting and financial administration.

## KAPLOAN

Students can get key information and advice about educational loans for college and graduate school through **KapLoan** (Kaplan Student Loan Information Program). Through an affiliation with one of the nation's largest student loan providers, **KapLoan** helps direct students and their families through the often bewildering financial aid process.

## KAPLAN PUBLISHING

Kaplan Books, a joint imprint with Simon & Schuster, publishes titles in test preparation, admissions, education, career development and life skills; Kaplan and *Newsweek* jointly publish the highly successful guides, **How to Get Into College** and **How to Choose a Career & Graduate School**. *SCORE!* and *Newsweek* have teamed up to publish **How to Help Your Child Suceed in School**.

Kaplan InterActive delivers award-winning, high quality educational products and services including Kaplan's best-selling **Higher Score** test-prep software and sites on the internet **(http://www.kaplan.com)** and America Online. Kaplan and Cendant Software are jointly developing, marketing and distributing educational software for the kindergarten through twelfth grade retail and school markets.

## KAPLAN CAREER SERVICES

Kaplan helps students and graduates find jobs through Kaplan Career Services, the leading provider of career fairs in North America. The division includes **Crimson & Brown Associates**, the nation's leading diversity recruiting and publishing firm, **The Lendman Group and Career Expo**, both of which help clients identify highly sought-after technical personnel, and sales and marketing professionals.

## COMMUNITY OUTREACH

Kaplan provides educational resources to thousands of financially disadvantaged students annually, working closely with educational institutions, not-for-profit groups, government agencies and other grass roots organizations on a variety of national and local support programs. Also, Kaplan centers enrich local communities by employing high school, college and graduate students, creating valuable work experiences for vast numbers of young people each year.

# Want more information about our services, products, or the nearest Kaplan center?

 **Call our nationwide toll-free numbers:**

**1-800-KAP-TEST** for information on our live courses, private tutoring and admissions consulting

**1-800-KAP-ITEM** for information on our products

**1-888-KAP-LOAN**\* for information on student loans

 **Connect with us in cyberspace:**

On AOL, keyword:"Kaplan"

On the World Wide Web, go to: http://www.kaplan.com

Via e-mail: info@kaplan.com

 **Write to:**

Kaplan Educational Centers
888 Seventh Avenue
New York, NY 10106

# Life is a series of tests.

# Some of them just count more.

Kaplan can help you score higher on the tests that matter. With Kaplan's private tutoring and live classes, you'll receive the expert instruction and personal attention you need to score your best. Find out why 3 million students have chosen Kaplan.

**Call 1-800-KAP-TEST to enroll today.**

## 1-800-KAP-TEST

### the leader in test prep

www.kaplan.com